THE REFORM IN OAXACA, 1856–76

THE
REFORM IN OAXACA, 1856–76

A Microhistory of the
Liberal Revolution

CHARLES R. BERRY

UNIVERSITY OF NEBRASKA PRESS
LINCOLN AND LONDON

Library of Congress Cataloging in Publication Data

Berry, Charles Redmon, 1932–
  The reform in Oaxaca, 1856–76.

  Bibliography: p. 253
  Includes index.
  1. Oaxaca, Mexico (State)—Politics and government. I. Title.
F1321.B47   972'.74   80–15378
ISBN 0–8032–1158–9

Publication of this book was aided by a grant from the
National Endowment for the Humanities.

DEDICATED TO—
Nettie Lee Benson and
Thomas F. McGann,
remarkable teachers, kind
critics, and good friends

CONTENTS

MAPS

TABLES

PREFACE

DURING THE DECADE following the achievement of independence from Spain in 1821, Mexico found itself torn by internal dissensions and struggling with grave problems. The difficulties centered on a malfunctioning economy; the absence of a political consensus; the carry-over of a colonial mentality, which emphasized privilege and which was reflected in institutions that were unable or unwilling to adapt to a new dispensation; unbridled militarism; and an unbalanced social structure in which a small, elite minority dominated and exploited the vast majority of citizens, who had little or no influence over policies and the course of events. After a brief period of euphoria, the ills of the nation soon became apparent, but deep, bitter political factionalism precluded any solutions.

These problems not only remained unsolved for a number of years but magnified to produce unhappy consequences that held out the prospect for a seemingly perpetual state of social and political instability and economic weakness. Before long, foreign powers began to prey upon Mexico, taking advantage of its debility, with the results that Spain, Great Britain, France, and the United States intervened to protect their citizens, take control of commerce, reduce the country to a debtor-client status, seize territory, or otherwise threaten the independence of the new nation. Private British firms loaned money to the Mexican government at high interest rates, soon came to dominate trade, and invested heavily in Mexican mines. Spain continued to sulk over the loss of its former colony, to rattle swords, and to intervene to protect its large number of citizens still residing in Mexico. France intervened in 1838 in an attempt to force the collection of claims owed to its citizens whose properties had been damaged or destroyed in internal Mexican political upheavals. And there was a growing dispute with the United States over commercial matters, rights of U.S. citizens living in Mexican territory, and the question of Texas, all of which culminated in war between the two nations in 1846–48.

Concurrently with this steady and seemingly irreversible plunge into chaos and economic stagnation, there developed a determination on the part of some men, active in state or national politics, to try to breast the tide and effect necessary changes in attitudes and structures that would result in the imposition of order and the strengthening of the nation. This sentiment became common during the dark days of the war with the United States. The progressive thinkers and politicians could point to the current situation as proof that the forces of conservatism and privilege, which had dominated much of the time since the winning of independence, were responsible for the lack of economic advancement, social development, political stability, and the significant loss of territory to the enemy.

The advocacy for change came largely from areas peripheral to central Mexico and the national capital. In the provinces, where the support for the federalistic structure of national organization was strongest, professional men, some landowners, some parish clergy, and others of the small middle-class groupings came to associate their federalist leanings with their support for liberal doctrines promoting change. Thus much of the substance and strength of the movement for imposing in Mexico a new order that would foster progress centered in the states of the union and their legislatures and governors, rather than in the congress or the executive branch of the national government. The provinces' federalism has long been recognized by historians and has received adequate attention, but there has been little attention paid to the groundswell of liberalism in the peripheral areas.

The Federalists-Liberals began to advocate many changes: a greater public works program; more attention to and support for education; a cessation of military involvement in political affairs; and a curtailment of the power and influence of the Roman Catholic Church, looking toward the disestablishment of the church, the disentailment of its urban and rural property holdings, and the sale of the real estate to private citizens. Throughout the 1840s and early 1850s, whenever Liberals were in control of state regimes, attempts were made to implement programs that would fulfill these goals and objectives.

Although the federalist-liberal groups spoke and wrote in terms of economic progress and political stability, their motives were not totally altruistic. At heart, they wished to forward their own cause and their position in government, to take control in order to promote their own advancement. They would be the chief beneficiaries of the disentailment of ecclesiastical property because they would be in an advantageous position to purchase the real estate put on the market, thereby strengthening their own financial base. Destruction of privileges could only improve the situation of those who were without privileges. The taming of the military would give the Liberals control over the army, which had heretofore acted to bar them from power. A people educated in the principles of liberalism would logically buttress the Liberals' status. Public works would serve to enhance trade, agricultural production, mining, and industry, which the Liberals would control. If their programs were implemented, they would profit immeasurably, both in concrete terms and in the less tangible, nonetheless important, realm of converting them into the directing class.

The Conservatives—privileged landowners, agents and representatives of foreign business firms, high-ranking military officers, and the hierarchy of the Catholic Church, the majority of parish priests, and members of the religious orders—all ensconced in positions of influence, protected by laws and the machinery of the state, thought that the changes fostered by the Federalists and Liberals would strike directly at their own power and privilege. Their posture grew increasingly rigid as they became more determined than ever to resist the liberal program. Their instruments were the military, the church, and high politics. In the early 1850s, in the aftermath of the war with the United States, they put all their hope in Antonio López de Santa Anna. They installed him once more in the presidency, made him a dictator, and created a highly centralized government, attempting to dominate the nation from their seat of power in Mexico City and the central region of the nation, where they had secondary strongholds in Puebla and Guadalajara. But Santa Anna, in attempting to repress the Liberals and their federalist political philosophy, went too far and provoked a rebellion, the Revolution of Ayutla of 1854–55, which toppled him from power and gave control of the government to his enemies. The Liberals then were in a position to enact their program of change. They were convinced that it would bring great progress to their nation, begin that long-delayed move toward modernity that had been expected three decades earlier when independence was achieved, and bring them material advancement and profit. This movement to effect change, revolutionary in concept and implementation, is known as *la Reforma*—the Reform—and it was to last for two decades, until 1876.

It is the Reform, viewed from the perspective of one of the strong-holds of liberalism, the southern state of Oaxaca, that is the subject of the present study, begun as a doctoral dissertation longer ago than I care to recall. When first conceived, it dealt exclusively with a tiny piece of territory and a small segment of the Mexican population in a crucial and important but nevertheless brief period of time: the Central District of Oaxaca during the years 1856–67. I intended to focus on that area in order to test some of the general theories and interpretations concerning the Reform program. I was convinced that the movement could best be understood and analyzed at the grass-roots level of society, and that the problems inherent in and emanating from the Reform, problems that, of course, would have national significance, could only be grasped fully when placed in this more human context. I felt somewhat at a disadvantage, despite my conviction that such an approach to Mexican history was valid, indeed necessary and long overdue, because I thought that it could easily be shrugged off by my coleagues as meaningless due to its very nature, the substance of which centered on the smallness of the sample. I also experienced some anxiety that my dissertation supervisor, Professor Thomas F. McGann, would find little to encourage in such a narrow study, since only a few years previously he had read and published a paper concerning research opportunities in Latin American history, in which he began by stating that he favored the "big topic."[1] On that count, I soon discovered that he was a remarkably kind and tolerant supervisor, giving me much encouragement at the time and in subsequent years as the original study underwent modifications and was broadened.

In 1965, I was not familiar with the terms macrohistory and microhistory. Undoubtedly they were in use, but I do not think they had yet become current and fashionable. Without realizing it, I was, in my own mind, trying to establish a case for a microhistorical approach to Mexico. In the following years, the terms became common as microhistorians began to speak out to justify their views and, more important, to publish works that quickly made that type of history respectable and exciting.

This new awareness of the importance of the smaller entity is the most significant development in the study of Mexican history in recent years. I need only cite such outstanding works as Womack's *Zapata and the Mexican Revolution,* González's *Pueblo en vilo,* Taylor's *Landlord and Peasant in Colonial Oaxaca,* Hamnett's *Politics and Trade in Southern Mexico,* Salamini's *Agrarian Radicalism in Veracruz, 1920–38,* Chance's *Race and Class in Colonial Oaxaca,* Altman and Lockhart's *Provinces of Early Mexico: Variants of Spanish American Regional Evolution,* and Powell's *El liberalismo y el campesinado en el centro de México (1850 a 1876),* all published within the last decade, to indicate the enormous strides made for subnational history. In addition, there has been considerable attention devoted to microhistory in scholarly meetings of Mexicanists. The third Conference of Mexican and North American Historians, meeting in Oaxtepec in 1969, set aside one session for a discussion of this approach; the following year, in Boston, the Mexicanist committee within the Conference of Latin American History chose to devote its single session to a consideration of subnational history. Luis González y González has become the major spokesman for microhistory, both in practice (with his study of his native village of San José de Gracia) and in theorizing, which he has done in several papers but most convincingly and eloquently in his article "Microhistoria para multiméxico," published in 1971.[2]

It is proper to echo González by pointing out that local and regional studies have long occupied a place in Mexican historiography, with precedents dating from the preconquest era. But in the modern period, the practice of micro- or subnational history too often has resulted in little more than chronicles compiled by local historians, usually by a process of transferring information from provincial newspapers of bygone days into their accounts, with some minimal use made of local archival materials—all fitted together to present a chronological development but with little reflection, meaning, or significance other than that they preserved information and made it more accessible. Only occasionally, that is, until recently, did a historian write local or regional history that broke with this general pattern.

In this study I have attempted a survey of the Mexican Reform from the subnational level. I originally chose the Central District of Oaxaca as my vantage point for several reasons. The archives of that area were relatively complete, in fair condition, and generally accessible to the researcher. It was far enough removed from the central plateau of Mexico so that the study would not lapse into an essay on the Reform as seen from the national capital, and yet at the same time it was close enough to the epicenter of events so that the repercussions from those occurrences were strongly felt locally. Furthermore, whereas the Liberals in Oaxaca focused their attention on the state capital, Oaxaca City, which was also the district seat, the activities there of several state leaders propelled them into national prominence to play major roles in the whole Reform movement. In short, Oaxaca seemed to offer a balance that could facilitate a microhistorical approach to the years of stress known as *la Reforma*. Through revision stimulated by the wise and kind advice of critics, I have now broadened the study to include the entire state and in some instances to continue my analysis to 1876, when the Reform faded into the Porfiriato.

Such an approach helps one to grasp the real meaning of the Reform. Its substance consists of much more than a series of laws and decrees announcing new programs, Liberals battling Conservatives, Mexicans fighting the French and Austrian invaders, while the somber, overpowering figure of Benito Juárez towered above the struggle. Instead, the essence of the Reform lies in the tribulations, fears, and insecurity, both physical and economic, of individuals caught up in an attempt to restructure basic institutions and patterns of life. It lies in political factionalism, which became so much of an impediment to carrying out the Liberal programs that in the end the Reform turned out to be something different from what was originally contemplated. The essence lies in the dilemmas forced upon various groups in society, ranging from clerics and nuns, who saw their old way of life virtually swept away, to politicians, who were tempted to commit treason in order to find some means of livelihood. It lies in the patriotic fervor and steadfastness of some as opposed to the doubts and wavering of others. By taking this view from the microhistorical level, one begins to perceive why the Reform evolved as it did, why it was concurrently a positive and negative movement, and what its accomplishments and its shortcomings were. Only then can one appreciate what the French historian Lucien Febvre meant when he wrote, "I have never known, and I still do not know, but one way to understand well, to place into context, the broader scope of history. This way consists of grasping in depth, in all its development, the history of one region, of one province."[3]

THE REFORM IN OAXACA, 1856–76

CHAPTER 1

OAXACA ON THE EVE OF THE REFORM

THE STATE OF Oaxaca encompasses an area abundant in resources but has so formidable a topograhy that modern technology has yet to conquer the terrain. There is no symmetry to the high mountains that crowd helter-skelter across the land; seldom do they give relief by separating to permit the level expanse of valleys. In one of those few pockets near the center of the state, the tall, dull blue and brown hills grudgingly pull apart so that the heads of three valleys converge. Near here, the Zapotec and Mixtec kingdoms took root and flourished in prehistory. Here, where the towering bulk of San Felipe Mountain sends out its spurs and almost succeeds in reaching Monte Albán, the bold Spanish conquistadors founded a town in 1523: they first called it Antequera after their Andalusian homeland.

THE CAPITAL

By mid-nineteenth century, the town of Oaxaca, as it came to be called, had grown considerably in population and area but still retained the stamp of its Spanish architects and colonial origin. The plat of the town, as laid out by its founders, continued to reflect the unity of man's spiritual, social, and economic activities. The business district was built around the central plaza, a large, open block only partially paved by 1850, devoid of trees and gardens, and dominated by a public fountain in the center. The north side of this plaza was bordered by the cathedral, the parish church of the Sagrario, and the administrative and treasury offices of the diocese. On the south side of the square was the unfinished Government Palace, the construction of which was begun in 1832 to replace an older building destroyed by earthquakes frequent in the region.[1]

1

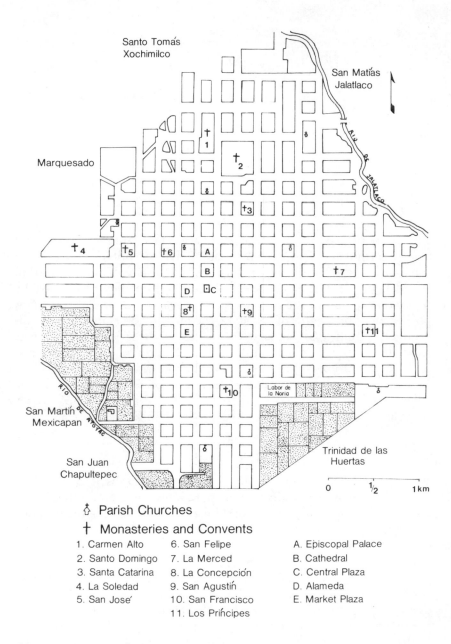

Santo Tomás
Xochimilco

San Matías
Jalatlaco

Marquesado

† 1
† 2
†3
† 4   †5   †6   A
B
D   C
8†   †9
E
†11
†10
Labor de
la Noria

San Martín
Mexicapan

San Juan
Chapultepec

Trinidad de las
Huertas

0   ½   1 km

⚲ Parish Churches
† Monasteries and Convents

1. Carmen Alto	6. San Felipe	A. Episcopal Palace
2. Santo Domingo	7. La Merced	B. Cathedral
3. Santa Catarina	8. La Concepción	C. Central Plaza
4. La Soledad	9. San Agustín	D. Alameda
5. San José	10. San Francisco	E. Market Plaza
	11. Los Príncipes	

MAP 1. The City of Oaxaca. *Source:* Based on a map drawn in 1848 by Count
Antonio Diebitech de Sabalkanski, commissioned by Governor Benito Juárez.

The structures on all four sides of the central plaza had covered walkways with opened arches fronting the streets, like the arched cloisters in a monastery. These were called portales, with those on each side of the square having their distinct name. The arcades on the south were called the portales of the Palace, and those on the north were designated the portales of the Clavería, the diocesan treasury offices. On the east and west sides of the plaza were business establishments, with the arched walkways called respectively the portales of the Shopkeepers and the portales of the Flowers, although the last was often referred to as the arcade of the Lord, because there in a niche above the entrance to one of the stores was kept a much-venerated image of Christ. This statue was honored by special religious ceremonies on the Fridays of Lent, when the plaza would fill with the faithful singing hymns to orchestral accompaniment and reciting prayers in homage to the Christ of the portales.[2]

Across from the front of the cathedral, which faced west, was the little park called the Alameda, with "shady trees, gravel walks, stone benches, lamps, and an iron railing for an enclosure," as one nineteenth-century traveler described it.[3] On the north side of the cathedral was the Episcopal Palace, one of the more impressive structures in the city, and next to it, the diocesan seminary.

Two blocks southwest of the central plaza was the large open space devoted to the market. This block was called the Plaza of San Juan de Dios because it was bordered on one side by the church of that name. The market square had galleries and stalls around all sides, which were designated *sol* and *sombra,* and sublet at various prices according to the amount of sun and shade they received during the day.[4] This plaza was owned by the ayuntamiento (town council) of the city, which rented it to an individual, who in turn subleased the stalls. In the mid-nineteenth century, an astute businesswoman, Josefa Bustamante, regularly contracted to rent the market from the council for 5,000 pesos per year.

From a source near the village of San Felipe del Agua, north of the capital, water was brought into the city by an aqueduct, built in 1755 but in poor repair a century later. The construction of this aqueduct made possible improvements in Oaxaca City by supplying water to the growing number of conventual establishments and permitting the laying out of a few public gardens. But the poorer sections of the town and the suburbs remained without water and their residents had to carry it from the nine public fountains or from the nearby rivers. Infrequently, repairs were effected on the aqueduct and then the flow was stopped until the work was completed. Once inside the city, water was diverted to the public fountains and homes and ran through paved ditches down the center of four of the main north-south streets. One of these trenches, spanned by narrow stone bridges, followed the street between the Alameda and the cathedral and along the west side of the central plaza.[5]

By mid-nineteenth century, there were 185 blocks within the city, fifteen streets running north and south and eighteen running east and west, most of them unpaved and deeply rutted. The city had the shape roughly of a diamond with the angles squared off and pointed toward the four cardinal directions of the compass. In 1852, to facilitate the levying and collecting of taxes, taking censuses, and maintaining order, the city was divided into quarters, each quarter to contain four sections.[6] The population was in the neighborhood of 20,000. (See Appendix A.)

Along the southern edge of the town flowed the Atoyac River, the course of which had been altered farther to the south in the early years in order to control flooding and make more acreage available on which the townspeople could grow their food crops. In the colonial era, Indian relatives of those natives in encomienda settled in this area. Their section came to be called Trinidad de las Huertas and even in the nineteenth century it still reflected its strong Indian heritage. Along the northern and northeastern edges of the city a creek, pretentiously named the Jalatlaco River, had scarcely any water most of the time but flowed tempestuously in the rainy season of some years. In an arc across the northern rim of the city were located the Indian villages of Jalatlaco, Xochimilco, and Tepeaca, and on the west lay the suburb of the Marquesado, or Santa María Oaxaca, all of which were contiguous with Oaxaca City by 1850 but remained separate political entities.

Prosperity came to Oaxaca in the colonial period because it straddled the route from the great central plateau of Mexico, 100 leagues to the northwest, to the Captaincy General of Guatemala to the southeast. Friars and nuns, petty bureaucrats and high state officials, soldiers and vagrants, convoys of mules and trains of oxen passed through from one area to the other, and Oaxaca City became the largest, most attractive way point along the route. Even more noteworthy as a factor of prosperity was the abundance of the nopal cactus and the tiny, red, spiderlike insects that fed on the plant. The nurture of these plants and insects and the manufacture of the red dye from the crushed cochineal insects became the most important industry of, and brought great wealth to, the region.

In the colonial era, then, many rich landholders, manufacturers of and dealers in cochineal, proprietors of mules and oxen, and merchants dwelt in the city. These wealthy people built magnificent homes, massive and solid, many using the beautiful green stone quarried from the nearby Indian village of Santa Lucía del Camino. But for the most part, the city consisted of one-story adobe and plaster homes, joined one against the other, so that someone walking down a street saw nothing but a solid and long wall, painted in various colors, pierced by grilled windows and heavy wooden doors.[7] Towering above the low dwellings were the many churches and monasteries. With their ornately carved facades and towers covered in tiles of white, yellow, and blue, which caught and reflected the sun, these structures could be seen from all directions.

The pace of life in Oaxaca City at mid-nineteenth century was slow and, to a remarkable degree, controlled by the institution of the church. It is difficult to realize now the extent of the influence of religion in the daily lives of Mexicans in the first half of the nineteenth century. The passing of the hours was tolled by the clock in the cathedral tower, the chiming of church bells to call the faithful, and the quiet, rapid recitation of prayers; the days were tallied on the liturgical calendar with its notations of feasts and abstinences, jubilations and sorrows. People arose early in the morning to recite the Rosary, some even getting up as early as 3:00 A.M. to march regularly in the procession that issued out of the Dominican monastery and wound through the streets for thirty minutes. These early devotions were followed by a light repast of chocolate. Then the faithful attended Mass at the nearest church at 5:00 A.M. After that, marketing and chores around the house were accomplished until 9:00, at which time breakfast was served. If it was not a holiday stemming from some church celebration, after breakfast those families that could afford to have their children in school sent them off, more than likely to an educational establishment operated by the church. The father went to his work, and the mother continued her tasks in the home.

At noon, a light meal of fruit was eaten, followed by prayers consisting of three Ave Marias. The family reunited at 2:00 P.M. for dinner, after which all retired for a siesta of an hour's duration. Following the afternoon rest, the men returned to their work while the women gathered in the veranda enclosing the patio to sew until time for evening prayers. The church bells pealed at dusk as a signal for these orisons—three Aves, followed by a Rosary, in which all members of the family and the servants joined. About 7:00, a light supper was served. An hour later, the church bells once more rang out in a *doblecito,* and all the family again said special prayers. For the remainder of the evening, the parents and children and other relatives stayed together for conversation. At 9:00, the cathedral chimes sounded across the still night, and the family went to bed.[8]

Visits and courtesy calls were made only by the wealthy few. Beginning about 1840, charades came to be a popular evening diversion within the family circle. Evening strolls were taken only on special occasions, such as the day of national independence (September 16) and the feasts in honor of the patron saints of the different sections of the city.

The houses, all of which had open patios in the center, were kept neat, clean, and well-ordered. The furniture, if not luxurious even in the wealthier homes, was adequate and comfortable, more utilitarian than decorative. The women learned how to read and to cipher— enough for their devotional books and household accounts—but that is about the only formal education they received. Informally, they were taught the crafts that they would employ as wives and mothers. Yet they were true mistresses of household affairs, sharp traders, and astute bargainers. The children were taught the fear of God, portrayed to them as an angry judge with a sword of fire that would strike down all who did evil. They were also taught to believe in an omnipresent devil, who appeared in different forms to lure the unwary into his clutches. The uneducated populace was superstitious and in the shadows of the night saw the black, beckoning forms of witches, Tío Pellejos, and worst of all, the Matlacihau, who devoured children. The fathers, even though they had faults and committed their peccadillos on the side, were always careful to conceal their small sins from their families and bring up the children to be upright and obedient.[9] In short, life was quiet, regimented; work was not burdensome and distractions did not dominate the daily schedule. But this does not mean that everyone was healthy, happy, and prosperous, or that no excitement ever broke the dull, unchanging routine.

To give protection to those inside homes and businesses, heavy grillwork covered all window openings and the glass panes were installed only in the upper half of the windows, the bottom half being covered with metal or wood. Municipal finances were so limited that only a small police force could be employed; security at night along the dark, unlighted streets was maintained by night watchmen, called *serenos,* who, in the early days of the century, were armed only with machetes but later received carbines. These watchmen sang out the hour and described the weather all through the night. To supplement their insufficient numbers, in time a volunteer night police patrol was organized by the alcalde, or supervisor, of each of the sixteen sections of the city. The thieves were especially fond of the area around the cathedral and central plaza for their hunting ground during the night. This area of the business district was therefore the first to be lighted when municipal funds permitted the expenditure to be made. By 1860, most streets had a few oil lamps, which hung from posts in the center of the thoroughfares.[10]

Manuel Martínez Gracida, a local historian whose active career spanned most of the latter half of the nineteenth century, compiled a two-volume chronicle of day-by-day events in and around Oaxaca City in which frequent mention is made of robberies and assaults. Many of these may be attributed to the political struggle between the Liberals and the Conservatives but a large number cannot be so connected. The frequency of such occurrences indicates the tenor of the times, the general lawlessness, and the lack of security.[11]

Although measures were taken to guard the health of the population, a large portion of the people were debilitated by intestinal parasites and respiratory disorders. Diseases of various types recurred frequently to plague the populace. Two terrible epidemics of cholera took heavy tolls in Oaxaca City and the Central District in 1833 and 1854. On top of that, smallpox came in epidemic proportions at not infrequent intervals. In 1851–52, 1,146 persons died in Oaxaca City and its environs from the disease.[12] The control and propagation of vaccine being a task of the town councils, the doctors were always solicitous that the serum be available in Oaxaca City. Mass immunizations were held often, and the newspapers of the epoch make frequent mention of measures to be taken in the cure of smallpox, the schedule of vaccinations, and gifts to the ayuntamiento of infected cows from which vaccine would be developed.

Hospital facilities within the city were poor. Three religious orders of hospitalers had been located in Oaxaca, well-endowed with rent-yielding properties, but these were in decline by the early part of the century and were finally suppressed by the Spanish Cortes just before independence. Their abolition left the area without any good infirmary. The municipal council took over the physical plant of the Bethlehemites' hospital but had insufficient funds to operate it adequately. In order to establish one good hospital for the city, frequent attempts were made over a long period of time to convince the diocesan hierarchy to regroup the assets of the three establishments that had accrued to the general treasury of the bishopric when the orders were suppressed, but to no avail.[13]

For entertainment, there was a theater, owned by a private citizen, which had opened in 1840. Although it was not a large building, it was elaborately decorated.[14] Occasionally, traveling companies of actors would come to the city to remain a few weeks (or even a month, if the response was encouraging), performing their repertoire of plays, many of which were currently popular in Mexico City. Or local musicians, of whom there were several, would come together to present an evening of salon music to benefit some worthy charity. In these events, the Alcalá family, father and sons, all talented on different instruments, would take active roles.

Then there were cockfights, cards, and games of dice. Bullfights were prohibited by the first state legislature in 1826 because they generated too much excitement and attracted too many beggars, thieves, and pickpockets and because the small police force could not control the crowds. Thereafter, the *corridas* were infrequent since special permission to hold them had to be sought from the state government. Some villages would go to such trouble in seeking permission in order to celebrate more vigorously the festivals of their patron saints. Dances and balls were not unknown, although not held very often, because, according to one traveler who visited the region, partisan feelings were so deeply ingrained in the people that seldom could they meet in a friendly, social attitude.[15]

The major entertainment was provided by the church festivals that marked the passing of the year. Some of these religious celebrations were more important than others, but all attracted their own following. Many involved elaborate, colorful processions, which included Indian musicians playing their drums and the strident flutelike *chirimías,* members of the religious orders, officers and soldiers of the military garrison, townspeople, and the ever-present flagellants. In addition to Corpus Christi in May or June, and Good Friday afternoon, which appealed to all of society, the Dominican friars celebrated New Year's Day, the feast day of Saint Dominic (August 4), the Day of the Rosary (the first Sunday in October); the Carmelites honored Saint Teresa of Avila on her feast (October 15); the Augustinians gave equal attention to the feasts of Saint Augustine and his mother Saint Monica (August 28 and May 4); the nuns of La Soledad convent celebrated especially the holy day of the Virgin of Soledad (December 18), whose miraculous image, dressed in black velvet sewn with pearls and precious stones, rested in their convent church; the Spanish Capuchinesses honored Saint Joseph (March 19)—all these and many more with their processions, floats, banquets, and carnivals.[16]

In the era before the Reform, the church in provincial Oaxaca, as throughout the Republic, was the common denominator of all segments of society, the one level on which all persons—rich and poor, soldier and priest, beggar and bureaucrat—could meet. And in the processions or in attendance at Mass, all were equal, despite the rags or the elegant clothes, the learning of some and the ignorance of many, the exalted positions of the high state officials or the humble stations of the vast majority of citizens.

Not only did the church give men and women some hint of equality and enliven their dull existence in provincial Oaxaca; it also accepted their obedience and support and in turn looked after their material welfare should they become down and out. Friars and nuns daily fanned out through the town to beg alms from door to door and on the street corners. The convents and monasteries took in orphan girls and boys and cared for them, provided employment and security for many domestics, and dispensed food and clothing to the unfortunate. Most active in these charitable works were the Dominicans, whose wealth permitted them to feed large groups of poor people each day, the only requirement being that the recipients stay to recite the Rosary after the meal.[17]

Despite what would seem to be a frozen world of the society of Oaxaca in the late colonial period and the quarter century following independence, there were subtle forces at work affecting the relationship between church and people. By the middle of the nineteenth century, the influence, wealth, and personnel of the church in Oaxaca had declined. The zenith of influence and opulence came probably in the third quarter of the eighteenth century, when new churches were begun, new orders came to the areas to found monasteries and convents, and there were enough secular priests to staff all the parishes in the state. This peak was undoubtedly closely connected with the wealth and affluence brought to the region by the cochineal industry. Money derived from the manufacture of the dye allowed the citizens to endow conventual establishments, contribute to pious works or create new ones, and pay the dowries to have their daughters enter the nunneries.

With the close of the struggle for independence, however, the church began to experience a slow, almost imperceptible decline in Oaxaca. A series of heavy economic blows had been struck, none of them individually devastating but cumulatively working to limit the activities and influence of the Catholic religion and its agencies. First there was the takeover of some of the ecclesiastical wealth of the church by the Spanish Crown in the first years of the nineteenth century, followed in succession by the forced loans exacted from the priests-administrators by José María Morelos when he invaded Oaxaca during the war of liberation; the expulsion in 1828–29 of the Spaniards, who were in general well-to-do merchants, cochineal manufacturers, and supporters of the work of the church; and the rapid decline of the cochineal industry.[18] In addition to these rather sharp losses, there set in a steady erosion of the strength of the church. The numbers of friars and nuns steadily declined from the period of the first Federal Republic in the mid-1820s to the beginning of the Reform era three decades latter. The income for several of the nunneries was barely sufficient, and in some cases not enough, to meet the expenses incurred in operating these houses. The friars of some of the orders fell into quarrels among themselves over offices, elections, and policies. The secular clergy likewise slowly declined in numbers and the priests became increasingly alienated from the parishioners. Arguments raged over fees the padres charged for their services.[19]

Just prior to the Reform, the diocesan seminary, founded in 1683, had undergone some revisions in curriculum and still maintained a large enrollment. In the mid-1840s, courses in criminal and civil law were added to the chairs of theology, canon law, philosophy, and Latin, and a few years later, French was being taught. Between 1831 and 1850, the enrollment increased from 250 to 379 students as a result of the addition of the law courses. No statistics are available on the number of students in the seminary who took holy orders, but available information would indicate that the attrition rate was high. In the second quarter of the nineteenth century, the young men were chiefly interested in obtaining a professional education, not in becoming priests. One need only read the biographies of men prominent in Oaxaca in the period of the Reform to see how many of them began their studies in the seminary, only to drop out just short of taking vows or to transfer to the Institute of Sciences and Arts.[20]

The decrease in the income of the church, the poverty of some of its conventual establishments, the diminution of its personnel, the disputes between priests and parishioners were not the disease itself but merely symptoms of the epidemic of secularism that had spread throughout the western Catholic world from its inception in France in the eighteenth century. Weakened economically and with its influence challenged in the realm of the spirit, the church was forced to fight a losing battle against men exhilarated by new ideas and concepts. This modern trend penetrated Mexico late in the eighteenth century; by the time independence was won, it had taken firm root and thereafter grew rapidly. In 1844, a Oaxacan priest, Dr. José Mariano Galíndez, summarized well what was happening in the provincial capital.

> Our church in bygone eras was the storehouse of the faith and was admired for its religious piety. I offer as an example so many convents where virtue and wisdom dwelled in a great number of persons; so many monasteries, the asylum of innocence and austerity; so many examples of worthy ecclesiastics, who have left us a holy memory of their virtues; the enthusiasm for spiritual practices which permeated all classes; the exactitude with which the church was obeyed; the devout attendance at religious functions; the pious works and charitable foundations; the reading of innocent literature; Christian education—in a word, good customs. . . . But let us turn our eyes to the present time. How different is the picture! We are disgraced that the most impious and licentious books penetrated even here: they were begun to be read with reserve, then passed on the same note from one friend to another, and then spread abroad with such untoward speed that they began to be sold without shame in our bookstores. Thus do we come to waver like children, letting ourselves be blown by any wind of doctrine, and even desiring to deify some men who deceive with cunning. The sentiments altered, teachers are sought who will make much of the new ideas. And what was the result here? What naturally ought to happen: the heart froze, understanding was obscured, customs were corrupted, and a modern philosophy became the mode. . . . Thus do we observe that fiestas are not blessed; that obedience to the church is left to children and pious old women; that abstinence is left up to the monasteries. Thus do we see men who, scorning the most edifying rites of the church, adopt the ridiculous ceremonies of a secret society and are honored to wear an apron. Today we feel that our solemnities are reduced to sterile works which do not produce the fruits of the spirit and the religion of the soul.[21]

The symbol of the new outlook of which Dr. Galíndez spoke, at least in Oaxaca, was the Institute of Sciences and Arts. It competed with the seminary for the minds of the youth and graduated many of the men who were destined to preside over the decline of the Mexican church. No wonder the priests referred to it as the "house of heretics" and the "house of prostitution" and to the students in attendance as "libertines."[22]

In 1826, the first constitutional legislature of Oaxaca, half of whose members were priests, decreed the establishment of the Institute; its doors opened in January 1827. The curriculum, as originally planned, called for courses in belles-lettres, English, French, rhetoric, logic, ethics, elements of mathematics, statistics, political economy, physics, geography, botany, chemistry, mineralogy, surgery, medicine, the natural history of Mexico, natural and civil law, public constitutional law, canon law, and ecclesiastical history. Still later, courses were added in pharmacy, Spanish grammar, and Latin. In 1835, this curriculum was somewhat modified to give more emphasis to science and training for professional careers in law and medicine. At the same time, the academic senate was organized, to consist of five medical doctors, five lawyers, and five theologians, plus the director of the Institute, the members being charged with the examination of candidates and the bestowal of the bachelor's degree. The senate also served as a scientific and literary group whose object was to promote the study of the various branches of learning.[23]

The chairs in these subjects through the years were held by capable men, many of whom were or became nationally prominent: Manuel Iturribarría, Manuel Ortega Reyes, José Antonio Gamboa, Justo Benítez, Porfirio Díaz, Félix Romero, Benito Juárez, José María Murguía y Galardi, Marcos Pérez, Manuel Dublán, to name only a few. In addition, four of the early directors, all priests, were among the most prominent clergymen in Mexico in their time. Friar Francisco Aparicio was prior of the monastery of Santo Domingo. Florencio del Castillo, a Costa Rican by birth, had represented his native province in the Spanish Cortes and afterwards settled in Oaxaca. Francisco García Cantarines, titular bishop of Hypen, had served as president of the first national congress. And Juan José Canseco was a lawyer as well as a priest and had been deputy and senator in various national congresses.

It would seem strange that so many priests were connected with the Institute either as founders, directors, or professors, in light of the general disrepute it came to have among the clergy. In the early years, though, it was closely allied with the progressive, forward-looking segment of the clergy, both secular and regular, and underwent what one later director has called "a prolonged theological period" of incubation, which lasted until the 1840s. The Institute was not founded to compete with the church but rather to extend ecclesiastical control over secular education. It was nurtured in its infancy by the clergy, or at least an important element of the clergy, only to break away gradually until by the mid-1840s or a few years later it had become the alma mater of men committed to the new way of thought. The break may have been closely connected with Benito Juárez's first term as governor, which began in 1848. Juárez had transferred from the seminary to the Institute in the early years, had returned to serve briefly as the director just prior to assuming the governorship, and as governor, showed a vital interest in both primary and higher education within the state.[24]

What was the quality of instruction within the Institute, and how effective was it? The physical plant was old and probably, in view of the chronic shortage of funds in the state treasury, always in need of repair. The first eight years were spent in a large building on the Calle de San Nicolás. In 1835, it moved to the old buildings known as the monastery of San Pablo, the first home of the Dominican friars in Oaxaca before they constructed Santo Domingo late in the seventeenth century. These facilities left much to be desired. Students who matriculated in the medical curriculum lacked instruments with which to work; cadavers were used when available, but most of the time a paper anatomical model was used. The hospital of Belem did have an amphitheater, however, where the students could watch their professors perform operations. There was no botanical garden where plants could be studied and analyzed, but private citizens gave the students access to their gardens. Some pharmacy classes were held in the professors' pharmacies, in order to give the young men practical experience in the mixing and dispensing of drugs. Connected with the Institute was a museum, "a rather impoverished little embellishment," as one writer of the period described it, as well as a library, which was "not the most abundant."[25]

There were three libraries in the city—those of the seminary, the Institute, and the monastery of Santo Domingo. The last was by far the largest and best, with hundreds of rare volumes. They lay collecting dust and unused by the diminished number of friars, who allowed learning to decline in that religious order. Efforts were made to obtain the prior's consent to lease the library to the Institute, where it would be cared for and used. Over the years various letters were exchanged between the government and the prelates, but no agreement was ever reached.[26]

For the time and place, the courses of instruction seem to have kept abreast of recent developments in the sciences. Texts by the great French pathologists and physiologists François Magendie and Claude Bernard were in use in the Institute at least as early as 1856. The students also studied the texts and works of Eugène Soubeiran for pharmacy, A. Bouchardat and the toxicologist Orfila for chemistry, François Arago for astronomy, and C. S. M. Pouillet for elementary physics. All these were important theoreticians and experimenters, contemporary with the period. In philosophy, the studies by the Spanish traditionalist Jaime Luciano Balmes served as texts. In law, older but nonetheless important writings were used, by the Swiss jurists Jean Jacques Burlamaqui (1694–1748) and Emeric de Vattel (1714–67), on natural, political, and international law; and by the German Johann Gottlieb Heineccius (1681–1741), on natural and international law. The last author was one of the earliest scholars to treat jurisprudence as a natural science with first principles rather than merely as a means for expediency in solving problems. Furthermore, the teaching was not static and unchanging. Textbooks varied over the years, indicating the wide knowledge of the professors, their ability to judge developments in their fields and select writings to be studied accordingly, and their desire to keep abreast of the times.[27]

That the teachers were professionals in their fields and practiced their law or medicine or pharmacy while holding lectureships in the Institute did much to enhance the value of the instruction received by the students. Practicing politicians also taught law, lectured on the state and national constitutions, and undoubtedly gave the students a valuable insight into the workings of government.[28] All the instruction was free, completely financed by the state, making it easier for any young man who so desired and who could be spared by his family to obtain a higher education, a principle in keeping with the liberal creed, which placed so much emphasis on the education of youth as the bulwark of democracy. Through the careers of its graduates, so far-reaching was the influence of the Oaxacan Institute of Sciences and Arts throughout Mexico that it elicits comparison with the role played by the National Preparatory School in Mexico City during the

Porfiriato. The former was probably the leading center of liberalism in the second quarter of the nineteenth century whereas the latter fostered the spread of positivism during the last quarter.

Primary education within the city was not compulsory and probably only the children of the upper classes of society benefited. There were four municipal schools, a few private academies, a commercial college operated privately, and a boarding school for girls run by the Catholic Church. This Colegio de Niñas Educandas, founded in 1686, was heavily endowed and in effect was a charitable institution as well as a school for poor girls. In addition to these, there was a Lancasterian school, founded in 1824 and for a time attached to the Institute as its preparatory academy. The instruction here was mutual; that is, a teacher taught students who in turn assisted in teaching others. This evolved into the state normal school in 1861. Subjects taught in all these academies followed the same general pattern: reading, drawing, writing, multiplication tables and numbers sense, Spanish grammar, some geography, perhaps the rudiments of geometry, Christian doctrine, manners, and the rights and duties of citizens.[29]

THE CENTRAL DISTRICT

The Central District of Oaxaca State, containing approximately 215 square miles, was the smallest but most densely populated of the twenty-five districts. It encompassed the valley encircling Oaxaca City; its boundaries ran along the ridges of the mountains surrounding the plain and crossed the valley floor where the hills approached each other.[30] The district approximated a county in geographical terms; politically it had much more significance, for each district was headed by a *jefe político* (a "political chief" or "boss") who served as intermediary between the office of the governor and the municipalities.

The changeable Mexican political situation between the time of independence and the beginning of the Reform movement, during which period Conservatives and Liberals, Centralists and Federalists were in and out of power, had brought about frequent alterations in the internal divisions of the states. Depending on which political group was currently in control, Oaxaca had been divided into departments varying in number from eight to eighteen. When Santa Anna was last in office (1853–55), the state had a strong centralistic goverment with a corresponding deemphasis on territorial subdivi-

MAP 2. The Central District. *Source:* Based on the *Mapa de las localidades del Valle de Oaxaca,* drawn by Cecil Welte of Oaxaca City.

sions within the entity. The Liberals who came to power with the Revolution of Ayutla in Oaxaca in late 1855 inherited the previous organization of eight departments, each headed by a departmental chief or governor who was appointed by the state governor. Not until two years later, in March 1858, was the territory of the state divided into twenty-five districts.[31]

The district was not in turn subdivided in legal terms, but in practical usage; that is, in the implementation of laws, in gathering statistics, and in making reports to the state government, a curious mixture of ecclesiastical and political subdivision was employed. To a resident of an Indian village, his municipio (roughly equivalent to the township in the United States) boundaries were the most important, if he knew them. Indeed, many municipios did and still do dispute their boundaries with neighboring villages.[32] To a cleric, the parish organization was the most important. Parishes were large, each usually containing several villages and churches. But for purposes of keeping records of births, deaths, marriages, and confirmations, there was only one parish church. Before the church's role in keeping the records of such vital statistics was abolished, governments necessarily had to place much emphasis on parochial organization. In the Central District, there appear to have been only six parish churches—two in the city, one each in the suburbs of Jalatlaco and the Marquesado, and one each in the villages of Tlalixtac and Cuilapan. To a politician, a combination of the two subdivisions mentioned above would hold importance. Decrees had to be promulgated in each municipality; the aspiring officeholder would have contacts in each village; in voting, the parish seat was the scene of the second balloting in a series of primary elections. Accordingly, the district had no real significance except for the convenience it provided the governor and perhaps the political party in maintaining close control on developments within the state.[33]

Within the Central District as of the date of its organization in 1858, there were twenty-nine towns and villages, including Oaxaca City and its suburbs, which were still legally separate from the capital; eighteen haciendas of varying sizes, none extremely large; fourteen ranchos or farms, usually devoted to cattle raising; three *labores,* or farms devoted exclusively to the cultivation of crops; two sugar mills; and three grain mills. (See Appendix B.) It is impossible to arrive at an exact figure for the population of this area, but it approximated 45,000. (See Appendix A.) The Valley of Oaxaca lay in Zapotec country, and the inhabitants of some villages continued to speak that language in mid-nineteenth century. A few of the towns in the Central District, such as San Andrés Ixtlahuaca, San Pedro Ixtlahuaca, and Santa María Azompa, were Mixtec in origin and spoke that language. Most of the pueblos, however, were predominantly Spanish-speaking by 1850.[34]

The economy of the Central District was based mainly on subsistence agriculture. Maize, beans, and wheat were the staple crops and probably ranked in that order in terms of the amount produced and the income derived. Sugarcane had been grown for a long period but never on a large scale. After the Reform period ended, the cane would become the large money crop of the valley. Alfalfa was produced in large quantities to supply feed for the cattle. A variety of other foods was raised, but not on a significant scale. San Pablo la Raya grew peanuts, for example, in addition to the maize and beans to supply the inhabitants of that village; three haciendas grew large amounts of tomatoes; and peas, sweet potatoes, avocados, and some citrus fruits were raised. The most diversified farming in the district was practiced on the haciendas, but even there the staple crops received major attention and all else was of secondary importance.[35]

Farming methods in the Central Distirct, as elsewhere throughout the state, remained unchanged from those employed in the colonial era; the Indians continued to sow and reap in the same manner as their forefathers, taking much from the soil and returning little, so that a large portion of the land was in the process of becoming exhausted. As a result, the area produced barely enough food to supply the needs of its own population. In addition to the low level of food production, the number of farm animals kept in the Central District was small compared to the population. In 1857, Lafond counted only sixty-six milk cows in the entire district. There were also 1,610 sheep, 1,433 oxen (the major means of transport), 1,400 goats, 611 pigs, and a few burros and other assorted animals. Although Lafond did not count beef cattle, their number undoubtedly would have maintained the same small proportion.[36]

Contrasted with the rather primitive methods used in growing crops, the system for distribution was well adapted to the region. Each village had its weekly market day, which always attracted Indians from surrounding towns to bring their products to sell and to buy their supplies. This system was used even in the capital, where Saturday was the day for major purchasing. A network of wagon roads and horse trails connected the villages with each other and with Oaxaca City and were generally kept in a good state of repair. The upkeep was a function of the municipios, but on some occasions the political chief intervened to order work done or obtained small amounts of money from state funds when the expenditures were too great for the pueblos alone to handle.[37]

Life within the villages of the Central District at best was dull.

Since the towns all had patron saints, there were usually annual church festivals, some of which lasted for several days and attracted residents of the capital to the merrymaking. For example, the last day in the Octave of the Feast of All Souls was observed in San Felipe del Agua with a day's celebration, the highlights of which were pantomime scenes performed by the local people. For two weeks following the Day of All Souls, there were daily festivities in Santa Lucía del Camino, not far from the eastern edge of Oaxaca City, which always drew large crowds.[38] In many cases, some portion of their communal lands, if the villages possessed any, were set aside for the purpose of financing the annual festivals.

But for most of the year, the inhabitants of the villages knew an immutable routine of occasional work in the fields interspersed with long periods of idleness. This and other factors led to occasional crime and drunkenness.[39] One town, Huayapan, was particularly noted for the bad sorts it turned out, and some roads leading to certain villages were considered dangerous to travel because of bandits.

Each village presented the same drab appearance—adobe huts and stores, some few of which might be whitewashed, crowded around a central plaza in front of the church. Some of the Central District pueblos, despite their indistinct appearances, retained different characteristics or specialized in certain products that served to set them off from the other towns. San Felipe del Agua, resting at the foot of the mountain, had a somewhat cooler climate than Oaxaca City and wealthier residents from the capital maintained summer homes there; San Antonio de la Cal produced little food but derived its livelihood from lime, which it supplied the capital and other villages for use in the preparation of corn meal; Santa María del Tule was frequently visited to view the large tree in the courtyard of its church; the two Coyotepec towns produced black pottery.

Education within the Central District was a sporadic affair. There were between fifteen and twenty primary schools, excluding those of Oaxaca City, scattered throughout the district. In some, only the subjects of reading, writing, and Christian doctrine were taught. The picture was rather desolate: the teachers usually possessed barely enough knowledge to set them above the students, the municipalities were chronically short of funds and could not meet the necessary expenses of operating schools, with the result in some villages residents had to contribute to pay the teachers' salaries, which were so low that good teachers could not be hired. In addition to these difficulties, the schoolmaster was frequently the secretary to the alcalde, or mayor, so that a poorly educated man held two jobs and could not devote full time to teaching the village youth. Enough students attended the schools to make the ratio between school population and total population compare favorably at that time with some of the most educationally advanced areas in western Europe, but quality and results left much to be desired. At that, schools within the Central District were far better than in areas farther away from the state capital.[40]

The production of handicrafts by the valley towns is a revival of ancient arts effected in the twentieth century. In the mid-nineteenth century, the arts of weaving, potterymaking woodcarving, cabinet-making, and metalworking were still carried on but only as shadows of what they had been in colonial times. There was little demand for these items except to satisfy individual and local needs—pots for the kitchen, blankets for the bed, wardrobes in which to store clothes. Throughout the ensuing Liberal regime, the leaders of the state continually lamented the fact that there were no schools in which the Indian artisans of the valley could be trained to apply their native talents to income-producing home industries.[41] Thus, save for few exceptions, the towns were not known, as they are today, by the handicraft wares produced.

THE STATE

In contrast to the mestizo-dominated Central Valley, with a substantial creole minority present in the state capital, the population of the remainder of the state was primarily pure Indian, with a small mestizo element also present. The population by districts is given in Appendix A, but figures should be taken as indications rather than as exact.

The Indian population was not homogeneous but was instead divided into some sixteen different groups, each speaking its own language. By far the largest in number were the Zapotecs, who occupied much of the central and eastern areas of the state. Second to them were the Mixtecs, who were found predominantly in the western region. The other groups—Nahua, Mazatec, Chontal, Zoque, Mixe, Chatino, Ixcatec, Ojitec, Cuicatec, Chinatec, Chocho, Huave, Triqui, Amuzgo—were all much smaller in number and as a consequence played a less important role in social and economic evolution of the state. In addition to the variety of Indian cultures, another

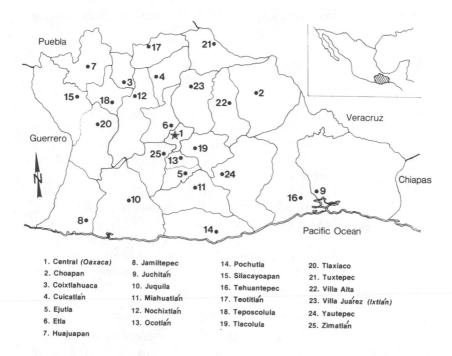

1. Central (Oaxaca)
2. Choapan
3. Coixtlahuaca
4. Cuicatlán
5. Ejutla
6. Etla
7. Huajuapan
8. Jamiltepec
9. Juchitán
10. Juquila
11. Miahuatlán
12. Nochixtlán
13. Ocotlán
14. Pochutla
15. Silacayoapan
16. Tehuantepec
17. Teotitlán
18. Teposcolula
19. Tlacolula
20. Tlaxiaco
21. Tuxtepec
22. Villa Alta
23. Villa Juárez (Ixtlán)
24. Yautepec
25. Zimatlán

MAP 3. The State of Oaxaca with the twenty-five districts created during the Reform. The district seats, represented by a dot, bear the same name as the districts in which they are located, with two exceptions: the seat of the Central District was also the state capital, Oaxaca City; and the district seat of Villa Juárez was Ixtlán. *Source:* Based on a map in *El estado de Oaxaca* by Matías Romero (1886).

characteristic of the population was the way in which small pockets of one group could be found completely cut off from the main body and surrounded by alien groups. The presence of the few Mixtec towns in the Zapotec territory of the Central District and the other parts of the three valley arms provides an example of this phenomenon.

The variety of the Indian groups and the persistence of the Indians in maintaining their cultures, as well as the isolated situations in which most of them lived, meant that there was little integration of any type—social, political, economic, or cultural—in the state. It was difficult for any government, of whatever persuasion or philosophy, to control closely and effectively the population of the state. Consequently, the vast majority of the Oaxacans, those living outside the

Central Valley area, were largely left alone except in times of national emergency or threats to the state's controlling faction. At such times, the Indians would be prevailed upon to support one side or the other, impressed into the armies of the contending factions, forced to form work gangs, robbed of their scarce agricultural and financial resources, or at least forced to share such resources with either or both sides involved in the disputes. On the whole, then, the Indians played only a passive, nevertheless important, role in the state and were brought into the political and military affairs when their muscle-power, numbers, or resources were needed. Otherwise, they remained uninvolved.

There were exceptions, depending on the circumstances and habits of some groups. For example, the Zapotecs of the Sierra region to the north of the Central District seemed to be inclined toward liberalism and in time played a crucial role in helping the Liberals maintain a foothold in the state after they had been expelled from Oaxaca City by invading Conservatives. Again, during the French Intervention and the invasion of Oaxaca in 1864–65, the Mixtecs, resentful of Liberal politicians and army officers, aided the imperial army willingly.

It would seem that most of the Indians were traditionalists, tenaciously holding on to their old ways and resistant to change. Such traditionalism undoubtedly was rooted in the early colonial period when the Indians became the wards of the state and the servants of their Spanish masters, who intended to Hispanicize and Christianize them. In this process, the Zapotecs appear to have been the most adaptable, but it would be difficult to determine whether this was because they were merely closer to a greater number of Spanish colonists by virtue of their location in the arms of the Central Valley, or because they found themselves in agreement with Spanish ways. In reading the colonial history of the region, one forms the impression that perhaps the Valley Zapotecs quickly learned that the best way to resist Spanish encroachment was to learn the ways of the Spanish colonists—to adapt only to the degree that would enable them to resist more strongly. This is particularly true in regard to land ownership. The colonial records show that, for a variety of reasons, the Valley Indians were able to hold on to much of their land throughout the colonial regime.[42]

After independence, the white-mestizo government and society in the state capital maintained contact with and minimal control over the population outside the Central Valley area through agents of the government—the department governors of centralist regimes and the political chiefs of the Liberal administrations—and through the institution of the church, which played a less important role than is popularly imagined. In the early colonial period, Dominican missionaries surged enthusiastically into Oaxaca in great numbers to evangelize the native population. The order built a number of monasteries throughout the region to serve as centers for their missionary work. So strong were the Dominicans and so significantly did they view their work in Oaxaca that of the four provinces of the order that came to be established in Mexico, one was contiguous with what came to be Oaxaca State when political independence was secured from Spain. However substantial the work of the missionaries in the early colonial era, much of what they accomplished tended to wither and die in the later period as the order declined in strength, numbers, and influence. By 1850, the monasteries established in Juchitán, Ocotlán, Petapa, Tehuantepec, San Mateo del Mar, Tlaxiaco, Teitipac, Yanhuitlán, Teposcolula, Coixtlahuaca, and Etla were either empty of monks and fast falling into ruins or had only small numbers of religious. Furthermore, as will be seen in the discussion of the disentailment of ecclesiastical properties, by the time of the Reform none of these establishments seemingly was well endowed with income-producing real estate.[43] On the whole, the influence of the religious orders in Indian Oaxaca was only minimal by the middle part of the nineteenth century, for none of the other regular orders present in the state had ever concerned themselves to any significant extent with the rural areas.

Nor did the secular church have much control over the Indians, and little influence, except in a residual sense, primarily because the number of priests was small compared with the size of the population ministered to by the church. This scarcity of priests was further accentuated by their tendency to remain in the state capital to enjoy the comparative comfort of the city rather than to live among their parishioners in the more remote, backward Indian towns and villages. Governor José María Díaz Ordaz reported to the state legislature in 1858 that there were 330 priests for the 140 parishes in the diocese.[44] Significantly, he used figures dating from over a decade earlier, in 1847. If we assume hypothetically that approximately a hundred priests habitually remained in Oaxaca City because of their duties or their predilections—and this figure does not seem extraordinarily

high when compared with earlier assessments—and if we assume that
the Central District's population was 45,000 out of a total of 548,000,
this meant that there were 230 priests for the remaining 503,000
Catholics in the state, or one priest for roughly every 2,200 inhabitants in the diocese.[45] But one must also take into consideration the
fact that those priests who lived among their charges would have
responsibility for several Indian villages in their large parishes and
would tend to remain in the parish seat for much of the year, thereby
leaving numbers of Indians without the services of the church and not
under the constant supervision of a priest. Thus the Indians were left
alone by the church to a large extent and, as a consequence, they
continued to practice their unique forms of religion, a highly syncretistic Catholicism, with little interference or direction from the
church. Controversies over fees for priests and the decline in the
produce of the tithe were as marked in the state at large as they were
in the Valley region.[46]

Few schools operated in the isolated areas.[47] The only hope the
Indians had for advancement in this field lay in their willingness or
ability to escape to the state capital, as some few managed to do. But
on the whole, the Indians grew up illiterate, suspicious of outsiders, in
poor health, and living in a subsistence economy.

All in all, Oaxaca state was in a period of depression by 1850.
Cochineal, the red dye, had brought great prosperity to certain regions, including the Central District, in the late colonial period; by the
1850s it was still being produced, but on a much smaller scale. In
earlier years, the fertile fields on the southern edge of Oaxaca City
had been completely given over to the cultivation of the cactus; by
mid-nineteenth century, the plants had disappeared and the fields
were being used increasingly to raise sugarcane. The peak year of
production of cochineal was 1774, when 1,558,125 pounds were
manufactured in the state. The price per pound that year was 2.18
pesos, yielding a revenue of 3,396,712 pesos. Then other areas in the
world, principally Algeria and Guatemala, began to cultivate the
nopal cactus and the insect that nurtured on it to produce the dye,
and still later a vegetable dye was discovered in Europe that gave the
same red colors. As a result, production declined in Oaxaca. In 1851,
only 866,400 pounds were manufactured, which brought 61 centavos
per pound for a total yield of 528,504 pesos. In some years the taxes
derived from cochineal production were not enough to finance the
office where the registry of the industry was kept.[48]

Nevertheless, some large fortunes had been made in cochineal. Among larger producers were the Esperón and Maqueo families, the latter of Milanese origin, who would buy comparatively large amounts of disentailed church property during the coming Reform. And Diego Innes, an Englishman who dealt in cochineal in the Miahuatlán area, was moneylender and financier in Oaxaca City in this period.[49]

Mining activity within the state, never very substantial in the best of times, was in a decline. During the colonial regime it had flourished to a degree, but after independence, foreigners gained control and began operations in the moutainous region to the north of the Central District. Through a series of mistakes—bad judgment and illegal methods—the company they organized went bankrupt. After the failure of that enterprise, mining was limited to small-scale activities, and the amount of gold and silver produced was only a fraction of the potential.[50] When mining flourished, Oaxaca City and the Central District derived considerable benefit, because there the materials needed in the mines were bought, there the miners brought their ore, from there the ore was transported to larger centers to be minted into coins.

Manufacturing, even of textiles, was nonexistent in Oaxaca, except for a few small factories turning out aguardiente and pulque, popular alcoholic beverages, and soap.[51] In 1843, the total imports of goods amounted to 1,779,572 pesos, while the exported products from the entire state brought in 1,182,662 pesos, leaving an unfavorable balance-of-trade deficit of almost 600,000 pesos.[52]

One of the major reasons for the depressed economy was Oaxaca's isolation from the rest of the Republic. The topography of the state made the construction of roads and their upkeep a mammoth undertaking. The route to Puebla and Mexico City was by way of an unimproved highway through Tehuacán. The road to the Istmus of Tehuantepec was likewise an irregular series of horse trails and wagon roads. In November 1857, work was begun on reconstructing the Tehuacán highway, but war would come along to interrupt the operations. On several later occasions, work would resume only to be interrupted again by war. Connections with Veracruz were somewhat better but left much to be desired. Roads to the state's Pacific ports were only trails much of the way. Mail was slow; stage travel to the national capital meant an arduous trip of several days' duration.[53] It is rather amazing that the economic activities carried on resulted in as high a level of production, exchange, and revenue as they did.

The internal conditions in the state—remoteness from the center and isolation of regions and groups from each other, widespread illiteracy, economic depression—meant that when the Liberals gained control and attempted to enforce their program of socioeconomic reform, they were faced with tremendous obstacles. In the first place, the influence of the Liberals outside their immediate areas of control in the state capital and in the Central Valley diminished markedly the farther one moved from these loci of power. Second, their program, which had its origins in the middle class and was bourgeoisie-oriented and -directed, naturally would have little appeal or meaning to the rural peasantry. In this regard, the Reform in Oaxaca was largely confined to the small central part of the state with only occasional, sporadic activity in other areas, activity that usually centered around military operations or attempts to redistribute property. Thus, in an important sense, Oaxaca during the Reform era was a microcosm of the larger Mexico, where the success of the Liberals was also most notable in the areas over which they had the greatest influence and where the implementation of the Reform measures lagged in peripheral regions.

CHAPTER 2

THE BEGINNING OF THE REFORM, 1856–57

THE REVOLUTION OF AYUTLA, which broke out in 1854, toppled Santa Anna from power. It brought home from exile in the United States a group of men who had been forced out of the country because of their opposition to the dictator. Among them was Benito Juárez, former governor of Oaxaca, staunch Liberal and firm democrat. In little over a year, Juárez was serving as minister of justice in the cabinet of President Juan Alvarez, around whom the opponents of Santa Anna had rallied and who had assumed the presidency when the old dictator fled the country. This revolution of 1854–55 was the most severe of Mexico's struggles up to that time, but because its center of operations was in the central plateau area and farther north, and because Oaxaca was isolated, the war did not greatly affect the southern state. In November 1855, however, there was a delayed reaction in Oaxaca. Juárez, as minister, had written a law, which the president promulgated, limiting the privileges of the military and the church in matters of trials and justice. When a barracks revolt broke out in Oaxaca City against the law, Ignacio Comonfort, who had quickly succeeded Alvarez, decided that Juárez should go there as governor in order to quell the troubles. The Oaxacan accepted the position and left the national capital for his native state late in December 1855. By this transfer, the movement known as the Reform was spread to Oaxaca.[1]

THE JUÁREZ ADMINISTRATION

With his characteristic diligence, Juárez began implementing his administrative program of reform even during the prolonged festivities staged to celebrate his return.[2] To a large degree, it was a matter of resuming what he had begun in his previous gubernatorial term, which had ended four years earlier. That interim period, filled with the hardships and dreams of his New Orleans exile and the fighting and planning of the Revolution of Ayutla, now seemed only a brief interruption to the sense of continuity his actions brought to the office of state governor. Once again he had the opportunity to begin new projects and to conclude old ones, all of them designed to improve the conditions of Oaxaca and the welfare of its people and to eliminate the arbitrary government of privileged interests.

One of his first actions, taken on the day after his arrival, was to set the date for elections of Oaxacan delegates to the national congress that would write the new constitution of the Republic. In the following weeks, he reopened the Institute of Sciences and Arts, closed during Santa Anna's most recent presidency, and placed his old friend Marcos Pérez in the rectorship; dissolved the permanent army in Oaxaca and strengthened the National Guard; elaborated a system of public health in the state and organized a hospital in the capital; and undertook various public works projects, all on a small scale but each one significant to the populace. Bridges were rebuilt, roads were reparied, work was begun once more to complete the Government Palace in Oaxaca City, a building was modified to serve as a prison.[3]

Besides local affairs, he was also involved in the national program of Reform that the Liberal administration was beginning to shape in Mexico City. That program was based on principles with their roots in the French Enlightenment and Revoltion and in the writings of Jeremy Bentham in England. In the process of transfer from Europe to Mexico and in the debates over the elaboration of the Liberal creed within Mexico in the turbulent quarter century following independence, certain ingredients were modified to fit the Mexican situation. Cardinal points of Mexican liberalism included social and judicial equality as opposed to privilege, individualism as opposed to corporatism, and an emphasis on the expansion of freedom as opposed to a limitation on rights.

The Mexican Liberals believed that all the troubles that had developed since independence could be blamed on a Conservative approach to nationhood. The Conservatives continued to focus on the cultural and political legacy that Spain had implanted in its colony during three centuries of control. In the Mexican Conservatives' view, although Spain had ruled by arbitrary decree, the arbitrariness was tempered by the mother country's concern for the well-being of the people. Thus the Indians were protected and the spiritual welfare of all was fostered by the Catholic Church. There was an "aristocracy of wealth and merit," which respected authority, guaranteed stability, and promoted advancement. The Mexican Conservatives had come to put their faith in a narrow, centralized government buttressed by the army and the church as instruments of control and regulation. They had allowed these two agents to maintain their privileges and, in the case of the church, its wealth, necessary for them to function as guardians against violent upheaval. It was only through such restraints that Mexico could become strong and take its place among the great nations of the world.

Opposed to this creed was the ideology of liberalism. The Liberals also desired a strong, respected, progressive nation. But the way to achieve this was not through slow, controlled, evolutionary growth under the auspices of a government run by a small elite who looked to the past for models and philosophy. All of Mexico's ills derived from the unwillingness of the Conservatives to realize that other groups and interests needed to be taken into consideration and had the right to share in both the responsibilities and benefits of government. The Liberals believed in popular sovereignty. Their democracy demanded that all citizens be given the rights to own property, to be free to achieve prosperity, to seek the benefits of education, and to have equal access to courts and elected office. The church and the army became the targets of the Liberals. The church must be forced to surrender its wealth, be denied its political influence and social control, and be relegated to the realm of caring for the spiritual welfare of its members. Mexico could advance only if the church's real estate and its financial reserves were tapped so that the property could be put in circulation through sale and thus be made available to individuals. This would give people a greater stake in the future and make them more concerned with governmental processes. The army must be restrained from interfering in political affairs. Thus it must be reduced in size and controlled by a civilian government. The most equitable form of government was a federalism that recognized regional distinctions and worked to harmonize those differences. Mexico should become more closely tied to the industrial nations through free trade; internally, all barriers to commerce should be eliminated. The Liberals' view of what Mexico should be was predicated on the idea that the state must protect rights and promote prosperity: that it had the duty to restructure institutions and reform practices in order to create a nation whose benefits would be given to all its citizens, not just the elite. Government and people cooperating in a program of hard work and thrift would in time realize the end goal of the Liberal philosophy—the perfection of man's estate.[4]

It was this program of social, economic, and political reform that the Liberals were committed to develop, now that they were in power after their Ayutla victory. Juárez himself, as author of the law on judicial reform, issued the previous autumn while he was a member of the cabinet, had already played a major role in forming that national policy.[5] Indeed, one of the reasons he had been sent to Oaxaca as governor was to put down an incipient rebellion in the national army contingents garrisoned in his native state, a rebellion that centered on a protest against the Juárez Law. This explains why, eleven days after his arrival in Oaxaca City, he decreed the dissolution of the permanent army in the state and replaced it with the National Guard. Soldiers were given the choice of mustering out of the army to return to their homes or transferring to the Guard. But this action was also in keeping with Juárez's policy in his previous gubernatorial administratin of deemphasizing the standing army and strengthening the National Guard. He believed that many of Mexico's ills, especially the frequent changes of government, were caused by military interference in civilian affairs. In his move to eliminate the threat posed by the army by organizing a civil militia, to be under the governor's command, he received the enthusiastic support of several leading businessmen and lawyers in Oaxaca City.[6]

After a few months in office, Juárez and his subordinates found that most of their attention was centering on implementing national policy as opposed to developing local programs. Two measures, a national decree that called for the alienation of real estate held in mortmain by ecclesiastical and civil corporations, and the promulgation of a national constitution, particularly required his attention, not only because of the reforms they embodied but also because of local opposition that developed to the new national charter and that required forceful action to contain it.

The sweeping measure alienating corporate properties was promulgated on June 25, 1856. Drafted by the Minister of the Treasury, Miguel Lerdo do Tejada, and consequently known as the Lerdo Law, the decree did not call for the expropriation of property but rather aimed at converting corporate wealth from real estate to liquid assets. Its provisions called for the sale of properties to tenants and stipulated a period of three months following the publication of the law in each locality for this process to take place. The sale prices of the properties were to be calculated on the rent paid as representing six per cent of valuation. If the tenants did not wish to purchase, they lost their right to acquire the property after the three months expired. The subrenter then received preference, and if the latter did not desire to buy the property, or if there was no subrenter, the real estate was to be put up for sale in public auction after being denounced before the local authorities. The purchaser then had to pay the denouncer one-eighth of the selling price, deducting that portion from the amount to be received by the corporation. This provision was included to encourage the ecclesiastical bodies to reveal their real assets so that they could receive the full price in payment. Aimed at the property controlled by the Church, the Lerdo Law also applied to properties owned and administered by civil corporations; that is, town councils and Indian communities.

The law was published in Oaxaca on July 3, and the regulatory statute of July 30 appeared in the state's official newspaper on August 15.[7] Within two weeks the adjudications began, with the few large haciendas near the capital receiving most attention. By the end of the month these had been sold. Other smaller properties were adjudicated during the remainder of the summer, but the end of the three-month period saw a real spurt of activity. On October 3, in the twelve hours between eight in the morning and eight that night, 191 pieces of property, mostly urban houses and lots, were denounced in Oaxaca City. The newspaper reported the activity "a highly satisfactory spectacle," and further commented:

> The Office of the Government of the Central District was full of all kinds of people who, grouping themselves around the chief officer, presented him their denunciations of urban properties, either to substitute themselves for the tenants who did not wish to adjudicate or to request the sale, each one wanting his petition to be received first so that someone else might not have the chance to denounce the property. There we saw merchants, brokers, lawyers, doctors, artisans, notaries, farmers, employees of all branches of the government, etc. Good! This fact shows that the public spirit is reborn, that there is life and movement, and with a public spirit the fatherland will advance. The houses denounced exceed 190.[8]

In the months following, there was a steady business conducted by the agencies of the state in receiving the denunciations, holding the auctions, and recording the sales and transfers. This process and the impact of the law will be discussed more fully in Chapter 6.

There was real fear among the Liberals in Mexico City that the Lerdo Law would provoke an outbreak of major proportions, if not civil war. In Michoacán, Querétaro, and Puebla, disturbances, risings, and isolated revolts by Indian communities, which were led to believe that their property titles were being taken from them and alienated, prompted José María Lafragua, the minister of Gobernación (interior), to take measures to ensure the peaceful enforcement of the law. On September 6, he wrote to Governor Juárez that President Comonfort had learned, to his profound disgust, that certain members of the ecclesiastical hierarchy had issued pastorals and circulars attacking the law and inciting the populace to impede enforcement. Such actions had to be stopped before they spread so that the national administration would not be forced into a position of having to punish the perpetrators. Juárez was ordered to prevent such circulars from being published and read in churches and to seize any that had already been printed. If churchmen caused any disturbances or incited disobedience, they were to be apprehended and turned over to the competent authorities. If this were not feasible, the offending clergy were to be forced to change their places of residence for some other location where their influence would not be so pernicious. As a last resort, they were to be sent to Mexico City where the national government would take proper action.[9]

Comonfort and his minister could have checked their anxiety regarding disturbances in Oaxaca. There were none. In the Central District, no priest protested publicly and the bishop remained silent. The policy of the Oaxaca diocese seemed to be one of passivity. In the sale of property, which continued apace, most of the members of the clergy who administered the real estate refused to hand over titles to the government's agents for delivery to the new owners, on the excuse that they had no authority to surrender them. But this impediment was easily overcome, for the law made provisions in such an event, and the agents merely interceded in behalf of the church and registered the titles in the names of the purchaser. One priest, the prior of the Carmelite monastery of Carmen Alto, decided to abide by the provisions of the law and notify the civil authorities of all the properties owned by his order in the city. The object of the prior was to receive the full sale price for the monastery's treasury rather than have an eighth-part deducted and paid to whomever might by chance denounce the property. This incident was publicized by the Liberal state newspaper, which used it to hold up the prior as an example of a good priest who was patriotic and law-abiding.[10]

In regard to the promulgation of the new national constitution, Oaxacan Bishop José Agustín Domínguez mustered his priests to oppose the charter openly and vociferously. Twelve months earlier, the constitutional congress had opened its sessions in Mexico City. It had the dual purpose of serving not only as a legislative body but also of writing a new fundamental charter. Its work was thus slow and the new constitution was not finished until a year later. There had been a long and heated debate midway through the year when the question of religious tolerance came up for discussion. Many groups sent letters and petitions to the congress asking that the principle not be included as an article in the constitution. Bishop Domínguez of Oaxaca wrote to the secretaries of the congress on July 15, 1856, having been requested to do so by his cathedral chapter. He asked that the proposed Article 15 be disapproved and reasoned that if religious tolerance were established, the majority of the population would return to idolatrous practices. Undoubtedly, behind his petition lay the realization that the large Indian population in Oaxaca, isolated to a great degree and with only infrequent contact with priests, was never far removed from the pagan practices passed down through the generations following the conquest; the church in that southern region could never be certain of the firmness of the faith of the Indians. Religious tolerance meant that Protestant missionaries would be free to operate in his diocese and they might have great success in winning converts among the Indians. This in turn would bring further divisiveness to an already divided nation.[11]

As a result of such arguments and pressure, the proposed article was returned to committee where it was permanently tabled in the closing days of the congress. This victory of the moderates of the Liberal party and the Conservatives was a limited one, however, for delegate Ponciano Arriaga then presented a resolution that became Article 123 of the constitution, giving the federal government the power to intervene in matters of religious observance and ecclesiastical discipline. This article, in addition to other threats to the church written into the constitution, forced the prelate in Oaxaca to take a stand, even though it was the Lerdo Law seven months earlier that had had the most immediate impact on the church but that had elicited no major response from the Oaxacan priests.[12]

Opposition by the Conservatives to this Constitution of 1857 took many forms. Rather than swear to uphold the charter, some government officials resigned their posts. It was reported in the press that these were few in number: in the entire state, only six or seven members of town councils, some brokers, a subaltern in the office that administered stamped paper, a postal employee, three magistrates on the state supreme court, three members of the council of government, one member on the health commission, and three other employees holding minor positions. Some of these resignations were, in fact, removals. Eight brokers were removed from the regulatory board of their profession because they refused to take the oath and were further prohibited from engaging in business. Those who were appointed to replace the Conservative officials were prominent Liberals.[13]

The great majority of priests were also opposed to the constitution. Among the events scheduled to celebrate the new charter was a Te Deum to be sung in the cathedral at noon on March 23, with all the state officials in attendance. On the 21st, Juárez had written to Bishop Domínguez a polite and formal note requesting that plans for the ceremony be made and asking the fee for the service so that the government might make arrangements to pay. Domínguez replied the following day, punctiliously and unenthusiastically, that he would arrange for the ceremony even though he disagreed with and had protested against certain articles in the constitution. The church service was held as scheduled, with the bishop in attendance, but an insult to the Liberals was intended by having a prebend and not the bishop sing the Te Deum.[14]

A week following the festivities celebrating the promulgation of the constitution, the churchmen in Oaxaca took a definitive stand against the new charter. The wavering of the past months abruptly ended. The bishop directed a circular to all the diocesan clergy on April 1, in which he warned them that since the constitution had been published, it could be expected that in the normal course of events demands soon would be made upon the priests to take the oath to uphold it. Not only were they prohibited from doing so, but they were to advise their parishioners against compliance. If any Catholic who took the oath later appeared at the confessional, he was to be told that absolution could not be granted until he abjured and the political authority before whom the oath was taken was so informed of the retraction. Similar actions were taken by all the Mexican bishops in their respective dioceses.[15]

On the same date that Domínguez in Oaxaca City was composing his circular, in the national capital Ignacio de la Llave, the Minister of Gobernación in Comonfort's cabinet, was also sending to all state governors a circular designed to counteract the bishops' move. The president had disposed, he reported, that any priest who abused the pulpit or took any kind of action to disturb the public tranquility was to be sent to Mexico City promptly for investigation and possible punishment.[16] Thus priests and populace were caught in a vise and the screw had been turned the first time. If civil employees failed to take the oath, they were dismissed and economic retaliation was forthcoming. If they took the oath, they would be opposing the dictates of the church and would suffer spiritual reprisals. Priests were faced with the choice of Caesar or God, with no middle ground on which to stand. Either they supported the government, only to be suspended as priests; or they supported the church, only to risk the threat of exile or imprisonment by the civil power.

In general, priests either remained loyal to the church or kept silent, whereas the civil employees took the oath; but there were isolated examples of those who dared to speak out one way or the other. One bureaucrat, José María Prieto, retracted his oath on April 25. Undoubtedly there were others. On April 9, a priest, Plácido Anaya, announced that in fulfilling his duties he had resolved to administer the Eucharist even to those who might have sworn to uphold the constitution, and that sick persons desiring to receive the rite of extreme unction could—"at any hour of the night"—send for him. The official newspaper printed this announcement under the headline, "A True Priest," and further commented: "The noble conduct of the enlightened Sr. Anaya is a relevant proof that, if in the clergy there exist men who through ignorance or the allure of social interests forget their evangelical mission, there are, on the other hand, those who do not heed the prohibitions of their prelates when such prohibitions are not in consonance with their duties."[17]

By the time these attitudes were becoming clear—attitudes that showed the Liberal government determined to have its way and the church determined to stand in opposition—the Easter season, 1857, was at hand. This gave some few priests a convenient and dramatic opportunity to demonstrate the depth of their convictions. Father

Anaya's declaration appeared in the press on Holy Thursday. On Good Friday, when the churches were filled with the faithful, one Franciscan friar and one secular priest in Oaxaca City preached inflammatory sermons against the latest actions of the government and almost succeeded in inciting their audiences to riot. Franciscan Friar Anselmo Ruiz was particularly angry. At the end of his sermon, in which he had tongue-lashed the government, he stepped down from the pulpit, strode over to a statue of Christ on the cross, removed the crown of thorns, pushed it hard onto his own head, and, as blood streamed down his face and neck, shouted: "Christ Jesus, this is the constitution we must swear to," and swung his arm toward the cross. "If you are truly religious, my people, rise up to defend your clergy and the Pope." Word of both disturbances spread quickly throughout the city and was brought to the attention of government officials, who held inquiries that same day. As a result, Ruiz was imprisoned. The other priest had ended his heated remarks with an apology for departing from the subject of his sermon and for this reason was not punished by the government.[18]

Easter week was chosen by the national government as the time to issue a third law of reform, which struck directly at the church and which further heightened the tension. On Holy Saturday, April 11, the minister of justice and ecclesiastical affairs promulgated a decree that regulated fees for various services, such as baptism and burial, performed by priests. This matter had long perplexed church-state relations and had been the cause of many disputes and ill will through the years. The decree included a schedule of fees, which varied from diocese to diocese. The poor were to be charged nothing—if they were, the offending priest would be fined triple the amount charged. Governors were to determine the subsistence wage in their states, and anyone receiving less than this amount would be considered poor and, therefore, exempt. If a parish priest refused burial because the family could not or would not pay the fee, the local political authority was empowered to intervene and order interment.[19]

On this occasion Bishop Domínguez was again conciliatory. Undoubtedly, he privately disputed the right of the state to interfere in such matters, but perhaps he recognized that regulation was necessary in light of the long history of disputes over fees. He instructed his priests to abide by the law, adding that they were not to participate in politics or preach sermons with political overtones.[20]

After April 1857, and for the following weeks, the battle shifted to the political arena within the state of Oaxaca. As an outcome of the shift, the Conservative press in the state capital was muzzled and the Conservatives were deprived of representation in the state legislature. To counterbalance the growing preponderance of the Liberals in Oaxaca, one of the Conservative leaders, Juan Bautista Carriedo, who had written two important books on the state's development, began publishing a newspaper, which he entitled *El Creyente* ("The Believer"). The second issue, which appeared on May 26, 1857, carried three articles by a religious, the deacon Ignacio Núñez Audelo. Two of the three pieces consisted of political commentary on the subject of religious freedom and on the new constitution. Since both these articles put forth the Conservative view, the government considered them seditious and fined the author 250 pesos. When Audelo declared himself insolvent, Carriedo had to pay the fine. This move effectively crippled the Conservatives' only organ in the Oaxaca press.[21] But the most important development related to representation in the legislature. Elections were held in May 1857, for delegates to the state assembly, the national congress, and for governor of the state. Fourteen men were chosen to sit in the legislature. Since this body would also write the state constitution in line with the national charter promulgated the previous March, the slate of representatives took on added significance. All but two were Liberals. All were destined to play prominent roles in the Reform.

Manuel Dublán, a lawyer, was married to the sister of Margarita Maza, the wife of Juárez. Félix Romero, twenty-six years old, with a distinguished career in journalism already behind him, had served as a delegate to the recent national constitutional congress and was an adviser to Juárez. Miguel Castro was of the same generation as Juárez and a close friend of the governor. Trained as a lawyer, he early began to acquire silver mines in the sierra and became not only a very wealthy man but the political boss of the mountainous region. José María Díaz Ordaz would loom large on the scene within a matter of months as successor to Juárez in the governorship. Juan N. Cerqueda, another lawyer, had been associated with Romero in editing and publishing *El Azote de los Tiranos* ("The Scourge of Tyrants"), which the eminent journalist Francisco Zarco termed the best Liberal newspaper in the Republic. Ignacio Mejía, another associate of Juárez, owned mines, was a professional soldier, and was currently serving as commanding officer of the Oaxacan National Guard. His brother, Manuel Mejía, was also one of the delegates. Cristóbal Salinas was the Liberal political boss of the Tehuantepec Isthmus and was likewise a soldier. Luis Fernández del Campo, a retired colonel in the regular army, had long served as head of the state treasury; once, briefly in 1853, he was interim governor of Oaxaca. Marcos Pérez, an uncompromising Liberal who had suffered imprisonment for his political beliefs, had been a fellow student with Juárez in the early days of the Institute. Luis María Carbó, a pharmacist by training, had given up his professional career in recent years to devote all his time to politics. Lately he had been serving as the political chief, or governor, of the Central Department of Oaxaca. José Esperón was a wealthy landowner, lawyer, and merchant, and in time would become the leader of the moderate faction of the Liberal party in the state.[22]

There were two delegates who had begun their political careers as Liberals, then became moderates with the passing of the years, and, as a result of the adoption of the Constitution of 1857, were finally propelled into the Conservative camp. These were Manuel Iturribarría, elected to the legislature as the delgate from Huajuapan de León, and Cenobio Márquez, chosen to represent the Etla District. Iturribarría had resigned as magistrate on the state supreme court the previous March rather than swear to uphold the new constitution. His had been a distinguished career in the service of his state—delegate to national congresses, director of the Institute of Sciences and Arts, frequent member of the state supreme court, and, briefly, governor in earlier years. He was one of the many Conservatives whom the ensuing struggle profoundly affected. As a result of the bitterness engendered by the Reform, he would eventually withdraw completely from politics. Márquez, a lawyer who had opposed Santa Anna and who had been instrumental in the downfall of the Santanista regime in Oaxaca during the Ayutla revolution, was Juárez's secretary in the first few months following the governor's installation early in the previous year. Two of his brothers were priests; one held a high position in the Oaxacan hierarchy. Márquez soon became disenchanted with Juárez and the attack against the church turned him into a Conservative.[23]

On June 20, in a preparatory junta held before the formal opening of the legislature, the credentials of the representatives came up for review. Quickly, and on a technicality concerning the balloting procedures in Huajuapan, the Liberal majority voted to nullify the election of Iturribarría. Then, when the time came to swear to uphold the Constitution of 1857, Márquez refused to take the oath in the prescribed form, adding a conditional clause that he would support the charter as long as there was no conflict with the doctrines of the church. The other members of the legislature voted to unseat him because of his refusal to conform. Thus the Conservatives were left without any representation in the body charged with writing the new state constitution.[24]

The following day, the legislature was formally installed. Custom and even law dictated that a Te Deum be sung in the cathedral on such an occasion of state. This year there was none, for Bishop Domínguez refused permission. As a result, the bishop and one of the cathedral canons were fined—and they paid promptly.[25]

This religious ceremony seemed to become the focal point of the sparring between the church and the Liberal government, as if it were a trophy to be awarded after victory in an athletic contest. Any astute observer almost could have guaged the growing hostility between church and state by the decline in the frequency of the Te Deums. When Juárez had returned to the governorship in January 1856, the occasion was marked by a Te Deum sung by the bishop. When the constitution was promulgated a year later, the church agreed to hold the ceremony, but under protest. Now, upon the installation of the new state legislature, the church refused to cooperate altogether.

The ceremony again became the object of controversy on June 30, when the formal installation of the governor was scheduled to take place. Juárez had been elected constitutional governor of the state by an overwhelming majority in the recent May balloting.[26] By custom, a Te Deum was to be sung on the day of his inauguration, but again Domínguez refused to allow it, writing to the governor on June 29 that it was impossible to separate being elected to public office from taking an oath to uphold and enforce the constitution; hence the cabildo and the bishop agreed that the church could not sanction a Te Deum on the occasion of the inauguration because it would violate the bishop's order "not to recognize with . . . religious acts the oath to the Constitution. . . ."

The following day, at ten o'clock, Juárez replied to Domínguez that the Te Deum *would* be sung that noon because a decree of 1829 stated that the installation of a governor should be celebrated by such a ceremony. An hour later, Domínguez penned his second note to Juárez. It was true, he wrote, that in times past the ceremony had been held with the church's full cooperation, but then there existed a mutual respect between church and state; now the former found itself attacked by the latter. And he reiterated his note of the day before, stating that for the church to lend its support to Juárez in his inauguration as governor would be tantamount to lending its support to the constitution, and this the church would not do. Upon receipt of this strongly worded refusal, the governor immediately replied with a note to the bishop in which he pointed out that the prelate was disobeying the law and for that reason was fined 100 pesos. Since the canons of the cathedral chapter unanimously supported the bishop, they too were fined the sum of 50 pesos each.[27]

This incident stuck in the mind of Juárez. In later years, when he wrote a brief sketch of his life for his children, he went into considerable detail about the confrontation with Bishop Domínguez, and he gave a somewhat different version of the events. In the autobiography, he described how the canons and bishop were angry with him for his law on judicial administration, which he had issued as a cabinet minister in November 1855. The real cause of the anger, as we have seen, was the Constitution of 1857. He further stated that the hierarchy intended to use the occasion of his inauguration as an opportunity to embarrass him by refusing to let him and the other officials enter the cathedral to hear the Te Deum. Thereby the canons hoped to make Juárez use force to gain entry into the cathedral, which in turn would make the canons appear the aggrieved party to the people and might provoke them into an uprising aimed at the defense of the churchmen. But Juárez was too astute to fall into such a trap. Instead of forcing the issue, as the canons desired, he simply ignored them and did not even appear at the cathedral, although he had sufficient support and could call upon enough force to make the canons comply with law and custom. In Juárez's way of thinking, he had by his actions turned what could have been a confrontation to good benefits; he had done away with the perfidious custom, which to him signified that past administrations governed in the name and with the blessings of the church. All of this was done out of the conviction "that the governors of civil society should not take part in . . . any ecclesiastical ceremony, except as men able to go to the churches and practice those acts of devotion that their religion may dictate to them. Civil governors ought not to have any religion, because, it being their duty to protect impartially the freedom of the governed to follow and practice the religion that pleases them, they could not fulfill this duty faithfully if they were sectarians of any."[28] By the time Juárez wrote his version of the controversy, a number of years had intervened to blur his memory. He had forgotten that up to the very last minute he tried to get Domínguez to hold the Te Deum ceremony.

THE DÍAZ ORDAZ ADMINISTRATION

The state legislature, installed in June 1857, completed its work of writing a new state constitution three months later. It was promulgated on September 15, the anniversary of Mexican independence, and gave the Liberals additional cause for celebration. In the selection of the prominent men who would give speeches on the occasion to commemorate independence and hail the new charter, four were chosen whose very presence on the rostrum was an insult to the Conservatives. Two former priests, Bernardino Carvajal and José María Cortés, both of whom had renounced their vows only recently to take their place in the ranks of the Liberals, were selected, as were José Antonio Gamboa and José María Díaz Ordaz.[29] Gamboa, a Oaxacan delegate to the national constituent congress of 1856–57, made there a long, impassioned, often-quoted speech in favor of religious tolerance. Díaz Ordaz, a member of the state constituent legislature, was a nephew of Bishop Domínguez and was one of the leaders of the radical faction of the Liberals. He would soon become govenor of the state.

Although proclaimed on September 15, the constitution was not to be put into effect until January 1, 1858. Opening with an extensive bill of rights, the charter set forth, among other creeds, the inviolability of property, which could never be taken except to meet a public need (and only then with just compensation), as well as the freedom from having to pay forced contributions to the government—both of which principles would be consistently violated in the months ahead, as if written in smoke. The document then proceeded to detail the structure of government: a governor elected to a four-year term; a legislature elected in totality every two years with no reelection possible; a judicial system composed of district judges and a state supreme court to which magistrates were indirectly elected for a term of six years; the division of the state into districts headed by political chiefs; and a local government that resided in the municipal councils, the size of which would be determined by the population of the towns. One feature stands out above the rest: a strong executive who had the

initiative in the formation of laws and who appointed the district
political chiefs. These officers were given wide powers and were the
direct representatives of the governor. They were charged with
promulgating and bringing about compliance with all the laws and
orders sent to them for enforcement; caring for the public tranquility
and security of people and property; overseeing the district judges
and treasury employees; enlisting, organizing, and disciplining the
National Guard companies billeted in their districts; and supervising
the logistics of troops on active service. They were the intermediaries
between the state government and the town councils.[30]

The legislature that wrote the constitution was to continue functioning until a new body was installed in September 1858. The current governor was to remain in office until December 1, 1861.[31] But
no sooner had the state constitution been published than Juárez resigned as governor. In the national elections held during the summer
of 1857,he had been chosen as the president of the Supreme Court,
which office succeeded to the presidency of the nation should that
post become vacant. But the national political situation led Comonfort
to invite him, on October 21, to join the cabinet as minister of gobernación. On the 24th, Juárez accepted, and the same day he was given
permission to absent himself from the governorship to take the
cabinet post. The new state constitution, while not yet in effect, called
for the regent of the state supreme court to become governor in the
temporary absence of the elected governor. Juárez's absence was to be
temporary: despite the fact that he had been elected president of the
national court, he asked for and received his leave only to serve as a
cabinet minister. The provisions of the new state constitution were
ignored, and instead of the interim regent's succession to the gov-
ernship, the legislature named José María Díaz Ordaz as interim governor. Díaz Ordaz was sworn in on October 25 and two days later
Juárez left Oaxaca, never again to set foot in his native state.

In the veins of the new governor there flowed the blood of conquistadors. Local historians trace his ancestry on his father's side to
Bernal Díaz del Castillo, Cortés's faithful soldier in the conquest of
Mexico, and Díaz's second wife and cousin, the sister of another captain, Diego de Ordaz. Born in 1821 to wealthy parents, he was a
lawyer and a large landholder, having recently increased his holdings
by purchasing the Hacienda del Rosario near Oaxaca City in the first
few weeks after the promulgation of the Lerdo Law. By a strange twist
of irony, he came to head the civil government during the reign of his

maternal uncle, José Agustín Domínguez, as bishop of the diocese of Antequera.[32]

The first weeks of his governorship were far from peaceful. To the opposition, intriguing questions arose concerning the attitude of the new governor. Would the nephew of the bishop be stern and uncompromising in his dealings with the ecclesiastical authorities, or could they count on his leniency? In other words, would his family connections attentuate his liberalism in his relationship with the church? Would he allow the hierarchy to regain some measure of their lost prestige? Would he give the church a breathing spell in which to recuperate?

The test soon came. In mid-November, a citizen, José Joaquín Rodríguez, lay gravely ill. Desiring the last sacraments, he sent a friend to fetch a priest from the Sagrario, the cathedral parish church. Padre José Pelagio Olguín refused to attend the dying man, nor would the other curate of the parish go to him, for Rodríguez had taken the oath to support the national constitution and under the law of alientation had bought property previously owned by the church. The priests made it clear, moreover, that the bishop, through his secretary, José Mariano Domínguez (brother to the bishop and uncle to the governor), had ordered them to follow this course of action. The prelate had previously heard of the serious state of Rodríguez's health and, anticipating his request for extreme unction, forbade the rite until an investigation revealed whether the sick man had retracted the oath and returned the property.

Díaz Ordaz, under date of November 19, wrote the Minister of Justice, Ecclesiastical Affairs, and Public Instruction, Manuel Ruiz, a fellow Oaxacan, summarizing the case. He stated that heretofore the governor would have handled the situation but now that the Constitution of 1857 was in effect, he was refraining from taking action and passing the information on to the national government. Ruiz's reply came quickly. On November 24, he reported to Díaz Ordaz that the information had been transmitted to President Comonfort, who had decided that in order to prevent any similar disputes from arising in the future, Padre Olguín should be exiled to Chiapas until he showed himself ready to comply with the law. Comonfort promised to investigate the bishop's role in the Rodríguez affair, and, furthermore, Díaz Ordaz was given the authority to exile any priests who might in the future refuse to obey the laws. Díaz Ordaz had acted decisively; the bishop now knew the temper of his nephew.[33]

By this time the situation was tense throughout the Republic. Rumor was rife of the government's imminent overthrow and conspiracy was in the air. On October 22, just as the change in the Oaxacan governors was taking place, in Cuernavaca an officer named Moreno had come out against the national constitution. Leaving that city for Puebla, he was joined en route by General José María Cobos, a Spaniard by birth, who had cast his lot with the Conservatives. These two men with their small army were soon defeated, but in retreat they invaded Oaxaca and captured Huajuapan. The goverment in the state capital took alarm. The National Guard quickly mobilized and plans were made to move the government offices into fortified monasteries and from there hold the city in case of attack. Soon word arrived that the Moreno-Cobos army had left Huajuapan, captured Nochixtlán, and then departed for the Etla Valley, which joined the Valley of Oaxaca. There were no forces available to stop their advance to the capital; indeed, it was feared that there were not enough guardsmen available to hold the city itself.

The impending crisis brought terror and confusion. When, on December 10, it was rumored that the Conservative forces were approaching the capital, the streets filled with people moving their belongings to places of safety. Soldiers dashed through the town, impressing men, mules, horses, and wagons to help transfer the files of the government offices into the walled monasteries of Santo Domingo and Carmen Alto and the nunnery of Santa Catarina. Each was a block apart and a few blocks north of the business district, the two monasteries sitting on a rise of land that gave them a commanding position. The Conservative army failed to appear, however, and calm settled over the would-be defenders.

In the next few days, the government of Díaz Ordaz worked around the clock to strengthen the defenses of the Liberal forces. Messengers were dispatched to other districts to order political chiefs to send detachments of the National Guard to the capital. Food supplies were brought into the fortified triangle. Barricades were thrown up and trenches dug in the streets. The governor decreed that a state of siege existed and imposed martial law. In the style common to all administrations, Conservative or Liberal, he decreed that the merchants and property owners in the city must contribute to an extraordinary "subsidy" of 30,000 pesos "to subvent the great sums that must be expended to save the social order." Despite the recent tension betweeen the church and the state over the Rodríguez affair,

Bishop Domínguez sent his nephew assurances that the clergy would not take part in the rebellion. This action on the part of the prelate serves to confirm the impression that he frequently wavered and changed his position, or otherwise displayed an indecisiveness, which may have been motivated by a desire to avoid a confrontation. In the long run, such a stance would not well serve him or his cause.[34]

General Ignacio Mejía, the most experienced soldier among the Liberals, arrived from the Isthmus on December 21 and assumed command. The following day, the crisis deepened. Word arrived from Mexico City that President Comonfort, a moderate Liberal, had supported a coup d'etat mounted against his own government by Conservative General Félix Zuloaga. Prompted by this news, the legislature hastily assembled to issue a declaration of loyalty to the Liberal cause and vote for a technical secession from the Republic until the Zuloaga rebellion was put down and the federal powers could resume their functions; in the interim, the state of Oaxaca reassumed its sovereignty and would govern itself through its special laws.[35]

Local Conservatives did not remain passive or inactive. By this time, some Conservative residents of the city had armed themselves and formed a band to go out to join the approaching army. They first went to the nearby villages of Xoxocotlán and Zaachila to the south of the capital to recruit others for their group, but with little success. En route to their rendezvous with Moreno and Cobos, they sacked the hacienda of Carmen.[36]

On December 22, the advance contingents of the Conservative army arrived in Etla, where they seized mules, horses, and food and demanded money from the citizens of that town. Six days later, Moreno and Cobos arrived in force and occupied the southern sector of Oaxaca City. For the next two weeks, there was sporadic fighting in the capital, accompanied by such intense looting that Moreno found it necessary to threaten his soldiers with courts-martial if they continued to pillage.

The situation deteriorated in the fortified triangle occupied by the Liberals in the northern sector. Rations were becoming exhausted and money to pay the guardsmen was running out. Governor Díaz Ordaz called a council of war, presented the facts, and called for discussion. Most officers favored an abandonment of the city and a retreat to the town of Ixtlán in the mountains to the north; a handful of the commanders opposed. When word spread among the guardsmen of the decision to retreat, they began to clamor for an attack. Díaz Ordaz then held a private conference with Ignacio Mejía in which the decision was made to attack. Porfirio Díaz wrote years later that the Oaxacan National Guard consisted largely of undisciplined men but that it was nevertheless a model army. "The soldiers fought like lions in Oaxaca but there was much resistance to leaving the state." There is a saying, he wrote: " '. . . the Oaxacans are valiant as far as the Marquesado.' "[37] Now that they were being called on to fight for their capital, they fought fiercely and well.

The attack took place on January 16, 1858. Within a few hours, the Liberals were victorious. The Government Palace, the last stronghold of Cobos's army, was stormed after its doors were blown open by cannon. The fight there was so furious, Mejía later reported, that "in the patio . . . the blood ran so thickly that the soles of my shoes were soaked." Cobos and Moreno fled, taking with them those of their men still alive and not captured, and who happened to learn of the retreat. Many were abandoned, however, and went into hiding in and around the city. As a result of the action of January 16, there were 58 Liberals dead and 48 wounded, while the Conservatives had 150 dead, 66 wounded, and 225 from among them were taken prisoner.[38]

In the two years and one week since Juárez's return to assume the governorship, the Liberal, constitutional, federal regime had become established and the onslaught against the entrenched position of the privileged groups had begun; the church became the primary target of the attack because it was viewed as the bulwark of privilege. Locally this struggle, despite its intensity, amounted only to a series of skirmishes, each one, considered separately, fought on a small scale and not very significant, but taken together, important in their totality. It has been necessary to trace in some detail the process by which the attack was launched and its overall nature in order to indicate how the Liberal Reform in Oaxaca was shaped from its very inception by circumstances peculiar to the state and how the conflict between the opposing sides in the struggle gradually grew in intensity and gained momentum to the point that military combat was the logical outcome.

In these initial months, sides were chosen and inroads against the opponents were made, only to be met with counterthrusts. The government clearly had the upper hand, not only because it was supported by a large segment of the population in the Central District but also because it had the means to command obedience to the reform laws. It had accomplished much: the national constitution was proclaimed, a state constitution was written and adopted, the Lerdo Law was enforced locally to deprive the church of much of its real estate. Juárez was propelled into national prominence by his election to the presidency of the Supreme Court—soon he would gain the highest office of the land. Díaz Ordaz held promise of being a firm governor, stubborn in the defense of the Liberal program. The Oaxacan National Guard, reorganized after several years of disbandment, was put to the test and proved itself well. Within the ranks of the Conservatives, some few men, primarily clerics, had spoken out against the Reform but, generally, the opponents to the Liberal policies seemed undecided on what course of action to follow.

Several trends emerge in this period as important factors shaping the course of events. One, which partially helps to explain the initial successes of the Oaxacan Liberals, was the wavering, hesitancy, and indecision of the local ecclesiastical hierarchy. Bishop Domínguez seemed unwilling or incapable of taking an unyielding stand against the Liberal goverment. Immediately following Juárez's return, the bishop cooperated with the Liberals. When the decree alienating property was implemented, there was little noteworthy opposition by churchmen. It was not until early 1857, fifteen months after the Liberals had seized control, that Domínguez took a strong position against the government program, occasioned then by the adoption of the new national constitution and the oath to support it required of all public officials. But even from that moment forward, there was a certain amount of confusion on the part of the bishop, perhaps growing out of his relationship to the governor. He did not look to Cobos and Moreno as saviors but instead advised his nephew that priests would not use the invasion by the Conservative army as an opportunity to forward the church's political interests. In effect, by such hesitancy Bishop Domínguez lost any initiative he otherwise might have had and thereby allowed the Liberals to make the gains they made.

A second factor that favored the Liberals was the manner in which they presented a united front in this initial period of the Reform. Such oneness of purpose and unity of action in themselves accounted for many of the accomplishments realized by the Oaxacan Reformers. This pattern of local cooperation was not, however, duplicated in the national capital. There the Liberals occupying high places in the administration were beginning to experience a divisiveness or factionalism, which culminated in the attempt of moderate President Ignacio Comonfort to avoid civil war and perhaps forward his own interests by dulling the sharp edge of the Reform program and enlisting the support of the Conservatives. But instead of avoiding civil war, this coalition of moderate Liberals and Conservatives provoked it. Such factionalism was not openly manifested until late 1857, and when it became a reality in the form of the Comonfort-Zuloaga conspiracy, a turning point was reached. From then on, as the contagion of factionalism spread, the moderate and purist or radical wings of the Liberal party seldom cooperated; the united front of the early months collapsed. In time, this would be reflected in Oaxacan politics. But for the moment, within the state, moderates and purists together enforced the Reform program. The Cobos-Moreno invasion, mounted in the closing weeks of 1857, was one result of the events that unfolded in Mexico City; indirectly, that incursion and the lingering threat of future Conservative intrusions into the state would serve to bring a change of directions in the politics of the Oaxacan Reform, changes bound to have an impact on local enforcement of the Reform and understanding and acceptance of the spirit of the program. The moderate Liberals in the state would attempt to seize control. Their success in this endeavor and the implications of the moderates' triumph in Oaxaca must now be examined.

CHAPTER 3

THE MODERATES IN CONTROL, 1858–63

THE ARCHIVAL MATERIALS relating to the rise to power of the moderate Liberals in the state leave many questions unanswered. Basic to the problem is a lack of correspondence among the various leaders of the factions, which might shed light not only on their philosophy but, more importantly, on the reasons for their actions; the economic, social, political, and personal factors determining their individual propensities for moderation or radicalism; and the organization and manner of operation of each group. Without such supporting evidence, one must enter into the realm of conjecture in analyzing the significant turn of events in Oaxaca by which the moderate Liberals came to control the machinery of government and to direct the implementation of the Reform program. However subtle or blatant the machinations of the state politicians, the moderates rapidly gained the ascendancy. Within six months after the defeat and expulsion of the Conservatives, they managed to take control of the state legislature, and within another half-year after coming to dominate the legislature they were able to oust the radical Díaz Ordaz as governor and replace him with Miguel Castro, a man they could at least influence and perhaps dominate outright.

BACK TO NORMALCY

The Cobos-Moreno invasion of Oaxaca and the nineteen-day occupation of the state capital by the Conservative army, surprisingly, had caused little damage. The governmental palace sustained the heaviest damages of any of the public buildings but private property generally remained intact within the city. The street lighting installed only a few

49

years previously was completely destroyed, and a special tax levy was imposed on property owners to rebuild the system. The aqueduct was quickly repaired. The greatest damage had occurred to the rural properties owned by Liberals in the Central District. The Hacienda del Rosario, bought by Governor Díaz Ordaz under the law of disentailment, was pillaged and all hacienda records were destroyed. Cattle, horses, mules, wheat, corn, and beans were carried off by the Conservatives. Likewise, the Hacienda de la Labor, belonging to the state treasurer, Luis Fernández del Campo, was pillaged and the big house burned—this during the flight of the Conservative army from Oaxaca toward Tlacolula on January 16.

There is no record of what happened to the large number of common soldiers captured by the Liberals; probably they were pardoned and allowed to return to their homes if they promised never again to take up arms against the federal republic. The tower cells and the cloister of Santo Domingo monastery became the jail of another type of prisoner: at least ten priests who disobeyed the bishop's order not to participate in politics and lent their aid to Cobos and Moreno; officers captured on January 16; and private citizens known to be in sympathy with the reaction. Some of these prisoners in time were pardoned and set free, some were returned home to recuperate from wounds or illnesses, and some few were tried and found guilty of treason. These were sent to Veracruz with a brigade of the Oaxaca National Guard, commanded by General Ignacio Mejía, who had been ordered to join the forces protecting the seat of the federal government.[1]

All in all, it took little time and effort to resume the normal pace of life and activities in the Central District. Schools closed during the siege were soon reopened, on February 8; the government files were moved back into the palace; streets were repaired; and busineses were opened.[2] Given the ease with which the state, and especially the capital, returned to normality after the brief, relatively undestructive Conservative invasion, it could be expected that political questions would again receive priority. In March 1858, the legislature, the same one that had written the state constitution the previous year, assembled for extraordinary sessions to deal with important business interrupted by the invasion. Four pressing topics were discussed in the assembly: subdivision of the state, defense, taxation, and elections.

Within four days after the sessions opened, the legislators adopted an organic statute setting forth the territorial division of the state. The old system of eight large departments, each with a governor at its head, subordinate to the state governor, was changed to a division of twenty-five districts, each controlled by a political chief appointed by the state governor.[3]

On April 20, Governor Díaz Ordaz took steps to reinforce the National Guard in Oaxaca. Some units of the Guard had recently returned from Tehuantepec, having pursued remnants of General Cobos's forces that far after the triumph of January 16. But no sooner had they arrived back in the state capital than a call came from Veracruz to send aid to protect that city from the Conservative army supporting the Zuloaga government. Oaxaca responded by sending a brigade, commanded by General Mejía, which departed on April 8. This left an insufficient number of troops in Oaxaca City and its environs to fight off another invasion should it materialize. Díaz Ordaz therefore decreed that a company of police should be organized, composed of five officers, five sergeants, eight corporals, and one hundred soldiers. This group, called the Police of the Capital, whose purpose it was to support the Guard in maintaining order, was put under the command of the political chief of the Central District. Only in extreme emergency could it be sent outside Oaxaca City.[4]

Since the government was short of money, the legislature had to deal with financial problems. In this matter, much opposition developed and some moderate leaders spoke out against the measures adopted. At the center of the financial crisis was the inadequacy of standard forms of revenue gathering to meet current exigencies arising from the civil war now raging throughout the republic. There were two kinds of taxes collected in Oaxaca that provided the major revenue. These were the property tax, called the *tres al millar* ("three per thousand"), and the *alcabala* ("sales tax"). All owners or rural and urban properties were to pay three pesos per thousand-pesos valuation on their properties. This taxation measure had been adopted first in 1850, but in the eight intervening years the valuations had never been completed. Only in three of the four sections into which Oaxaca City was divided for tax purposes had the cadastral surveys been carried out, while in remote areas of the state the property tax was in chaos and virtually impossible to collect. Many officials believed—in all likelihood they were right—that the valuations did not represent the real value of the property.

The sales tax applied to various kinds of transactions—foodstuffs, merchandise transported within the state, and lately, the transfer of property titles resulting from the adjudications and sales under the Lerdo Law of Disentailment. The property transfer *alcabala* was 5 per cent of the selling price and a portion of this fee was to accrue to the states. On all taxes collected, certain percentages were deducted to pay the collectors and to operate the offices of collection. Although there was a central accounting office for all governmental incomes and expenditures, there was probably a considerable amount of money paid in taxes that never found its way into the state treasury. Now that the nation was in the throes of civil war, the shortage of state funds was a grave problem, because there was not enough money available to pay the officers and men of the National Guard, to meet the regular state expenditures, and to repair the damage done by the invasion of the Cobos-Moreno army. Thus, the government found itself in the position of having to rely on emergency forced contributions, loans, and special taxes, despite the injunction against such practices in the recently adopted state constitution.[5]

When a 30,000-peso contribution was levied against the merchants and property holders of Oaxaca City in December 1857, to support the besieged Liberal government and the garrison of soldiers protecting it, the money was paid quickly and with little grumbling. On April 21, 1858, the government again found it necessary to decree an "extraordinary contribution" to "subvent the expenditures required at present by the department [*ramo*] of war." This contribution was to apply statewide and amounted to 80,000 pesos, but Oaxaca City and its suburb of the Marquesado were to supply more than one-fourth of the total. In the state capital, the ayuntamiento was charged with levying the quota to be paid by each property holder. The payments could be made in three installments—on the first days of May, June, and July. Inconsistently, eleven days after the first payment was due, the government decreed that those citizens who wished to pay the first two installments on the date the first payment fell due would receive a 12½ per cent discount from their quotas, and if they made all three payments at once, they would receive a 25 per cent discount.[6]

The complaints made before the ayuntamiento are indicative not only of the resistance in Oaxaca City to the payment of this tax but also of how poorly the property records were kept. José Esperón, the leader of the moderate faction of the Liberal party, protested that his quota was based on property owned by his deceased relative, Lucián

Esperón, that he, José, had not inherited this property, and that he did not even know who the present owners were. Esperón, who was a lawyer, also protested in behalf of three of his clients. Mariano Mantecón, he reported, was assessed a sum based on ten houses, but he owned only four of those ten. Perhaps the other six had been owned in previous years by Mantecón's dead uncle who had the same name as the nephew. Isidora Peralta had one house valued at 5,265 pesos and José Jáuregui had a house valued at 7,234 pesos. They were each assessed 285 pesos, an amount entirely too high based on their holdings. Besides that, neither of these two clients lived in Oaxaca City. José Regules, a Spainard, claimed he had been assessed 145 pesos on his business establishment, although he had disposed of his merchandising firm two years previously. Instead of his owing money to the government, he countered that the national treasury owed him large sums, for in times past he had given Mexico enormous amounts of money. During the recent occupation of the city by the Conservatives, General Cobos had robbed Regules of all his savings so that he had nothing with which to pay his assessment.[7]

With such resistance to this forced contribution, it is little wonder that there was difficulty in collecting. The due date for the first installment was continually being extended and notices inserted in the newspaper calling for the payments to be made. On August 25, the political chief of the Central District announced that September 2 was the absolute deadline for making the first of the three payments, and that if the amounts due then were not forthcoming the fines provided for in the decree of April 21 would be levied.[8] Undoubtedly the purists or radicals received the major share of the blame for the taxation measure and it may be supposed that the resistance that developed to paying provoked a considerable amount of grumbling against the radical leaders.

Other than problems of financing and administering the government and providing for its protection, the legislature also had to devote its attention to the matter of elections. At last, the state governorship was to be put on a constitutional basis. Juárez's election in 1857 as president of the national Supreme Court of Justice was now recognized by the legislature (in fact, Juárez was currently serving as chief executive of the federalist government in Veracruz) and it was therefore necessary to hold an election in the state to fill the governorship; in October 1857, Díaz Ordaz had been named interim governor only. In the balloting that took place throughout the state on

May 9, Díaz Ordaz carried the state, although he failed to win in the
Central District where Marcos Pérez, of the same political persuasion,
received a majority of almost 7,000 votes.[9]

RADICALS AND MODERATES

The gubernatorial elections of May were followed in July by balloting
to select delegates to the state legislature, the first to be elected under
the constitution. In these elections, the Liberal moderates, or *borlados,*
as they were called locally, won seven of the fourteen seats in the
unicameral assembly. Two *rojos* (radicals or purists), members of the
group that up to now had controlled state politics under the leadership of Juárez, Marcos Pérez, and Díaz Ordaz, won seats, while the
remaining five delegates were committed to the Liberal party but
belonged to neither faction and would therefore remain an unknown
quantity in partisan issues. If these five consistently voted with the
purists, the legislature would always have a tie vote. But the borlados
could count on some of the uncommitted members to side with them,
giving the moderate faction a majority.[10]

The basic difference between the two factions was that of
method. The moderates believed as firmly as the purists in the necessity of restructuring the nation with an abrogation of the ancient
privileges long enjoyed by certain small but powerful segments of the
population in the highly stratified society of the Mexico of that epoch.
But the moderates wished to proceed slowly and cautiously in
eliminating the privileges and reshaping society along democratic
lines, chipping away bit by bit the incrustations of the ancien régime.
The purists, on the other hand, were less patient. If the moderates
wished to tear down the thick wall of privileges with a chisel, the
purists wanted to demolish it at once with a wrecking ball. The
moderates feared that the radically innovating proposals of the
purists would catapult the nation into demagoguery.[11]

One other distinction between the two groups may be made: the
radicals were more the men of action who took to the field to fight for
the principles in which they believed. Among the Oaxacan purists
there were at least five soldiers who played major roles in defending
the state against its enemies. These were José María Ballesteros,
Tiburcio Montiel, José María Díaz Ordaz, Ignacio Mejía, and Porfirio
Díaz, the last two of whom reached national prominence as a result of
their military activities. The moderates, on the other hand, were more

the men of talk, of backroom political manipulations, of deals. In the art of politics, the borlados excelled.

The moderates could count on the wholehearted support of Manuel Dublán, Bernardino Carvajal, José Esperón, Manuel Velasco, Esteban Maqueo, Ramón Cajiga, Cristóbal Salinas, and Juan de Mata Vázquez among the leaders. The titular heads were Esperón and Dublán. In the ranks of the radical faction were Marcos Pérez, José María Díaz Ordaz, Luis María Carbó, Félix Romero, Justo Benítez, Porfirio Díaz, Ignacio Mariscal, José María Ballesteros, Ignacio Mejía, and Tiburcio Montiel. They were led by Marcos Pérez and accepted the young Díaz Ordaz as their second in command.[12]

Governor Juárez seems to have catered to both groups in an attempt to maintain party unity, and with much success. In fact, part of the problem would seem to center around the figure of Juárez as Liberal administrator. Several of his biographers have pointed out that during his previous gubernatorial term and even earlier in his days as a rising politician in Oaxaca City, he was more moderate than radical, more willing to seek a modus vivendi with Conservative groups, particularly the clergy, that would allow him to develop a program of evolutionary, gradual reform without polarizing the various factions contending for control within the state. It was only as the agent of the Liberal Reform, from early 1856 to the autumn of 1857, that he began to appear more radical. He realized by that time that there could be no reconciliation between Conservatives and Liberals and at that point his previous attempt to govern by consensus was abruptly changed to government on behalf of the progressive majority. That majority, however, represented many shades of opinion, ranging from center to left, from moderates who still hoped to see cooperation with the Conservatives to purists who wished to eliminate the opposition. Since Juárez himself had traveled along this route from moderation toward radicalism, he could identify with all shades within the Liberal spectrum and seems to have had remarkable success in keeping the Oaxacan Liberals free from the factionalism that was so evident elsewhere.

The essence of the binding nature of his leadership can best be seen in the personal relationships he developed over a long period of time with men from both the major factions as well as the centrists. For example, one of his closest associates from the early days was Marcos Pérez, whose friendship dated back three decades to the days when they were together at the Institute of Sciences and Arts. Pérez had always been inclined toward radical Liberalism. Another close friend, and of Juárez's same generation, was the wealthy and politically powerful Miguel Castro, a confirmed Liberal but partisan of neither extreme. Juárez had given encouragement to the young Díaz Ordaz, a radical, and had counted on his enthusiasm and support in building up the National Guard. At the same time, the governor drew into the ranks of the party the former priest Bernardino Carvajal, who, when he affiliated, joined the moderate faction. Juárez's brother-in-law, Manuel Dublán, who headed the governor's secretariat, was a moderate. Such a complex of political, personal, and family ties and friendships served to bind together the two extreme factions and those in between into a cohesive party while Juárez was present in the state as governor.

Although the records are silent, one suspects that the factionalism that developed after Juárez's departure in late 1857 did not arise simply from differences of philosophy and methods. Undoubtedly, there were personality clashes or deep animosities, which could not be covered up forever. Realistically, it seems more than likely that the borlados were disturbed at what was happening locally, particularly in regard to taxation and the intensification of military operations as the civil war came closer to affect more areas and more people. This could only result in an upset of business and threaten security and property. When such a point was reached, the moderates were stimulated to take control and to conduct affairs at a less intense level of operations, thereby hoping that economic interests would not be threatened.[13]

Translated into terms of political realism, it was natural then that the borlados should attempt to take control of the state legislature and through it try to control the radical governor, Díaz Ordaz, as well as the degree and rate of implementation of the Reform program. Failing this, they would have to seek to oust the governor and replace him with a borlado candidate or with someone more sympathetic to their views. As far as the Reform was concerned, this meant the borlados would implement the national decrees and measures to the extent it pleased or suited them to do so. In the borlado government of the next five years, a direct ratio can almost be perceived in the moderates' approach to the Reform: the more the civil-political strife heated up, the more economic interests were threatened, the less vigorously the borlados would prosecute the Reform. The lesser the threat, the more vigorous the implementation of the decrees.

Part of the borlados' dissatisfaction with Díaz Ordaz lay in his idealism and his willingness to make every sacrifice—and to demand such sacrifice from others—to see his principles upheld.[14] They did not dispute these principles but wished to control the procedure and pace by which they would be implemented. Their strategy for accomplishing this by limiting the actions of Governor Díaz Ordaz through the moderate-dominated legislature failed, however, and then they began to conspire to remove him from office. The opportunity to do so soon appeared.

Late in the autumn of 1858, President Juárez in Veracruz called on the governments of Oaxaca and Puebla to mount a campaign against the Conservative armies operating on the borders of those states in order to eliminate a possible threat of an attack upon the port city. Oaxaca acceded to the request and began to prepare for the expedition. Díaz Ordaz decided he would command in person, assembled the National Guard, and was given permission by the legislature to leave the state. Miguel Castro, one of the neutral legislators, was named to serve as governor pro tempore while Díaz Ordaz was away. Leaving Oaxaca City on December 23, he led his army of 700 guardsmen to Teotitlán del Camino where he incorporated the contingents under Colonel Cristóbal Salinas into his force. Plans called for joining a brigade under General Anastasio Trejo so that the combined army would then have sufficient strength to combat the Conservatives who were commanded by General José María Cobos. But the rendezvous with Trejo failed to materialize; Díaz Ordaz, fearing that the Conservatives greatly outnumbered him, retreated without a battle. When the legislature heard of this, they decided to oust the governor. The borlados, acting with the support of a few disappointed radicals, commissioned Bernardino Carvajal to travel to Díaz Ordaz's headquarters, convince the National Guard to mutiny against its ineffectual commander, and give their allegiance to Colonel Salinas, a moderate. The former priest accomplished his mission well. Díaz Ordaz hurried back to Oaxaca City to demand the governorship but the borlados refused to deliver it to him. He then went to Veracruz—this in February of 1859—to try to get President Juárez to exonerate him of his military failures and intercede in his behalf in Oaxaca. But Juárez was in no hurry to become that involved in local politics, for he had other matters on his mind: the defense of Veracruz against the Conservatives and the prosecution of the Reform program.[15]

THE MODERATES' REFORM

By early 1859, then, the moderates were in firm control of the affairs of Oaxaca. It fell their lot to enforce, in their own manner and at their pleasure, the Reform program, which, during the summer of 1859, was given major impetus by the national Liberal government in Veracruz. In many aspects of enforcement, the moderate leaders of the state proved as fierce and uncompromising as the radicals would have been. In two matters, however—regulation of nunneries and support of the war effort—their cooperation fell far short of what was demanded by law or of what was expected by the struggling national government. Their mixed record of achievement was determined by their own view of national issues and local conditions.

It is necessary to discuss in some detail the Reform decrees of the summer of 1859 in order to analyze their impact in Oaxaca and the manner in which they were enforced locally. On July 12, 1859, the president issued a decree usually referred to as the Law of Nationalization of Church Property. Since the clergy had resisted all attempts by the government to regulate the temporal affairs of the church in such diverse matters as parish fees and property, and since churchmen everywhere had continued to support the Conservative rebellion against the legal government, strong measures were needed, it was believed by the Liberals in Veracruz, to weaken the power of the ecclesiastical authorities. The law of July 12 proclaimed that all property administered by the church in whatever form belonged henceforth to the nation. In addition, the decree called for the complete separation of church and state, with the government being limited to the protection of the public worship of any religious faith, Catholic as well as Protestant.

The details of how this property was to be transferred to the civil authorities and how, once transferred, it should be disposed of, were left for a subsequent regulatory decree, which followed the next day, July 13. This second decree is more properly the real law of nationalization, while the first decree, that of July 12, is devoted almost exclusively to striking another blow at the church—by the closing of the monasteries, the limiting of the number of churches open for worship, and the close regulation of convents by the state.

Article 5 of the decree of July 12 called for the immediate suppression of all the regular orders, confraternities, and brotherhoods. From there, step by step, the details followed in terse language. The establishment of new regular monasteries was prohibited, no priests could wear the habits of the suppressed orders, regular clergy would become secular parish priests subject to the ecclesiastical ordinaries of the dioceses. Regulars who obeyed the closure law were to receive 500 pesos for their support, and old and infirm friars unable to serve as secular priests were to receive an additional 3,000 pesos. But all regulars who continued to wear their habits or to live in the monastery were to be sent into exile.

The law called for inventories to be made of all furnishings within the monasteries, the lists to be turned over to the diocesan bishops. Books, objects of art, and antiquities were to be confiscated and placed in public museums and libraries. Finally, upon petition by the bishops, state governors were to designate which churches of the suppressed orders would remain open for public worship.

Nunneries would be allowed to continue operating and observing the rules of their cloisters, but those convents subject to the spiritual jurisdiction of the regular monastic orders would now come under the control of the bishops. The lifeblood of the nunneries was cut off, however, for all novitiates were suppressed and present novices would not be allowed to take their vows. The law also contained provisions that encouraged professed nuns and novices to leave the convents and return to the secular state. Any who left were to be given back their dowries; if they belonged to a mendicant order and did not give a dowry upon entry into the convent, they would nevertheless receive 500 pesos each upon departure. Each nun who elected to remain in the convent was to be given back her dowry in the form of rural or urban property, which she was to hold personally and dispose of as she deemed best, even by willing it to relatives. The convents, even though a major portion of their wealth was thus taken away from them, were to be left with enough funds to meet daily operating expenses, the upkeep of buildings, and the support of the festivals of their patron saints. The mothers superior and chaplains were to draw up budgets of their expenses within fifteen days and submit them to the state governors for review and approval. All other property of the nunneries reverted to the nation.[16]

The regulatory decree of July 13 gave the details for the transfer of church property to the nation and how this property was to be disposed of. The state offices of the national treasury were charged with directing the confiscations. The physical plants of the monasteries were to be inventoried and then divided into lots, which would be evaluated and sold at public auction. Excluded, of course, were those monastic churches designated for public worship. The minimum bid acceptable in the auctions was two-thirds of the appraised value, one-third to be paid in cash and one-third in securities of the national debt. If the property failed to sell in auction, provisions were made for private or conventional sales.

Mortgages held by the clergy, whether originating from property sales carried out before the Law of Disentailment of 1856, or resulting from that law, had to be redeemed by the mortgagees. Failure on their part to do so within a thirty-day period meant that they forfeited their right of redemption, and any person could then gain the right to redeem the mortgages within the next ten days by paying off the debt. At the end of forty days after the publication of the law, all unredeemed mortgages were to be sold in public auctions. These provisions were difficult if not impossible to implement because the redemption of such mortgages implied a mobilization of cash, which very few people had in abundance. In addition to the foregoing provision, the decree stipulated that all church property not yet alienated under the Lerdo Law was to be sold at auction. No sales tax was to be levied against the sale of these properties as an inducement to move them into private hands. Anyone who brought to the attention of government officials church property not yet alienated or mortgages owed to the clergy and not yet redeemed gained the right to acquire title by paying 70 per cent of the value in government securities and the remaining 30 per cent in cash in forty equal monthly installments.

As a means of encouraging the states to prosecute the property sales and mortgage redemptions under this law, there were provisions stating that one-fifth of all money collected from the sales and redemptions would go into state treasuries to be used to improve roads and other means of communications and to undertake other projects that promoted the general welfare. In addition, treasury officials and administrative offices were to keep 5 per cent of all money collected to support the officials and finance the process. As a result, the national treasury was to receive only 75 per cent of the income derived from the nationalization of church property.[17]

These two decrees were published in Oaxaca on July 23. Two days later Bishop Domínguez died. The common version was that he died of a broken heart brought on by the promulgation of the Law of Nationalization. The fact was that he had been ailing since Easter week, when he fainted at the altar while blessing the sacred oils on

Holy Thursday. Perhaps, too, his spirit was broken by the sad plight of the church in such dark times.[18]

In another time and place, left to his own devices, José Agustín Domínguez might have gone down in history as one of the few great Mexican bishops, because his early actions on the eve of the Reform had given evidence of a desire to strengthen the church through remolding the clergy into a new image that would make them respected by the people. But the Reform backed him into a corner, distracted him from his aims and goals, and left him bewildered. At times fighting back with all the resources he could summon, at other times giving in and accepting the erosion of the power his institution had come to take for granted and often abused, he gives the impression of wavering and being unable to take a stand. No matter what he did, his enemies were on all sides. If he stood unflinching in the face of the Reform, the Conservatives would be satisfied while the Liberals would become fierce, unsatiated opponents. If he allowed himself to be swept along in the current of the Reform, the Liberals would court him, holding him up as an example of an enlightened clergyman, wisely adapting to the modern world, while the Conservative faithful would become estranged members of the flock he was charged to keep. The dilemma was too great for him; he resolved it by trying to satisfy both groups and ended up by pleasing neither, leaving behind a picture of a man who could not make up his mind.[19]

It is ironic that the announcement of his death, briefly stated, appeared in the same issue of the Oaxaca official newspaper that published locally the first installment of the Law of Nationalization of Church Property.[20] There followed thirty turbulent days in Oaxaca City, marked by the most intense attack against the church in the local annals of the Reform, with the government ever watchful and moving swiftly to suppress any opposition. At this moment, it suited the borlados in control to move rapidly to carry out the provisions of the July decrees. Perhaps the primary motivating factor was the prospect of the additional properties and the large number of mortgages being made available to them for purchase, although this is impossible to determine with accuracy. Also, it should be pointed out that there was no direct, immediate military threat to the central region of the state at this time. Not only did the state government act quickly to confiscate the properties of the church, but it also made it plain that it would tolerate no opposition from clerics. In this latter regard, several members of the hierarchy fell victim to the borlados' sternness.

To fill the vacancy created by the death of Domínguez, the cathedral chapter elected Vicente Márquez, one of the canons, as vicar capitular, who in turn appointed the young Father José Sáenz de Enciso as his secretary. Márquez was destined to govern the diocese for just over a week. During his brief administration he took two significant actions, one showing his concern for the plight of the diocese and the other demonstrating his hostility to the government. On August 4, he wrote the dean of the cathedral chapter saying that all the ecclesiastical administrations but most especially the seminary had been hard hit by the Law of Disentailment, that all were in need of aid, and that he would soon propose a plan to use what available, scarce resources there were to bolster all the administrations in such perilous times. The following day, he issued a circular to all priests of the diocese, fulminating against the Law of Nationalization and the regulatory decree. He declared in force the circular issued by Domínguez in April 1857, forbidding priests to give sacraments to those who supported the Reform measures. Nor were priests to cooperate with the civil authorities by surrendering property titles or mortgages or signing inventories. This circular was countersigned by his secretary, Sáenz.[21]

General Francisco Iniestra, who had recently assumed military command of Oaxaca, considered this circular subversive and issued orders for the arrest of the vicar and his secretary. Márquez hid in the Indian Capuchinesses' convent of San José, but Sáenz was caught and imprisoned in Santo Domingo monastery. When the vicar learned of his secretary's capture, he emerged from hiding and surrendered. Both were exiled to Veracruz.[22]

The cathedral chapter then elected José María Alvarez y Castillejos as the vicar capitular. Obstinate in his opposition to the laws of July 12 and 13, he too refused to cooperate with the civil authorities in the nationalization procedures. At first fined, he was then exiled on the night of August 18, when he refused to sign the inventories. Accompanied by his mother, he went on to Panama, arriving there on October 17. A month later he was dead.[23] Once again the cathedral chapter, now reduced in number, met to select a member to take charge of the diocese in the absence of a bishop. Nicolás Vasconcelos, the canon so chosen, managed to hold on to the office of vicar capitular, temporizing and avoiding any confrontation with government officials but also, as subsequent events would prove, biding his time until a turn of events would allow him to demonstrate his true sentiments.

It was during this period of confusion, while the cathedral chapter was trying to provide leadership for the diocese, that the law of July 12 in that part pertaining to the monasteries was put into effect in all its vigor. On August 11, the monasteries were closed by direction of Félix Romero, district judge at the time. Twenty-eight friars were locked out of their homes and put at the mercy of their secular brothers and an unyielding vicar. The records show that only one, the Dominican Margarito Maldonado, asked for the 500 pesos due him for obeying the Reform laws. The Liberal sympathies he had long nourished now came to the fore and he enlisted enthusiastically in the cause of the federal government. There seems to have been little repercussion or anger on the part of the populace, although one Franciscan priest who fled to the Oaxaca border to join the army of Cobos, operating on the frontiers of the state at the moment, claimed that the people poured into his monastery weeping and wailing over the turn of events. It appears that one friar, a Franciscan, was allowed to remain in his monastery in the position as chaplain of the attached church, which was one of the conventual chapels designated for use in public worship.[24]

By the action of closure, the government came in control of the properties of the monasteries of Santo Domingo, Carmen Alto, San Francisco, San Agustín, La Merced, and the Oratory of San Felipe. Going a step further, Romero also took over the Episcopal Palace and the Conciliar Seminary in the name of the government.[25] Not only did the government gain property, but the libraries of the monasteries and the seminary, all negligible except that of Santo Domingo, went to the library of the Institute of Sciences and Arts. There are accounts of the hiding of jewels by the friars and superiors so that they, too, would not fall into the hands of the Liberals.

Alvarez, the vicar capitular when the monasteries were closed, was unbending in his opposition to the measures being taken against the church and in no mood to make the transition easy for the regular clergy shut out from their cloisters and forbidden to wear the habits of their orders. On August 10, he issued a circular to his secular priests insisting that any friars who presented themselves to the parish priests to celebrate Mass in the secular churches would be refused permission to do so unless they were dressed in their habits. Nor would they be allowed to hear confessions or bless objects unless they wore their habits.[26] This placed the regular clergy in an awkward position: if they wore their habits they were subject to exile by the civil government; if they did not wear them, they could not perform their priestly duties.

Nor was it a simple matter to assign the excluded regulars to churches as secular priests. The income of the parishes and consequently the livings of the secular priests had diminished so sharply that few if any churches could support one cleric, much less take on the extra burden of providing a living for another. The secular priests were all too often the uncharitable, avaricious, jealous guardians of their small realms, unwilling to share with their unfortunate and displaced brothers.[27]

In regard to the provisions of the nationalization law pertaining to the nunneries, no action was taken at this time in Oaxaca for reasons unexplained by contemporary documents. It is certain that action was contemplated, however, for on August 9, 1859, Governor Castro wrote to President Juárez asking for clarifications on certain points of the laws of July 12 and 13. In response, Minister of the Treasury Ocampo replied that Juárez had disposed that all governors were to make surveys of the convents within their states, such surveys to include the number of professed nuns, novices, servants, and other persons serving the nunneries, the conventual incomes, and capital assets, including rural and urban properties. With these statistics in hand, the local authorities should then set up a budget for each nunnery. Governors were to appoint one or more administrators for each convent and these officials were charged with collecting the incomes and products for the conventual establishments. If the income was not sufficient to cover the operating and maintenance expenses, the difference would be made up from public funds. But beyond Castro's inquiry no further action was taken, which was in keeping with the moderates' approach to the Reform statutes. Convents were being valuated in this period but under a property taxation decree of May, 1857, rather than under the Law of Nationalization. The question of the return of dowries was not brought up again until 1862. Despite the law of July 12, therefore, the nunneries in Oaxaca were left alone for the time being.[28]

One can only speculate why the moderates chose to ignore the provisions regulating the nunneries. Probably the principal reason was the social attitude toward women in general and nuns in particular in the nineteenth century in Mexico. Nuns were considered gentle ladies who did much good for orphan girls and widows in their care. To limit their operation in any way would cause the women much hardship. A Mexican gentleman could not easily bring himself to enforce such a harsh provision as that demanded by the nationalization law.

The reform program did not end with the Law of Nationalization of Church Properties. To it and the 1855 law overhauling the judicial system (Juárez Law) and the 1856 Law of Disentailment (Lerdo Law) were now added in rapid succession most of the other statutes constituting the Reform code: July 23, 1859, the Law of Civil Matrimony; July 28, the Law of Civil Registry; July 31, the Law of Noninterference in Cemeteries; August 11, the Law Regulating Religious Holidays. One by one, the privileges of the church were being denied it; the Liberals were demolishing "the worm-eaten structure," as Juárez called it.

The Civil Matrimony Law was published in Oaxaca City on August 4. The official newspaper greeted it with enthusiasm. "The nation is about to embark on the road of true progress, and although the reforms that are being planted at present might not produce an immediate result they are nevertheless the only means of reaching that future of exaltation and freedom to which Mexico is called." The law declared that matrimony was a civil contract, which must be made before a civil official. The marriage ceremony, to be legal, would henceforth be performed by the civil registrar in the presence of an alcalde and two witnesses. The couple could then have a religious ceremony if they wished in order to satisfy their own scruples, but this was secondary and had no legal standing.[29]

The Civil Registry Law was promulgated in Oaxaca on August 16. In order to maintain the independence between church and state, the record-keeping function of the former was to be assumed by government-appointed civil registrars. The church would no longer be the sole keeper and repository of vital statistics, important data to a Liberal regime believing in progress and needing figures on population to guide the nation in its development. Details were set forth to establish registry offices throughout the republic. Where these offices were to be located and who the judges of the civil registry would be were left to the state governors to decide. To register acts of birth, marriage, and death, fees were to be charged that would in part finance the offices, but the indigent were exempted from payment.[30]

Through the centuries, it had been customary to bury the dead under the floors and in the walls of churches. This practice, naturally, gave the clergy a deciding voice in interment regulations and had led to many disputes, particularly over fees. To take this matter from the control of the church, the law of July 31, published in Oaxaca on August 30, commanded the clergy to cease interfering in the matter of burials, which could no longer take place without the knowledge of civil authorities. The civil registry judges were charged with overseeing cemeteries. In order to maintain impartiality in matters of religion, the ministers of all faiths were to have easy access to all burial places and would be able to perform graveside services. Fees for any religious service connected with interment were private matters, to be arranged by the interested parties and the ministers.[31]

On September 17, 1859, the Law Regulating the Official Holidays was promulgated in Oaxaca. Designed to cut down the large number of days Mexican government workers could take off from their jobs, it also indirectly limited the influence of the church since most holidays were connected with religious festivals and holy days. As a consequence, only the patriotic holiday of September 16 and the religious days of New Year, Holy Thursday, Good Friday, the Thursday of Corpus Christi, the Days of All Souls and All Saints, the Feast of the Immaculate Conception, Christmas Eve day (later changed to Christmas Day), and all Sundays were to be observed officially as holidays. On all other days, businesses and government offices would remain open.[32]

Thus by the end of the summer of 1859, there were on the statute books all the Reform laws except one, all aimed directly or indirectly at denying the church the influence it formerly held over the economic, political, and social affairs of the entire populace of Mexico. Not all the measures emanating from Veracruz, where Juárez and his cabinet were doggedly holding on, could be put into effect immediately in all areas under Liberal control, but the foundations were laid. In the short space of fifty-seven days, July 23 through September 17, Oaxaca had seen drastic changes made in the way of life of its citizens. They received additional encouragement to purchase property formerly locked in mortmain, the church could no longer serve as banker to individuals or the state since its economic stranglehold had been broken, religious denominations other than the Roman Catholic Church would henceforth receive protection, burial customs had been altered, marriages were made civil affairs instead of religious acts, and days of leisure had been significantly reduced. That these laws gained full acceptance overnight could not be expected, but the insistence of the Liberal creed demanded them as goals to be achieved and the changes wrought would be sure signs of a nation emerging into the modern age.

THE SECOND COBOS INVASION

Throughout 1858 and the first half of 1859, Oaxaca had served as a recruiting center for the Liberal army as the War of the Reform or the Three Years' War between the Liberals and the Conservatives raged farther to the northwest in central Mexico. Brigades raised in the state were sent to Veracruz to protect the seat of government from the attacks of Miguel Miramón and other Conservative generals. By the second half of 1859, however, victory seemed so imminent to the Conservative forces in the central area of the nation that they could turn their attention to knocking out Oaxaca, reputedly one of the strongest supports of the besieged Liberal regime.

By late October 1859, the Conservative army under General José María Cobos, operating on the Puebla-Oaxaca frontier, had grown in strength. To counter the Cobos threat, Governor Castro had seen to the restrengthening of three battalions, financed by still another contribution in the form of a commercial and industrial tax of 1 per cent on property.[33] Despite opposition to this measure, the arms, uniforms, and provisions were gathered, the troops recruited and trained, and on October 7, two thousand strong, they left the capital to seek out and defeat Cobos. Only 247 military, including a fraction of the Juárez Battalion of the National Guard and the police force, were left to garrison Oaxaca City. Since it was a major expedition and the stakes were high, the senior ranking and most experienced officer in Oaxaca, General Ignacio Mejía, was placed in command. On October 30, at Teotitlán del Camino in the Upper Mixteca region, he engaged the enemy, was soundly defeated, and completely routed. Mejía led the remnant of his troops by a circuitous route to Tuxtepec, where he notified Juárez of his defeat and in turn received orders to go to Veracruz to undergo an investigation.[34] The inquiry was not terminated until February 6, 1860, with the exoneration of Mejía, but by then Oaxaca had been lost.

On November 2, Governor Castro learned of the battle of Teotitlán and its somber outcome. All had been gambled and all was lost. There were no more forces to call upon to stop Cobos; there was no alternative but to evacuate the city and flee to Ixtlán in the fastness of the sierra to the north. After issuing a proclamation telling the citizens of the defeat, declaring Oaxaca to be in a state of siege, setting up a Tribunal of Public Safety to maintain order in the city and try all crimes under martial law, plans were made to leave the capital. The activity was feverish; terror gripped the populace; commerce came to a standstill. On November 4, a rag-tag caravan pulled out in carts, wagons, on horseback, walking, pushing, carrying, dragging their belongings, and strung out along the dusty road that climbed up into the steep foothills and onto the mountain barrier. In the line was Margarita Maza de Juárez, wife of Benito, astride a burro with her three children riding in baskets hung on the little animal's sides.[35]

In a last act before departing, Castro appointed three prominent private citizens who were staying behind to act as commissioners to deliver the city to Cobos. So bad did lawlessness become in the capital that on the afternoon of the 4th the commissioners, instead of awaiting the appearance of General Cobos, directed a note to him begging him to hurry his arrival to restore the rapidly decaying order in the city.[36]

On November 6, General Marcelino Ruiz Cobos, cousin of José María, arrived in the capital where he was greeted jubilantly by the Conservatives who now predominated in the city. Several of the towns of the Central District also accepted the arrival of the Conservative army with festivities while many of their men hastened to enlist in Cobos's army. Two weeks later, on November 19, General José María Cobos arrived. To show their enthusiasm, the general's sympathizers in the city pulled his coach from the Marquesado to the Government Palace. Significantly, he took up his residence across from the Alameda and near the cathedral and the capitol so that he could keep an eye on both.[37]

The churchmen in Oaxaca welcomed General Cobos, greeting him as their deliverer. The military began to enforce the Zuloaga Law that Conservative President Félix Zuloaga had issued the previous January, which declared null and void any transactions regarding church property carried out under terms of the Lerdo Law. Cobos also repealed the 1857 law regulating fees paid to priests for services rendered to their congregations. The Episcopal Palace and the seminary were returned to the church and all monasteries were reopened.

Nicolás Vasconcelos, the vicar capitular, ordered that a Mass of thanksgiving be celebrated on December 5, announcing that once more the church "has begun to breathe, after more than three years during which impious demogoguery has oppressed it . . . ."[38]

But a quarrel soon developed between the general and the priests over money. Cobos was hard pressed for funds; the church was wealthy, he thought. Why not seek a loan from the hierarchy? In early December, he asked for 100,000 pesos. Vasconcelos replied that he realized that the money was necessary to sustain Cobos's government but that such a large amount was not readily available. It would have to be paid in installments, properties would have to be sold, and mortgages redeemed in order to make up the full amount. A few days later, Cobos demanded some cash immediately. Through great effort, the vicar capitular managed to find 10,400 pesos, in addition to an earlier personal loan he and a layman had made as partial payment of the first installment on the 100,000 pesos. Ironically, the Conservative army was taking on the responsibility of destroying the last vestiges of the wealth of the church in Oaxaca, which it had come to save and restore to its former position of opulence and influence.[39]

The clergymen were not the only ones who experienced the avarice of General Cobos. Taxes were levied throughout the territory under his control and many abuses were committed in the collection. Forced loans were levied against individuals, many of them Liberals. Another form of robbery was practiced against those Liberals who had chosen to remain in the city rather than go to Ixtlán. Many of these were put in jail and then forced to contribute money to Cobos or contribute rifles to his army in order to gain their freedom. Many of the arrests were made because the Liberals had been caught writing to their friends and members of their families in the sierra.[40]

In Ixtlán, the Liberal government found itself in dire circumstances. The large numbers of soldiers, government employees, and private citizens who had fled from Oaxaca City on November 4 drained the area of all its food supplies. Some wives who had remained behind in the capital managed to send a trickle of supplies by circuitous routes to the government, but hardly enough to provide sustenance for a long period of time.[41] The shock of defeat seemed to pervade everywhere in the sierra, morale was low, and as the stay became prolonged, the Indians of the region began to grumble about the way all the food was going to feed their uninvited visitors. The government leaders could not decide on a course of action; whereas a few urged an attack against Cobos, more opted for going to Veracruz to join Juárez.

José María Díaz Ordaz, who had been in Veracruz for some time, succeeded finally in convincing the president to send him back to Oaxaca and allowing him to resume the leadership of the state government. Cleared at last of culpability in his retreat from the Cumbres de Acultzingo, which had taken place almost a year earlier, he left for Ixtlán and arrived there on December 20, 1859. Juárez had written ahead to Miguel Castro telling him to turn over the office of governor to Díaz Ordaz, who, in order to unite the factions, made Castro the head of his secretariat. The governor once more assumed military command, taking over from the borlado Colonel Cristóbal Salinas. Many moderates were displeased with the changes made on Juárez's instructions. Dublán, Castro's secretary, resigned and left for Veracruz, as did Bernardino Carvajal, the second man in Castro's secretariat, who departed for Tehuantepec where he hoped to convince Porfirio Díaz, the new governor's second cousin, to rebel and proclaim himself the leader of the state. Having second thoughts, however, Carvajal stopped in Villa Alta, where he served a while as parish priest, illicitly, then returned to Ixtlán to offer his services to Díaz Ordaz. The governor, possessed of outstanding qualities of leadership, was able to unite the Liberals temporarily and by carrying forward plans to recapture the capital managed to raise the morale of all the refugees. Supplies and funds also began to arrive at this time from Veracruz—rifles, ammunition, and some reinforcements.[42]

Before long, plans for the campaign were complete. Porfirio Díaz was to march from Tehuantepec, unite with the forces of Díaz Ordaz at the foot of the Sierra, and together they would attack Cobos. Díaz had only 170 men, some of them Chiapans, but Díaz Ordaz had 1,240 under his own command. Before the rendezvous took place, however, many soldiers in Díaz's small contingent mutinied and Díaz was attacked by Marcelino Ruiz Cobos, the second in command of the Conservative army in the state. As a result, Porfirio was forced to retreat.[43]

Ill-luck struck the larger Díaz Ordaz column also. En route to the rendezvous point at Tlacolula, they met the main force of José María Cobos at the village of Santo Domingo del Valle, lying at the base of the mountains on the rim of the valley floor between San Felipe del Agua and Tlacolula. The battle was long and bloody, but victory lay with the Liberals. In the closing moments, however, Díaz Ordaz fell

from his horse mortally wounded. Rumor was rampant that the borlados had assassinated him, using the confusion of battle to hide their
crime. He died the next day while being carried back to Ixtlán.

From observing Díaz Ordaz's features, one would readily conclude he was a writer of romantic novels, a philosopher, a poet, or a
musician. The aristocratic background is evident. His face betrays the
characteristics of an idealist who would not come to terms with the
world, who could not be satisfied with reality, and who wished for a
better life for all men. And perhaps one would not be wrong in
forming such an impression. It was Díaz Ordaz's dissatisfaction with
the present state and his desire for a better world that made him the
great man of the Reform in Oaxaca. He lived in a realm far removed
from the machinations of local politicians; he became involved in their
backroom deals only as their victim. When he tried to lead them to
victory as an amateur soldier, brave and persevering but untrained,
the enemies within his ranks saw to it that even then he was entangled
in the brambles of politics. Whether he was murdered by his political
opponents who counted on the confusion of battle to hide their crime,
or whether he was killed by a shot from the Conservative side, neither
of which can be disproved or proved, is of little consequence. One can
be sure that, as the smoke of battle lifted from the field, many men
were glad to receive the news that their leader had fallen.

The death of the commander prevented the Liberals from following up their victory by pursuing Cobos to the capital. Instead, they
turned toward Ixtlán to resume their exile, joined by Porfirio Díaz
and his diminished, defeated troops. Marcos Pérez, as regent of the
supreme court, succeeded to the governorship and Salinas took over
military command. Their strength, however, had not suffered from
the battle of Santo Domingo del Valle; before long, they regained
their morale and again poured out of the mountains to lay siege to
Oaxaca City in early February. Their number was not large enough to
work a complete encirclement; they had to be satisfied with investing
the northern edge of the town and occupying the heights overlooking
the Marquesado and the northeastern section of the capital. Pérez, the
radical governor, could not work with Salinas, the borlado military
leader. Clash of personalities and opposing ideologies prevented the
close cooperation necessary for success. President Juárez sent General
Vicente Rosas Landa, a graduate of the military academy and a
former Conservative, to take command and direct the siege.

In the city, Cobos had become a tyrant. Residents of the capital and the nearby valley towns and villages were taxed, forced into work gangs, impressed into the Conservative army, imprisoned for the slightest infraction and then forced to pay heavy ransoms to gain their freedom, and had their food supplies and farm animals confiscated. By late spring, 1860, even the clergy were disgusted. Vicar General Padre Cházari, who had greeted Cobos's arrival so enthusiastically in November, was sent into exile on February 10. His crime was making an opening in the wall between his house and that of one of the Esperón brothers, all of whom were prominent borlados. Priests were forced to make contributions and failure to pay resulted in imprisonment. Through influential prelates in Mexico City, complaints were lodged concerning the huge sum of money Cobos was extracting from the Oaxacan church and the members of the priesthood, but the complaints never reached the government: the Oaxacan hierarchy was advised to be patient.[44]

As a result, Cobos may not have been beloved of the people but by his ironfisted policies he was able to make the city into a formidable fortress. Streets were cut by trenches, barricades, and even moats. The Conservative army was concentrated in the central section of the capital within a rough quadrilateral whose redoubts were the monasteries and convents. Sacks of earth protected the rooftops of the churches where cannon had been hoisted into place. The Spaniard had more men, more ammunition, more supplies, more artillery than the Liberals.[45]

General Rosas Landa and his staff arrived on February 13 to take command of the Liberal army besieging Oaxaca City. Aloof, strictly military in all matters, he immediately became unpopular with the rough Oaxacans who were accustomed to a greater spirit of camaraderie between officers and troops than Rosas Landa was willing to lend himself to. He was so disliked by all the Oaxacan soldiers from the very beginning that, in a negative way, the shared hatred brought together for the moment the radicals and moderates in a determined spirit to win victory despite the poor leadership.

For his part, the general was dismayed when he surveyed the situation and found what he had to work with: a treasury low in funds, no food supplies except those that could be foraged on night patrols, little ammunition, a cavalry too small to mount an attack, cannon with a range too short to permit firing upon Cobos's positions, and, worst of all, undisciplined troops numbering some 1,500 officers and men, many of whom came and went as they pleased. The military academy had not prepared him for such a command. Except for orders issued to strengthen the fortifications, he immediately lapsed into inaction on the excuse that he first had to train his army in methods of warfare.[46]

In March, he managed to capture the Marquesado, holding that position along with the forts on the heights above. This gave him a better base from which to seek supplies and launch an attack against the city proper: but again, caution and delay. And the citizens of the suburb complained to the general that not only had their food supplies been seized by the Liberals but their men had either been impressed into the army or had run away, leaving the populace unprotected.[47]

Then in early May, word reached the Liberals that General Miguel Miramón had raised his siege of Veracruz after months of trying to take that city, thereby freeing the Conservative army for operations elsewhere. A large contingent was en route to reinforce Cobos. There was nothing left but to withdraw once more into the sierra. The Liberals were so angry that a group of them, headed by Luis María Carbó, tried to assassinate Rosas Landa on the retreat, but Porfirio Díaz protected him and saved his life. On May 14, the general sent a dispatch to the minister of war in which he reported that that very afternoon his staff was turned upon in the mountain town of Villa Alta, the assault being urged on by the renegade friar Margarito Maldonado who was "drunk, giving shouts of death and calling them and me traitors . . . ." On May 18, the haughty general wrote to Juárez that he was on his way to Veracruz, having received from the Oaxacans the greatest outrages imaginable.[48]

The Liberals, still apparently in their cooperative mood as a result of their mutual dislike of Rosas Landa, were determined to show Veracruz that they could defeat the Conservatives on their own initiative, that they were good and resourceful fighters despite the disparaging reports sent throughout the spring by the recently departed general. In Ixtlán they spent June and July in reorganizing their forces. On August 4, they left the sierra for Oaxaca City where they formed when they reached the northern outskirts. One battalion, commanded by Ramón Cajiga, occupied the Hacienda of Dolores, while another occupied the Hacienda of San Luis. Marcelino Ruiz struck at the first hacienda and was repulsed; his cousin attacked the second; he too was unsuccessful. Meanwhile, Porfirio Díaz had hit the center of the Conservative army, which retreated into the city and occupied Carmen Alto and Santo Domingo monasteries. The Liberals formed two columns to pursue the retreating army and upon reaching the city surrounded the fortresses. Cobos managed to break out of Santo Domingo with 800 of his men and escape. The Liberals then poured into the monastery and Carmen Alto soon surrendered. Once more the state was saved for the Liberal cause.[49]

CHURCH AND STATE

When the Liberal army reoccupied the city on August 5, 1860, its major effort was devoted to putting the machinery of the administration back into working order. All that the Cobos cousins stood for collapsed, for the time being, when they escaped before the attacking army. Toward the end of September, less than two months after recapturing the capital, the Liberal government was functioning smoothly, and on the 23rd, a grand ball was held to celebrate the rapidity with which the transition had been made. Three months later, the civil war was terminated in victory for the Liberals. Mexico, it was hoped, could be at peace.

But all was not well among the Oaxacan Liberals during the last weeks of the Three Years' War. Marcos Pérez was, like his predecessor Díaz Ordaz, an unbending radical. The borlado faction held a majority in the legislature and was dissatisfied with Pérez as the leader of the state; soon the moderates began to plot his removal, as they had done earlier with Díaz Ordaz. When the governor failed to make his annual report to the legislature, as required by the state constitution, his opponents were provided with the technicality they needed to oust him from office. The legislature met in a secret session, voted his removal, and replaced him with one of their number, Ramón Cajiga, who in turn appointed José Esperón, rich merchant, property owner, lawyer, and leader of the borlados, as head of the governor's secretariat. Pérez's supporters were too few in number to modify the course of events. His strongest advocate, Porfirio Díaz, was out of the state participating in the final campaign to wrest Mexico City from the reactionary government. So he was forced out of the governorship, remained completely discredited by the moderates, and died eleven months later.[50] Cajiga, desirous of giving his appointment as governor the stamp of constitutionality and in order to bring about public sanction of the manipulations of the borlados, called for statewide gubernatorial elections for January 20, 1861. He won handily over the rojo candidate, Luis María Carbó, and was inaugurated in office on February 20.[51]

To the moderates, then, fell the task of completing the program of the Reform, now that the Three Years' War was at an end. The borlados would retain control of affairs in the state for three years, from November 1860, to December 1863. Their record in this undertaking is, as before, a mixed one and indicates again the manner in which they looked upon the Reform. In regard to the attack against the church, they continued to compromise on some points but pursued a determined policy on others when it suited their purposes. Their overall efforts brought about a triumph; yet the victory was due not so much to the vigor of their attack as to the momentum generated in previous years and the devastating, cumulative effect of the Reform on the church.

Enhancing the prospect of victory, the Oaxacan church in the autumn of 1860 became conciliatory. Nicolás Vasconcelos, vicar capitular of the diocese for the past year and supporter of General Cobos, suddenly resigned. When the cathedral chapter met to choose a new head on October 24, 1860, the members elected a moderate, Rafael Hernández. He immediately notified the state governor of his selection in the belief that it was his duty to do so, and sent out a circular to the priests of the bishopric informing them of his election to the vicariate. A graduate both of the Oaxaca seminary and the Institute of Sciences and Arts, Hernández had just turned forty-four. The official press greeted his selection with the anticipation of a détente in church-state relations, pointing out that the new leader, while orthodox, was neither a reactionary nor a fanatic and that he would bring about a clerical regeneration.[52]

In several matters, he showed himself to be interested more in the spiritual welfare of the faithful of the diocese than in political confrontations. He labored to provide the seminary with more funds with which to operate, prohibited the unauthorized veneration of certain images, forbade lay persons from hearing Mass from the altar, stopped the practice of collecting money for charitable purposes during the Mass, and suspended priests who abused their vows. When the government requested that no church bells be sounded during the celebration of independence in September 1861, he acceded and cooperated.[53]

While the Liberals and churchmen in Oaxaca were managing to live together in this period of brief and guarded peace, the national

government continued its frontal attack against the church with the issuance of the Law of Religious Liberty—the measure that had caused so much heated debate in the constitutional congress of 1856–57 and that failed to gain acceptance at that time. Not many weeks later, the bishops of the Republic were ordered into exile because of their support of the reactionary cause in the recent war and to prevent their further meddling. And, finally, on February 1, 1861, the minister of justice notified all state governments that President Juárez had decided to reduce the number of nunneries in order to bring about an economy in their operations, partly financed by national treasury funds since July 1859. The convents had been left alone after the law to nationalize church property and suppress the monasteries was put into effect. By the measure now resolved upon, religious orders with similar rules were to be moved together into designated convents. Once the nunneries were vacated, local treasury officials were to send reports to the national government and action would then be taken to dispose of the buildings.[54]

The moderates in charge of the government of Oaxaca state, following their pattern of compromise and delay, chose to ignore the decree concerning the nunneries for over a year. There was no great stir when the Law of Religious Liberty was promulgated—it evoked no editorial comment in the official press of the state. And since there was no bishop in Oaxaca at the time the order of expulsion was issued, there was no official comment on that measure.

Despite his good record, Hernández was allowed to remain as head of the Oaxaca church only slightly longer than a year. On November 21, 1861, José Vicente Salinas announced by circular to the priests of the diocese that in Rome Pope Pius IX had confirmed a new bishop for Oaxaca, José María Covarrubias y Mejía, and until he should arrive in his see to take charge, Salinas had been designated chancellor.[55]

Salinas, who, like Hernández, was a native Oaxacan and who was also in his early forties when named to the office of chancellor, was one of the bright stars in the diocesan hierarchy. Extremely intelligent, he early showed a talent for leadership and, ever since his ordination in 1842, had moved rapidly upward in positions of importance: by 1848, when he was only twenty-nine years old, he was serving as one of the canons of the cathedral chapter.[56]

By the time these hierarchical changes were made, the Oaxacan church was prostrate. The stringent measures taken to regulate its income from fees, deprive it of its real estate, suppress the orders, and generally limit its influence among the people had forced it to the ground. Cobos, in demanding the large contribution of 100,000 pesos, delivered the coup de grace, so that the recent actions of the national government were only blows on a lifeless body, as far as Oaxaca was concerned.

Specific evidence of the difficulties of the local church are not abundant, but the few that do exist are eloquent testimony of the miserable depths to which it had sunk as a result of the Reform program. For example, when the bishops were exiled, there were no prelates left within the nation to consecrate the holy oils used in the religious ceremonies. Hernández sent out a notice to priests that the oils had arrived in Oaxaca on July 2, 1861, from the Archbishopric of Havana, Cuba. The traditional time for consecration always comes at Easter, which means that it had taken three months for the sacred ointments to reach Mexico and be distributed to the various dioceses. Hernández had also spoken of the "sad and very critical" state of the seminary in Oaxaca City and the lamentable situation in the parishes. When Salinas became chancellor, he found it necessary to order the curates to return a large portion of their conciliar pensions to the coffers of the church in order to provide money for the operations of the diocese and to help support the two mendicant orders of Capuchinesses in the city. But most telling of all was the official newspaper's description of Easter week, 1863, in the capital city of the state:

> It [Easter week] passed dismally in the inquietude of the situation [the War of Intervention]: The Catholic celebrations were cold, the churches with an appearance of poverty even to the point that the silver adornments and the jewels of the images had disappeared, not without marked intention and calculation. On Holy Saturday there was not the procession of people in the plaza which had attracted so many persons the previous year in the Alameda.[57]

In March of 1862, furthermore, the borlados had decided to make use of the decree of February 1 of the previous year calling for a reduction in the number of convents. The capital of the state was without adequate jail facilities, nor did the town council have a permanent home. The idea was advanced to confiscate Santa Catarina convent of the Dominican Sisters and remodel it for a jail and municipal offices. The ayuntamiento petitioned President Juárez that the city be ceded the convent, Juárez granted the request, and on March

4, at midnight, with all the security possible, the Dominican Sisters, thirteen in number, some of advanced age, were removed to the convent of La Concepción, there to be housed with the Conceptionist nuns. "The most profound silence shrouded this solemn act," reported the newspaper. "The nuns left their old habitation full of resignation, of holy respect, and were conducted in carriages to La Concepción where their companions received them cordially." All the furnishings were shifted with the nuns; even the plants within the convent were uprooted and moved. No incident marred the transfer, but a few days afterwards, workmen who had already begun the remodeling of the nunnery discovered a cache of rifles and gunpowder, leftovers from the Cobos regime, buried beneath the latrines. This was a good propaganda piece and it was fully exploited. The convent was thrown open to the public for a few days so that the curious could see the arms that had been hidden, while the official newspaper fulminated against the supporters of General Cobos and derisively wrote of the guns as "those sacred relics hidden in a convent of virgins."[58]

The excuse given for the delay on the part of the state government in its implementation of the decree regarding the consolidation of the nunneries was that the move had to be well planned in order to avoid incidents. It should be noted that the borlados stopped short of full enforcement, for they did not consolidate the orders of Capuchinesses located in Oaxaca City. After the confiscation of Santa Catarina convent, the government finally acted to attempt to return to the nuns their dowries. Felipe Sandoval, a notary and a Liberal, was commissioned to ask the nuns individually if they would accept their money, but when he went to the various convents on March 25, each nun refused to receive her dowry. The large sum of 200,000 pesos was involved. Governor Cajiga requested that the national government allow the state to place this amount on deposit until the nuns should decide to accept it, meanwhile letting the public instruction committee use the money to improve education. The matter was brought to the attention of President Juárez, who decided that the local officials should try once more to convince the nuns to accept the money the government had set aside for them. Again, on September 19, Sandoval visited the convents and talked with each nun; again they refused. On October 22, the governor forwarded the results of the second interviews and repeated his request that the money be used for educational purposes. A month later, Juárez, through his minister of relations, Fuente, wrote Cajiga that the dowry money was to be treated like all nationalized property. He further stipulated that since perhaps the Oaxacan nuns may have been influenced in their decisions in order to attract sympathy for their plight and thereby become the nucleus or symbol of a plot or demonstration against the government, no one would be allowed to solicit charity for the ladies. Then in January 1863, it was decided to allow the state to grant 100,000 pesos of the dowry money to the Escuela Central, which had recently been established to educate the youth of the state who wanted to prepare themselves as teachers or who could not attend the Institute of Sciences and Arts.[59]

This was not the only manner in which the state became the beneficiary of the property taken from the church. Despite the provision in the 1859 law suppressing the regular orders, which called for dividing the monasteries into lots to be sold, some of the closed monasteries in Oaxaca City were ceded—on May 24, 1861—to the state government to finance the construction of a road from Tehuacán to Huatulco. Along with Santa Catarina convent, the municipal government of the state capital received four confiscated houses to be used as schools. On March 15, 1862, the state asked for the former residence of the bishop, the Episcopal Palace, to be used as the location for the new Escuela Central, and had its request granted a month later. On June 30, 1862, San Pablo monastery was given to the state for the Institute of Sciences and Arts and San Agustín monastery was likewise ceded and was to be divided into lots and sold, the income from the sales to go to endow the Institute. This was the only cession stipulating division into lots. San Francisco monastery had already been turned over to the state and Governor Cajiga recommended it be converted into a school for artisans. The Institute was occupying the buildings of the seminary, which the national government likewise gave to the state. Cajiga also recommended that a girls' school be established to occupy the House of Spiritual Exercises of the Oratory of San Felipe Neri. Santo Domingo and Carmen Alto monasteries were being used as barracks, stables, hospitals, and jails for political prisoners, as the situation demanded. The monastery of San Juan de Dios, next to the market, was in the receivership of the state and was soon turned over to the town council to be used as an extension of the market plaza. Thus the procedures adopted in Oaxaca to dispose of the conventual houses present a noteworthy and important exception to the methods used elsewhere in the Republic by which such real estate was placed in private hands or converted to public purposes.[60]

In other areas, the principal method of disposal was sale to individuals.

WAR

Now began a long period in which attention was taken up with military matters: recruiting and enlistment, marches and counter-marches, the battlefield and the home front. Spirits were high, desertions few in this moment when the passions of patriotism took hold. The nation was threatened, not by internal revolts but by foreign invasion. The defeat of 1848 and the long night of gloom that followed it still fresh in their minds, the Liberals once more rallied to support their republican government, to preserve the gains made in the recently terminated, terrible War of the Reform.

Although the Conservatives were defeated in the three years' civil war, which had ended in December 1860, they had not given up the struggle. They decided next to seek support in Europe for their cause. Many of the Conservatives were convinced that reestablishment of a monarchy was the only solution to the problems confronting the nation. At the same time, England, Spain, and France were concerned about mistreatment of their citizens residing in Mexico and financial questions revolving around loans, bonds, and claims. There was a conjunction of interests in 1861—Conservatives looking for a second chance, Mexicans living in exile agitating for monarchy, some European states showing sympathy for the defeated faction and expressing distrust of the Juárez government, Catholics manifesting concern over the treatment of the Mexican church, and Napoleon III desiring to extend his empire to include Mexico as a satellite state. By late 1861, the consensus among many of the Conservatives was that they should take advantage of these currents to impose a monarchy with a European prince on the throne supported by European powers. At the same time, France, England, and Spain agreed among themselves to intervene in Mexico to seize the customhouses in order to force settlement of claims and to collect debts.

The Spanish fleet appeared off Veracruz. When word reached Oaxaca City on December 18, 1861, Governor Cajiga made a show of putting the state on a war footing. He issued a stirring proclamation informing the citizenry of the threat to the Republic, declared a state of siege, assumed extraordinary powers, and summoned to active duty the National Guard, only recently reorganized and diminished in size.[61]

The Spanish force landed at Veracruz and was later joined by large British and French armies. Learning of France's ulterior designs on Mexico, Britain and Spain soon withdrew from the joint enterprise. To block the French army from penetrating the interior, the republican army converged. A convention was signed agreeing that no advance by either side would be made and was quickly broken. Puebla became the strategic point, guarding the approaches to the central valley, and the contingents from Oaxaca moved toward that city to join with the other defenders. And then—tragedy.

Ignacio Zaragoza commanded the Army of the East, the force charged with stopping the trim, efficient French army. He ordered his third division, led by General Ignacio Mejía and composed mainly of Oaxacans, to San Andrés Chalchicomula, in the eastern corner of the state of Puebla, some 100 miles due east of the city of Puebla and 75 miles west by northwest of the important town of Córdoba. The first brigade, arriving on the afternoon of March 6, bivouacked around the colecturía, or tithe barn, the largest building in the town, where 46,000 pounds of gunpowder had been stored. Food vendors came out to sell their tortillas and beans while the loyal women started their campfires. The slight breeze caught a spark, carried it inside the colecturía, and the air suddenly filled with the great thunder of explosion. One thousand forty-two soldiers, 475 women, 30-odd vendors were killed instantly. Two hundred men lay wounded, most them with limbs blown off, or blinded. Few of the first brigade escaped; in seconds, Oaxaca had lost 1,500 of her sons and daughters.

An eyewitness who viewed the town on the following Sunday reported that every nine or ten yards along the streets bonfires burned to purify the air of the acrid pall that still hovered over the area. No persons ventured outside but remained in their homes, many of which had been used as hospitals and morgues and were still covered with blood. Carts were filled with the putrifying bodies of the unburied dead; the air was so fetid that one could only enter the town with a soaked handkerchief over his face. Ungathered arms and legs could be seen scattered over the ground.[62] Without the aid of a contingent of French doctors who came to the aid of the victims, the loss undoubtedly would have been greater. Thus the War of the Intervention arrived in Oaxaca early, not through invasion of the territory of the state but through the loss of a large portion of the army she furnished the Republic.

Word of the explosion reached Oaxaca City on March 9. The entire city wept, for scarcely a family remained untouched by the tragedy. *La Victoria*, the official newspaper, rushed a special edition onto the streets giving the details of the colossal accident. Immediately, a committee of charity was formed to collect money for the families of the victims. One of the canons of the cathedral, Father Ignacio Merlín, was appointed to this committee, but he refused to let himself be associated with the charitable work, perhaps because only a few days previously he had witnessed the removal of the Dominican Sisters from Santa Catarina convent. The Liberals used his refusal as an opportunity to point out the deficiencies of priests: ". . . Señor Merlín, a faithful representative of his class, refuses to belong to a humanitarian society, not because he lacks time but so that the world might be convinced that it is not to the clergy to whom one should run when the business is that of succoring the unfortunate . . . ."[63]

Despite the tragedy at Chalchicomula, the republican army held and managed to stop the advance of the Interventionists at Puebla in May 1862. The French withdrew toward the coast, to wait for reinforcements and a second chance to invade central Mexico. Thus the war continued. Consequently, the home front in Oaxaca City became extremely active. Recruiting was carried on by the state government and various private citizens and the women of the city mobilized their talents to aid the war effort, principally through their organization known as the Sociedad Zaragoza, named in honor of the defender of Puebla who had died shortly afterwards of typhoid fever.

The women's society originated in Mexico City in September 1862. Its main purpose was the collection of supplies for the military hospitals, but it carried on other activities, such as sewing for the soldiers in the field and raising funds to support the hospitals. In December 1862, a branch of the organization was formed in Oaxaca City, with Juana Maza de Dublán, the sister-in-law of President Juárez and wife of Manuel Dublán, serving as president. Other officers included the wives of Luis María Carbó and Miguel Castro and the aunt of José Sáenz de Enciso, the young priest who had been exiled to Cuba in 1859 for his opposition to the Reform laws. Within a week after its organization, over a hundred women had joined the society. Members were required to donate some articles of underclothing or bed linen upon joining the group and thereafter to contribute weekly either a small sum of money or cloth and thread. The women met frequently to decide how best the contributions could be used and to sew for the soldiers.[64]

An outgrowth of the program of the Sociedad Zaragoza in Oaxaca was the life injected into cultural and entertainment activities, for it sponsored events of various types, the income from which financed its work and supported the military hospitals. The benefit performances consisted of such varied entertainment as dramatic productions, equestrian acts, and concerts, all staged by local talent.[65]

In May 1863, the interventionist forces tried again to take Puebla. The second attempt was successful and the way was opened for the French to enter the great central valley and occupy the national capital. Of the many prisoners captured with the fall of Puebla, General Porfirio Díaz managed to escape while being transferred to Veracruz but another Oaxacan, General Mejía, was shipped to France where he was held for several months before being repatriated. Díaz, after his escape, made his way to San Luis Potosí, where Juárez had established his refugee government. Here plans were formed to reorganize the armed forces of the Republic into different geographical groupings in order to hold those areas that had not yet fallen to the French. It was decided to establish the headquarters of the Army of the East in Oaxaca City with General Díaz in command. He was to have jurisdiction over Veracruz, Chiapas, Tabasco, Yucatán, and Campeche, in addition to Oaxaca, later to be extended to include Tlaxcala and Puebla. He was given 2,800 men to take south with him.[66]

Leaving San Juan del Río near Querétaro on October 6, 1863, the Army of the East began its long march to Oaxaca, fighting various skirmishes and battles along the route, which led through the mountainous states of Mexico, Michoacán, and Guerrero. On October 28, Díaz attacked Taxco and pillaged it. The poor condition of the troops, the lack of enthusiasm among many who had been impressed into the ranks and were watched as prisoners, the harsh terrain over which they had to march, and the lack of supplies caused many difficulties for Díaz. The entire Second Brigade, the Sinaloans, not desiring to go so far from their homeland, attempted a desertion en masse but the general found out about it in time to prevent it. By the time Díaz reached Huajuapan on the Oaxacan frontier in late November, he had lost almost one-third of his troops through desertion.[67]

Porfirio Díaz had never wavered from the strict Liberal creed taught him by his friend and mentor, Marcos Pérez, and therefore had no sympathy with the moderate politicans who were controlling the affairs of Oaxaca. Besides that, he was convinced that Cajiga and Esperón had entered into negotiations with the French to the end that a secret agreement had been worked out that neither the French army contingents that had occupied the border areas of the state after the fall of Puebla the previous May would advance further into Oaxaca nor would republican troops in that state attack the invaders pending a settlement of the difficulties between France and Mexico. It was well known that Cajiga had not proscuted the war effort in Oaxaca to the fullest extent after the first surge of patriotism in 1861–62 had grown tepid and that the men recruited and the supplies gathered and forwarded to the war zone had only begun to tap the potential available. Furthermore, Cajiga had gradually reduced the number of National Guardsmen on active duty and had consistently disarmed republican guerrilla bands seeking refuge in the state. In December 1862, President Juárez had sent Félix Romero, at the time serving as chairman of the permanent deputation of the recently closed national congress, to Oaxaca City on a special mission to try to convince Cajiga to send more troops and supplies. Romero was successful but each bit of aid forthcoming from the borlados in Oaxaca had to be cajoled and begged and forced, and then was as frequently refused as granted.[68]

Just before the arrival of Díaz in Oaxaca City, Cajiga and Esperón met secretly with the moderate-dominated legislature to decide what course of action they should take if the general was empowered by Juárez to demand the governorship of the state. They concluded that under no circumstances would Cajiga relinquish his office. When Díaz arrived and the governor learned of his instructions, Cajiga addressed a note to Díaz informing him that he considered the general's grant of powers unconstitutional and inquired if Díaz would use force in removing him. The general, who was never one to mince words, replied that force would be employed to defend the nation against all foreign invaders and traitors and that anyone who resisted complying with the orders of the federal government was a traitor. Cajiga and Esperón both took the hint and quickly resigned. Accordingly, on December 1, 1863, Díaz himself assumed the civil governorship and appointed radicals to key positions. At the same time, he retained command of the Army of the East. The burden soon proved too heavy, however, and on February 16, 1864, he appointed General Ballesteros civil governor. Félix Romero headed the secretariat for the governor while Justo Benítez served as secretary of the general staff of the army. Clearly, Ballesteros was only a figurehead who merely promulgated and enforced the orders issued by Díaz.[69]

From the moment of his arrival in Oaxaca, Díaz began to put the state on a more active war footing by recruiting men to serve in the army and National Guard; establishing court-martials to prosecute deserters, thieves, and other criminals; reworking the tax structure to provide more financial support for the war effort; requiring medical students to work in the military hospital in the city; taking over the properties still unsold from the nationalization of church real estate to sell them at lower values and use the income to finance his military operations; sending detachments to neighboring states to bolster the republican cause in those areas; prohibiting the exportation of lead, gunpowder, and saltpeter; establishing a munitions factory to cast cannons, mold bullets, and rework old rifles; and exiling all trouble-makers who opposed his policies.[70]

The moderate Liberals were in control of Oaxaca from late 1858 to late 1863, a perido of five years, except for the months taken up with trying to defeat the Conservative army under General Cobos and expel that force from the state. Parenthetically, it is significant that when actual fighting was involved against the Conservative army in 1859–60 and that when armed struggle loomed on the horizon as it did in late 1863 and early 1864 with the prospect of the invasion of the state by the Imperialists, the national Liberal government under Juárez insisted that radicals should hold the chief military and civil positions in the state—first in the return of Díaz Ordaz and then with the sending of Porfirio Díaz half the length of Mexico to assume command.

Although no materials have been found that relate specifically to the national regime's preference for radical leadership in Oaxaca in time of war or threat of war, the very fact that radicals were pushed into positions of leadership at such times of extreme emergency indicates indirectly that the national administration trusted the purists more and considered them to be more faithful than the moderates. This can be explained by the process of radicalization that the national leaders had undergone through the years of civil war and invasion by European powers. Juárez and his associates were having enough trouble from intraparty struggles and strident opposition from the moderate Liberals and had themselves become so radicalized that it was natural for them to feel an affinity and express a preference for purists of similar resolution, perseverance, and will at the state level.

The moderates simply could not be trusted to carry out with unquestioning loyalty the measures deemed necessary by the national radical leadership nor was there present in the actions of the borlados the sense of urgency demanded of them in meeting the various crises besetting the Republic. In enforcing the Reform program, the record of the moderates in Oaxaca was uneven. In regard to most of the orders emanating from Veracruz in the form of decrees and statutes, the Oaxaca moderates complied and showed themselves determined to uphold the Liberal position. But in one important aspect, the restrictions placed on the convents, the borlados were dilatory in doing their duty. As will be seen later, when in 1863 the national government finally ordered the closure of all convents and the exclaustration of all nuns, the borlado administration in Oaxaca ignored the order by silently and discreetly filing it away and forgetting about it.

In another important matter, the support of the war effort, the record of the borlados in Oaxaca was likewise mixed. The state was in a position to provide vital aid for the Liberal and republican war machine that operated in the central part of Mexico, but what support was forthcoming was marked by fecklessness and fickleness much of the time. It is no wonder, then, that Porfirio Díaz was sent to oust Cajiga and Esperón from their entrenched position on the eve of the French invasion of Oaxaca. The moderates could not be counted on to fight; indeed, there was fear expressed that instead of fighting they would negotiate some form of surrender. This fear, probably well founded, explains why General Díaz acted so swiftly and decisively in turning Oaxaca into a fortress, and why, in doing so, he alienated so many of the residents of the state capital, people who had grown accustomed to the moderates' policy of doing no more than what was absolutely necessary to stay in power.

Oaxaca City became, in those first months of 1864, a veritable military depot and fortress. It was well that Díaz acted with such resolution and foresight, for the French, now that Mexico City was in their hands, had designs upon the southern state.

CHAPTER 4

THE INTERVENTION IN OAXACA, 1864–66

WHEN PUEBLA FELL in May 1863, Juárez's republican administration fled northward. The French army occupied Mexico City and plans were made to invite Austrian Archduke Maxmilian von Hapsburg to become the ruler of a Mexican empire, created by Napoleon III in agreement with Mexican Conservatives. From the Valley of Mexico, the interventionist army, reinforced by Austrian contingents and including a considerable number of Mexican Conservative units, began a campaign to extend its control over other parts of Mexico.

For several reasons the French were compelled to turn their attention to Oaxaca. If Maximilian were to be emperor, he had to have an empire, extensive in size and united in loyalty to the throne. At the time of the Austrian's arrival in the early summer of 1864, the southern part of Mexico was the only important area still supporting the Liberal cause and, therefore, it had to be forced to adhere to the monarchy. Justo Sierra, in his *Political Evolution of the Mexican People*, described Oaxaca as "the last stronghold of the armed Republic," and added that only in that state was there "a solid core of resistance, slowly being firmed up by the most earnest of the young republican chiefs, General Porfirio Díaz, and preparing for the tempest that was sure to come."[1] Throughout 1864, detachments sent out by General Díaz from his headquarters in Oaxaca City menaced the French lines of supply and communication from Veracruz to Puebla and on toward Mexico City, a threat that had to be eliminated. Finally, since all other important areas had been captured by the French and Conservative Mexican armies, there was a large available force that needed to be kept employed.

87

In July 1864, one month after Maximilian's arrival, Marshal Achille-François Bazaine, commander of the interventionist forces, issued orders preliminary to undertaking the campaign against Oaxaca. General Henri Agustin Brincourt, division commander at Puebla, was instructed to move forward enough men to tighten the arc around Oaxaca State, thereby restricting the area in which Díaz's detachments could operate. Then construction of a road along the proposed invasion route began, for none existed capable of handling the heavy artillery, supplies, and large contingents of troops the French would be moving toward Oaxaca City. The new road was to proceed from Puebla via Acatlán and Huajuapan, the route followed today by the Pan American highway. At the same time the trail from Puebla via Tehuacán was widened and improved. Since the engineering difficulties were tremendous due to the rough terrain, construction took several months. Díaz attacked the road in August, defeated the French forward positions, and then retreated. Brincourt followed as far as Nochixtlán, where he was ordered to halt, although he could have gone on to Oaxaca City easily with only his infantry and cavalry. The road was completed as far as Yanhuitlán in late November, built by the Mixtec Indians who lent their aid willingly to the French because they were disgusted with the treatment they had received from the detachments of Díaz's army during the previous twelve months.[2]

General Courtois d'Hurbal was given command of the column that was to move over the new road. This column, formed in Acatlán, was composed of large detachments of troops from Orizaba, Puebla, and Mexico City. They reached Yanhuitlán on December 12, but since the road beyond that point was not yet ready, d'Hurbal left all supplies and field artillery there and moved on with only his infantry and light cavalry, arriving in Etla, near Oaxaca City, six days later.[3]

THE FALL OF THE CAPITAL

Bazaine decided to direct the attack against Oaxaca in person. He left Mexico City on January 3, 1865, bringing with him reinforcements, and arrived in Etla on the 15th.[4] In the meantime, all supplies had been moved forward and the preparations for the attack were almost complete. The marshal established his headquarters at Hacienda Blanca near Etla. Under his command he had approximately 8,000 men.

Lieutenant colonel Brissonet, commanding officer of the corps of engineers, had already conducted a reconnaissance of the area immediately surrounding the city on January 11, and had devised a plan of operations that was closely studied by all commanders. On the 14th, d'Hurbal approved it, writing amplifying notes and directions on some points. Lafitte, the artillery commander, also approved it. And when Bazaine arrived, he too accepted it in general terms, stipulating that further details should be developed from more reconnoitering expeditions.

Since the city had been strongly fortified and Díaz's troops were behind a formidable quadrilateral, of which the major points of strength were, as usual, the monasteries and convents, Brissonet emphasized that an immediate and direct attack would result in a block-by-block fight with the loss of many men. It would be better to encircle the capital, then capture the hill forts the Liberals held, from there bombard the central section where Díaz's soldiers were concentrated, thereby weakening the enemy's garrison, and next, if necessary, attack the city proper. It was believed that the proposed heavy bombardment of the Liberals' position from the heights overlooking the town would bring about surrender or so weaken the opponent that a frontal attack would be of short duration and result in victory. Except for a few minor details, this was the plan adopted, and the days following Bazaine's arrival were taken up with putting it into effect.[5]

Díaz's strength was considerably less than that estimated by Brissonet, who put his garrison at from four to five thousand men with fifty pieces of artillery. The French even had a report from a "very intelligent" deserter from the city who, about January 21, gave out the information that Díaz had 7,000 men.[6] The exaggerated estimates caused the invaders to be unduly cautious. At the beginning of the siege, the republican army numbered approximately 3,000 troops; by the time it ended, Díaz had fewer than 1,000 men. His food rations, furthermore, were low, and his ammunition was in short supply, partly due to an explosion that destroyed the improvised munitions factory in Santo Domingo monastery on January 12, in which Colonel Juan N. Almogabar, the officer in charge of the works, was killed.

Desertions mounted daily. Díaz seems to have been a commanding officer who had little talent for holding together an army when the odds were against him. One eyewitness reports that the officers were haughty, taking little notice of the conditions of the men under them, and that deserters escaped in large numbers. Not even quick courts-martial followed by immediate executions—"each eight days one to five men accused of desertion were executed"—hindered the flow of men leaving the doomed garrison. The greatest blow came when Joaquín Treviño, sent out to defeat Bazaine's column of rein-forcements before it could unite with the main force at Etla, con-vinced the San Luis Lancers and the Legion of the North to desert instead of attacking, thereby depriving Díaz of his cavalry, except for his brother Félix's small detachment. When Treviño deserted, Díaz was automatically committed to accepting the siege; what mobility he had possessed was gone.[7]

Worst of all, however, was the ill-will the republican general had earned from the populace. When it became evident that Oaxaca City would be besieged, Díaz had set his men to work constructing the defenses. Not only were the usual barricades thrown up and trenches dug across the streets but all houses lying outside the quadrilateral were leveled in order to deny the French army any cover and to give the Liberal defenders a clear line of fire in case of a frontal attack. All houses lying along the defense perimeter had large holes knocked in their side walls to give cover for the movement of men and to facilitate communications.

Few Conservatives were to be found among the residents of the state capital, so battered had they become throughout the previous long months of the Liberal campaign to circumscribe or eliminate the Conservative party. The great majority of the inhabitants were by now avowedly Liberal in their sentiments, but it must be remembered that among those who counted—the property owners, merchants, lawyers, bureaucrats—allegiance lay with the borlados. The arrival of Díaz in late 1863 spelled gloom for the moderate majority. They were dis-mayed that he had come, displeased that they were forced to make so many sacrifices throughout 1864 as Díaz prepared for war, and now that it had come and they saw their city turned into a fortress at their great expense, they were angry. Many residents had fled to the rela-tive safety of outlying villages as the siege began, but those who stayed in the city were completely hostile to and alienated from their republi-can defenders.[8]

On the night of February 1, the French completed their encir-clement and then seized the hill forts. On the 4th, at dawn, the bom-bardment began with fury and continued for twenty-four hours. Dense clouds of acrid smoke rose from the gun emplacements and hung over the valley to cut off vision of the surrounding hills. The scene was one of desolation. On the 8th, Bazaine ordered an attack, the final assault, for the following day. At that same moment Díaz was coming to the decision that surrender was the only course of action open to him, for his ammunition was gone, desertions had left him with only 700 men, provisions maintained by the few remaining families in the city were exhausted. the citizens were complaining loudly, and the defenders were completely demoralized.[9]

Towards midnight, he rode out with Colonels Apolonio Angulo and José Ignacio Echeagaray, was fired upon by a French outpost, convinced the officer in charge of his identity and mission, and was led to Bazaine. In the following hours before sunrise, Díaz negotiated the surrender with the French marshal. At dawn, Colonel Echeagaray returned to the Mexican fortifications to order the defenders to lay down their arms, and after sunrise, Díaz himself went back into the city, escorted by French troops.[10]

At the plaza in front of the government palace, the defeated republican army formed for the ceremony of surrender. Díaz was crushed: ". . . scarcely could his voice be heard, choked with a suffering that was evident in his face with the indefinable traces of pain," one soldier present recorded. Then Díaz and the other officers were taken to Montoya Hacienda on the outskirts of the city, Bazaine's headquarters since February 1, where they had breakfast with the French marshal. From there, under close escort, they began their long march to Puebla and prison.[11]

Bazaine reported the fall of Oaxaca in a matter-of-fact tone to both the minister of war in Paris and to Maximilian in Mexico City. The Mexican emperor replied, "I am happy to see terminated so pacifically a siege that occupied so many of our valiant soldiers and forced [us] to postpone so many other necessary operations."[12] The note of bitterness couched in the congratulatory message gives indication of the strained relations developing between the emperor and his general, for Maximilian viewed the campaign in Oaxaca as a drain upon the treasury and thought that the victory could have been won at least five months earlier. The caution exercised by the French and the delay in bringing about the capitulation of Porfirio Díaz was to become a bone of contention, one of many, between the emperor and Bazaine. Some weeks later, Maximilian wrote to Napoleon III: "The capture of Oaxaca, for instance, had cost ten million francs, whereas many soldiers stated that the city could have been taken in August by General Brincourt with only a thousand men."[13] Indeed, many im-

portant officials in the imperial government, Maximilian and Charlotte included, doubted the necessity of the Oaxaca campaign since
such large sums had to be expended to bring it off, making it virtually
impossible for the treasury to meet the claims of France as well as its
remaining financial obligations.[14]

BEFRIENDING ENEMIES AND LOSING FRIENDS

It was the policy of Maximilian to appoint Mexicans to supervise and
manage the territories incorporated into the Empire. These appointees were given various titles and ranks—political prefects, imperial
deputies, and imperial visitors—depending on the size and strategic
importance of the areas placed under them and the types of duties
assigned to them. For the overseer of Haujuapan, the emperor had
designated Juan Pablo Franco political prefect. Then, as the French
pushed farther south and in anticipation of the fall of Oaxaca, by
September Franco had been named the prefect of Oaxaca with headquarters in the state capital, which he entered on February 9 in the
train of General Bazaine.

Born in Chiapas in 1816, Franco was a lawyer who had spent
most of his career in the far south of the Republic. He married into
the wealthy influential Chiapan family of the Larrainzars. When the
Revolution of Ayutla came, General Juan Alvarez appointed him a
district judge, but he was not allowed to assume the post because, in
his words, he had the reputation of being a firm and formidable
opponent to the widespread contraband operations in Chiapas, and
malefactors known to be involved in the illegal trade created so much
turbulence over his appointment that he had to leave. In 1856, he
moved with his family to Oaxaca City, practicing there his legal profession unsuccessfully, dealing in tobacco unsuccessfully, and es-
pousing the Conservative line. Perhaps urged by his in-laws, who were
opposed to the Liberal program and who would in time lend
wholehearted support to the Empire and the French Intervention, he
went over to the Conservative side. Although he did not actively support Cobos during either of the periods of reaction in Oaxaca—that
is, he did not hold any positions in the Cobos government—he
nevertheless later thought it prudent to deny publicly his affinity for
the Conservative cause. In January 1861, he appeared before the
political chief of the Central District to protest his innocence: he was,
he said, a simple merchant who did not indulge in politics, who had

taken no part in the Cobos invasion, and who wanted only to obey the law of the land. Belatedly Franco swore to uphold the Constitution of 1857. Sometime between that date and the summer of 1864, the Chiapan left Oaxaca and moved to Mexico City, for on June 16, 1864, he was among a sizeable group of Oaxacan Conservatives living in the national capital who signed a letter declaring their loyalty to the Empire and welcoming Maximilian and Charlotte upon their arrival. He probably owed his appointments as political prefect of Huajuapan and then of Oaxaca to the influence of Manuel Larrainzar, his in-law, whom Maximilian had made an imperial counselor.[15]

To Franco, then, fell the enormous tasks of rebuilding the severely damaged city, which would take months; of holding the former Liberal stronghold for the Empire, which, given the citizens' disaffection with Díaz, was not as difficult as might be expected—as long as Porfirio was in a Puebla prison; and of satisfying his overlords, which was to be his heavy yoke and would prove impossible.

The first order of business was to clean up the city. The town council of Oaxaca discussed plans for this in their session of February 21, and it was announced by Manuel María de Fagoaga, an old Conservative who had been appointed municipal prefect or president of the ayuntamiento, that 400 pesos—a pitifully small sum considering the extent of the damages—had been set aside for the operation and that workers from the surrounding villages would come into the city the following day to begin filling in the trenches and removing the barricades. Manuel Ortega Reyes, Porfirio Díaz's brother-in-law (and later his father-in-law), a member of the council, brought up the question of the holes that had been knocked in the walls of the private homes of citizens, but it was decided to begin work on the streets and let individual owners take care of their own property.[16]

This proved to be too great a task for private owners and gave Maximilian an opportunity to display magnanimity and generosity, which he seized, thereby winning over many adherents in Oaxaca to himself and his throne. His official newspaper, *El Diario del Imperio,* on March 9, carried the following description of Oaxaca City:

> Incredible is the state of ruin and misery to which the city has been reduced by the dissidents, who worked destruction in it. . . . Thousands [of the inhabitants] are without homes and resources of any kind and wander through the streets dressed in rags and dying of hunger, and the new authorities cannot remedy so much misfortune, notwithstanding the measures they have taken.

To provide some relief, the paper reports, the emperor is contributing 6,000 pesos from his personal funds and the empress 4,000 pesos
from hers. Then 10,000 pesos were added from public funds, and on
March 28, the 20,000 pesos arrived in Oaxaca. It was decided to
alleviate the hunger by distributing one-fourth of the gift among the
poor, whether or not they had suffered property damage, and the
remaining 15,000 pesos would go to the poor who had lost their
homes and who had no money with which to rebuild. Within a month,
adobe bricks were being manufactured on a large scale to supply the
materials for reconstruction. Not only did Maximilian provide money,
but he also ordered meat distributed among the poor of the city and
those who were working to clear the roads of the district. The workers
from the villages were rewarded and made happy by having the bells
from the village churches returned. These Díaz had confiscated,
thinking to use them in the manufacture of arms or to fill with gunpowder and grapeshot for use as mines in one grand explosion if the
French had made a frontal attack.[17]

Even during the siege, special care had been taken to deal sym-
pathetically but firmly with the Oaxacans. Resistance to the French
and the Empire was punished, cooperation gently encouraged and
rewarded. When the aqueduct bringing water to Montoya Hacienda,
Bazaine's headquarters, was cut in three places, the three Central
District villages near where the cuts were made were fined for having
been parties to the operation. On the other hand, all villages that sent
workers and supplies to aid the French army were exempted from the
capitation tax. When the republican guerrilla leader Ladislao Cacho
entered into negotiations with Franco preliminary to surrender,
Bazaine sent him congratulations and a safe-conduct pass.[18]

The people of Oaxaca City quickly made friends with the French.
By early March, they were returning to the capital daily in large
numbers. Their motives for accepting the situation gracefully were
probably mixed. They had to provide sustenance for themselves and
their families, and there were positions to be filled in the bureaucracy
in which many of them had spent most of their careers under the old
administration. For many citizens, including the borlados, it probably
brought little pain to accept the monarchy.[19] Franco's policy seems to
have been one of compromising the men of the Liberal party as much
as possible by offering to them and insisting they fill the government
positions, thereby bringing about adherence to the Empire in a subtle
manner. By mid-April, such men as Manuel Dublán, Colonel Luis

Mejía, Miguel Castro, Ramón Cajiga, Luis María Carbó, Manuel Ortega Reyes, the notary Juan Rey, Juan Cerqueda, some of the Esperón brothers, and José Inés Sandoval were working in the government offices.[20] Also, many had become so angered at Díaz's destruction of their property that they accepted the Intervention as a means of expressing their animosity to the republican general and all that he stood for. Another probable motive lay in the very fabric of Mexican history of the postindependence decades, when, as a result of the rather constant turnover of governments, it became fashionable to some and a necessity of survival to others always, or as often as possible, to be associated with the winning side.

On the lower level of society there was also acceptance. Had not the good emperor provided food and money in time of need? The relations between the native Oaxacans and the foreign garrison were so free and easy that some officers feared their men would lose allegiance. Colonna D'Ornano of the African brigade reported to General Mangin, who had taken command of the city upon Bazaine's departure:

> There exists perhaps, from the point of view of the demoralization of the troops, more danger in Oaxaca City than in the countryside. Old statistics show that before the fall of the city there were eleven women to one man. This proportion has doubled since the arrival of the French in Mexico. . . . The houses frequented by our soldiers and the houses where they spend the night without permission ought to be closely watched. The sale of brandy will be reduced as much as it can be, putting into force a police ordinance fallen into disuse that closes all saloons at six in the evening.[21]

To maintain the loyalty of the newly captured territory and to insure peace, the society of Oaxaca was for a time closely regulated and watched by the French, Austrian, and Mexican officials charged with administering the area. Citizens were prohibited from owning or hiding rifles or firearms, a curfew on merchandising establishments was decreed, restrictions were placed on the sale of liquor to soldiers, and the military authorities maintained close surveillance of some individuals, requiring them to obtain passes to enter or leave the city. An Austro-Mexican police force was organized to support the regular police in maintaining order in the city.[22] Probably the most severe measure taken was the implementation of Maximilian's decree of October 1865, calling for courts-martial to try anyone opposing the Empire. But even this was nothing new when promulgated, for courts-martial to try criminals, especially highwaymen who were operating throughout the nation in this disturbed era, had been decided upon by the emperor over a year previously as the only means available of stemming the lawlessness. Soon after the surrender of Oaxaca City, these courts were set up. On March 9, 1865, Cirilo Castro, convicted of armed robbery, was executed in the state capital. Two weeks later a deserter from Félix Díaz's cavalry was tried for his participation in sacking the village of Santo Domingo del Valle and sentenced to twenty years at forced labor. But there is little evidence that the courts-martial were widely used in Oaxaca to suppress the Liberals, or became oppressive to the people, or created ill-will on the part of the citizens toward the government imposed upon them. The local populace was undoubtedly glad that something was being done at last to deter the lawlessness that was so widespread.[23]

Many Oaxacans welcomed the French and accepted the Empire because previous governments had been unable to bring peace to the land. A typical Conservative viewpoint was expressed locally by Luis B. Santaella in his speech given on the program of September 15, 1865, to celebrate the independence of Mexico. All good Mexicans, he declared, understand that since the character of the people precludes self-government through republican institutions, ". . . only the monarchical institution can save us," for it alone could rise above political parties to "dominate them and make of Mexico a nation of true brothers, without hatreds or animosities . . . ."[24]

For this reason, and others, the invaders found the population docile, ductile, and if not enthusiastic, at least willing to cooperate. Typical of the cooperation given was the example set by the ayuntamiento of the capital. No outstanding republican leaders were members—these held higher posts—but there were Liberal republicans among the twelve regidores (council members), including Roberto Maqueo and Manuel Ortega Reyes. And Francisco Vasconcelos served as secretary. The transcripts of the sessions of the council throughout 1865 and 1866 indicate that only routine business was conducted, suggesting that the initiative lay in some other body or in some person outside the ayuntamiento. Only routine communications came from Franco. There was never any mention of disturbances or demonstrations against the French or Austrians garrisoning the city. There was a frequent turnover in personnel with several members moving up to higher positions in the bureaucracy. All in all, the regidores seem to have been conscientious about their duties and did not

try to subvert the imperial government. In short, they were collaborators, but nearly everyone else was, too.[25]

The one segment of the population in Oaxaca that failed to accept the French intervention and the Mexican Empire was, ironically,
the church. Coming to the Diocese of Antequera soon after the fall of
the city to the invaders was the new bishop, José María Covarrubias y
Mejía. A native of Querétaro who had spent most of his life as a priest
in Mexico City, he had almost moved to Oaxaca a quarter of a century
earlier when a bishop-elect of that diocese had appointed him his
secretary; but the bishop died before he was consecrated. So Covarrubias stayed on in Mexico City, gaining the favor of Archbishop
Posada and his successor, Archbishop Garza y Ballesteros. He became
a member of the cathedral chapter in the national capital, and in time
Garza appointed him vicar general of the metropolitan see. When
Garza and the other bishops were sent into exile in 1861, Covarrubias
accompanied them. In Europe, he spent time in Rome, visited
Maximilian at Miramar, and was in Barcelona when the archbishop
died. Before his death, Garza nominated Covarrubias to fill the vacancy created by the death of Domínguez two years earlier. Pius IX
accepted the nomination and proclaimed him bishop of Oaxaca in
June 1861. But Covarrubias remained in Europe more than two years
after his consecration before returning to Mexico. Even then he dared
not go to Oaxaca where the Liberal regime controlled by Porfirio Díaz
would not have welcomed him. Bravery was not one of the bishop's
virtues. When the French took Oaxaca City, he left the imperial capital and arrived in the seat of his diocese on March 28, 1856, forty-nine
years of age, undistinguished in appearance.[26]

Covarrubias seems not to have concerned himself deeply with the
spiritual needs of his diocese. Bazaine ordered that the Episcopal
Palace be returned to the bishop; the seminary was moved back into
its old location; and the Conceptionist nuns, evacuated during the
siege, returned to their convent of Regina Coeli near the capitol.
These were the only material restorations allowed by the interventionist government to the Oaxaca Church. The bishop also reissued
the 1854 edict of his predecessor, Domínguez, regarding the conduct
of the clergy. He ordered prayers to be said in the Mass against the
persecutors of the church and for peace. And, finally, he put forth
some effort to try to channel more money into the support of the
seminary.[27] Other than these measures, he assumed a negative role,
that of opposing the program the government was trying to put into

effect, rather than laboring to strengthen the spiritual resources of a diocese that had suffered from the Liberal onslaught.

One week after his arrival in Oaxaca City, the new bishop wrote to Maximilian endorsing the protest recently made by the archbishops of Michoacán and Mexico against the emperor's policy of religious toleration.[28] The truth was, Maximilian had turned out to be as liberal as the government he came to displace: he accepted in principle nearly all the measures the Juárez regime had promulgated. Thus the emperor recognized the sale of ecclesiastical property by the Juárez government, stipulating only that the transactions made under the republican government be reviewed in order to ferret out any illegalities; established a civil registry; and decreed that while Catholicism would be protected as the religion of the state, there also would be a wide, frank tolerance of all religions within the nation.[29]

Covarrubias was one of the first bishops to protest the registry law of the Empire but virtually all of them did protest eventually. The Oaxaca prelate's opposition was expressed in a long exposition addressed to Maximilian on January 11, 1866. In general, Covarrubias based his arguments on the fact that marriage was an institution divinely ordained, a sacrament of the church, and this the civil law by its very existence denied.[30]

Regarding the religious toleration decreed by Maximilian, Covarrubias's protest took the form of a pastoral letter. Issued ostensibly to warn the faithful of the dangers of the modern world and to publicize Pius IX's *Syllabus of Errors,* more than half of the long epistle dealt with the dangers and pernicious influence of Protestantism. Considering that no protestant activities were evident in Oaxaca at the time—missionaries would not arrive until 1870 or 1871—it is strange that the prelate deemed it necessary to lash out so strongly on this subject. He was merely following the lead of bishops farther to the north whose dioceses were already invaded by the Protestants and who were witnessing rather large sales of Bibles sponsored by foreign Bible societies. These bishops, Covarrubias included, were using Maximilian's declaration as an excuse to show that the faithful were in jeoardy and that one of the principal unifying factors of the Mexican nation, Roman Catholicism, was in danger of being destroyed, with its destruction sanctioned by the Austrian Catholic duke who had come to bring about peace and unity.[31] From the very beginning, then, the Oaxacan church, which should have provided the strongest support locally for the foreign ruler, balked at cooperation with the interventionist regime.

ADMINISTRATIVE DIFFICULTIES

While Maximilian was having troubles with the Oaxaca bishop, his imperial visitor, Franco, was becoming increasingly embroiled in disputes with the Austrians who had taken over the job of garrisoning Oaxaca. The difficulties had diverse roots—overlapping authority, clash of personalities, differing interpretations of instructions, and varying concepts of policies.

To begin with, the key to the difficulties lay in the administrative structure as it applied to the territories incorporated into the Empire. This imperial territorial division was established by Maximilian in March 1865, just after the capture of Oaxaca and when the Empire reached its greatest extent. Centralistic in form, it was composed of fifty departments, each under a superior political prefect who generally reported directly to the emperor and received orders directly from him and his ministers. The republican state of Oaxaca was broken up into four of the fifty imperial departments: Tehuantepec, Ejutla, Teposcolula, and Oaxaca. The last department had its capital in Oaxaca City and the highest ranking official in that subdivision was Prefect Franco.[32] (See Appendix D.)

This Conservative was promoted from superior political prefect to imperial visitor on September 5, 1865, and put in charge of the Departments of Oaxaca, Tehuantepec, Chiapas, and Tabasco. From that date on, the superior prefecture of the department alternated between Juan María Santaella, a lawyer of Oaxaca City who had long been a Conservative, and Colonel Manual María de Fagoaga, who also had the position of municipal prefect, until General Carlos Oronoz, the division military commander, took over as superior prefect on August 6, 1866.[33]

Militarily, the Empire at its zenith was divided into eight divisions under the command of division or brigade generals or colonels, who were subject to instructions agreed on by Maximilian and the minister of war. In matters of an emergency nature demanding immediate action, the division commanders were to consult with the imperial deputies in their areas and were to lend the aid of the armed forces if solicited by the deputies or superior prefects, whenever the security or preservation of public tranquility so demanded. Under the eight-division arrangement, Oaxaca was placed along with the Departments of Veracruz, Tuxpan, Puebla, Tlaxcala, Teposcolula, Ejutla, and Tehuantepec in the second district with the Austrian General Count Franz Thun as commander, headquartered at Puebla. As time passed, Franco found this arrangement unworkable, especially in light of his difficulties with General Thun, and presented to Maximilian a plan for creating a ninth military division. The emperor adopted the suggestion and on May 30, 1866, decreed the change. The Ninth Military District was to include the Departments of Oaxaca, Tehuantepec, Tabasco, and Chiapas, with headquarters at Oaxaca City. General Carlos Oronoz, a Mexican, was given command.[34]

It is seen, then, that there was some flexibility in the chain of command, some latitude for playing off the civil against the military branches, and some freedom in bypassing certain authorities in cases of emergency. Such maneuverability could be highly advantageous at times but at other times confusing and undesirable. Franco, generally possessing a certain spirit of independence of action, was always inclined to interpret his authority as cutting across both military and civil jurisdictions to give him the widest possible powers.[35] He derived his authority directly from the emperor, who had appointed him for the specific purpose of pacifying the Departments of Oaxaca, Tehuantepec, Chiapas, and Tabasco. It was he, or so Franco thought, who should command these operations, and all other officials, military as well as civil, were subordinate to him in accomplishing this goal.

Troubles developed beginning in late August 1865, when Colonel Casimiro Aceval, commander of the Mexican cavalry Franco had labored to organize, complained that the Austrian commandant of Huajuapan had insulted him and thrown him in jail.[36] Then in September Franco set out to pacify the towns of Jayacatlán, Atatlanca, Nacaltepec, and Cotahuixtla, which had given aid to republican guerrilla forces operating in their vicinity. The towns were completely destroyed, no thanks to the Austrians, who refused to participate in the campaign. While at Nacaltepec, Franco began receiving complaints against Austrian excesses and outrages. He wrote to Bazaine asking him to have General Thun issue orders restraining the Austrian superior commandants in the Department of Oaxaca. He noted the many complaints that had reached him and wrote that he was forced to ignore them in order to maintain harmony and avoid a conflict.[37]

Such complaints continued, however. On September 19, the interim subprefect of Teotitlán del Camino wrote to Franco's secretary, Noriega, about an incident that had taken place three days earlier. Liberal guerrilla forces had appeared near Teotitlán and Austrian detachments moved in to disperse them. The Austrians demanded corn and forage for their horses. When the citizens protested that they barely had enough for their own needs, the Austrian commander ordered the maize fields cut. Beams and doors from houses were taken and cut up for firewood, horses and burros were stolen, and the people were terrified. Complaints to the commander by the subprefect brought no satisfaction.[38]

While these troubles were brewing, a change of command took place in Oaxaca. Major Klein, the Austrian subcommandant, was ordered back to Puebla and was to be replaced by Major Hotze, who had not yet arrived. Klein therefore turned over his command to Captain Thindeis, the officer in Huajuapan who had torn up Franco's orders to him and thrown Aceval into jail. The imperial visitor wrote Thun a long letter, acknowledging the relief of Klein and welcoming the appointment of Hotze. Then he explained point by point all the difficulties he had experienced with the Austrian subcommandants, placed all the blame on the officers, and denied having meddled in military affairs except in certain cases where the Austrians refused to do anything.[39]

On September 28, Klein turned the command over to Thindeis without informing Franco. The first news the imperial visitor had of the actual change was a note received from the arrogant captain ordering Franco to assemble all the Mexican troops on the 29th for a review. Franco immediately sent his adjutant to see Thindeis and present him with Franco's credentials as well as pertinent communications from the minister of war. Thindeis received the intermediary but refused to examine the documents, saying that he, too, had his instructions, that he was in command, and that if Franco failed to comply with his order regarding the review, compliance would be forced at rifle point.[40]

A crisis was building up. Franco regarded the Mexican troops he had organized as being directly under his command and at his personal disposal. The local citizenry had come to look upon Franco as their intermediary with and protector from the surly Austrians, and when word spread of Thindeis's contemptuous attitude, the entire city became aroused. On September 29, Franco's in-law, Federico Larrainzar, wrote a long account of the situation to his uncle in Mexico City.

> The too-well known antecedents of Thindeis, his audacity, his severe and brutal disposition [genio] made one fear that, working at his own discretion and arbitrarily, he might dictate violent measures, which, compromising the situation, would disturb the peace of the department and leave the citizens without security and guarantees. The indignation and discontent were so profound that several reputable and well-known persons advised Juan [Franco] to abandon the city before he let his decorum and dignity be abused, and many others had resolved to ask for their passports and quit a city where a miserable captain was going to make himself lord in rashness and military despotism. The excitement was such that all the Mexican officials, without a single exception, as well as a multitude of influential private citizens, urged him not to comply with an act that so diminished and mocked public authority, suggesting that he meet force with force and strike at the Austrians, if necessary, in which case perhaps the entire town would arise en masse to aid him.

But, he goes on, Franco had decided to avoid a showdown, and acceded to Thindeis's demands. On the morning of the 29th, the review was held in the plaza. In the presence of all, Thindeis bluntly insulted the government of Oaxaca with a thousand insolences. "The city is overcome with stupor," Larrainzar reported in a second letter to his uncle. How can a mere captain intimidate the authorities set up by the empire and subject higher Mexican officials to his will?[41]

That same day, Thindeis dispatched a group of political prisoners, among them Colonel Cristóbal Salinas, to Puebla, afoot, some sick, in bad weather, with orders to the Austrian escort to shoot all if the column were attacked by guerrillas. On the way, the foreign soldiers committed depredations at the Hacienda of Dolores, property of Noriega, Franco's secretary.[42]

The imperial visitor submitted and the crisis vanished when Major Hotze arrived. The minister of war confirmed Franco's command of the Mexican troops, which Thindeis had tried to take away from him. Before many months had passed, however, the imperial visitor was again having trouble with the new commander. In the meantime, two events occurred that heightened the tension. Porfirio Díaz had escaped from jail in Puebla and had raised guerrilla forces in the area of Oaxaca fronting the state of Guerrero. Second, Franco had tried, without sucess, to form a military expedition to go to Chiapas and pacify that area. He received little cooperation from the Austrians in either combating Díaz or preparing the campaign in the south.

In February 1866, Frano wrote to Bazaine of new difficulties, enclosing copies of his recent correspondence with General Thun. The Austrian had written from Puebla that the imperial visitor should abstain from any participation in military affairs and should therefore turn over the troops destined for Chiapas to Major Hotze. Franco has confessed, Thun reminds him, that he knows little of military matters, and the professional soldier urged the amateur to stop meddling before a serious defeat was incurred and he damaged his reputation.

Franco replied to the Puebla commandant that if he took such advice, the mission Maximilian had given him would be nullified. He reminded the Austrian that the very title imperial visitor meant that the recipient was given a special task, but Thun had denied him the facilities for carrying out his mission. By special concession of the emperor, Franco had complete freedom of action in civil as well as military matters to do whatever he deemed necessary to accomplish his goals.

> To obligate me to pacify four departments and deny me the right to dispose the military elements of the same departments, to name me the representative of His Majesty and make me subaltern to a major, to order me to direct expeditions and to disallow me the right to move troops are certainly contradictory.[43]

Maximilian, aware of the growing dispute between Thun and Franco, and realizing that, if not halted, there would be disastrous consequences, asked Bazaine for his opinion. The marshal recommended that the principle be established that imperial visitors, as well as prefects and subprefects have command only over the rural police forces. If it should be necessary for them to have other troops to meet emergencies, a written requisition should be presented to the military commander. In this manner, interference by civilian authorities in military affairs would cease.[44]

The epistolary exchange among Franco, Thun, and Bazaine was seemingly a tempest in a teapot but in reality had far-reaching repercussions in that the dispute over jurisdictions and prerogatives and the lack of cooperation between Mexican officials and their French and Austrian overlords so debilitated the administration that when a true crisis arose, no effective action could be taken. Herein lies the fundamental reason why the Liberal Republic triumphed and the Intervention failed.

For the moment, the dispute in Oaxaca ended, only to flare up again a month later. Porfirio Díaz was threatening the strategic town of Jamiltepec, from which the Austrian contingent had withdrawn. Franco stepped in and sent 600 troops to reinforce the Austrians in their new position near Juquila, and at the same time sent another detachment to Miahuatlán. "With the forces at my disposal," he wrote,

> I believe with certainty that not only can we resist any thrust of Porfirio Díaz but also destroy him and eject him for a second time from the department; but I should frankly state that the enemy, for me, is not in the south. I possess sufficient energy and enthusiasm to resist all the forces of the Alvarezes [of Guerrero State, who were supplying Porfirio Díaz] in defense of the Empire. The evil lies in internal discord, since the Austrian high command and General Thun, due to mere questions of form and pride, set aside the most sacred interests of the Empire, and in their conduct not only can dampen the enthusiasm which I have tried to create in the department for the Empire but also strengthen the enemies.

Hotze had refused to lend support in parrying Díaz's thrust, saying that he commanded only the Austrian garrison in Oaxaca City. To try to get matters straightened out, Franco announced that he was sending his relative, Federico Larrainzar, to Mexico City as his commissioned agent to present to Bazaine and the court a clear, detailed picture of affairs in Oaxaca and the difficulties with Thun and Hotze.[45]

Larrainzar left on March 28. He had an interview with Maximilian on April 13, who sent him to José Salazar Ilarregui, a member of the cabinet. The confidential agent wrote a memorandum summarizing his interview with Salazar and forwarded it to Bazaine. In the session with the minister, Larrainzar presented three alternatives to the solution of the problems: remove the Austrain garrison and replace it with four or five hundred French soldiers to guarantee the security of Oaxaca, thereby leaving Franco free to proceed with his plans regarding the other three departments; or, order the Austrian garrison to take part in the campaign against Díaz, after which Franco would go to Chiapas to begin operations there and leave Hotze in command, with a free and in Oaxaca; or, give Franco the means to organize new forces in Oaxaca, enough to garrison the capital city and at the same time pacify the southern departments.

Bazaine approved the first alternative, Hotze the second.[46] None was adopted. By this time, Napoleon III had become disenchanted with his Mexican venture and was looking for a way to back out. Plans were already being made to evacuate the French army. With the moral support and military aid of the French vanishing, the Empire was beginning to collapse, slowly. Larrainzer's subsequent interviews with General José María García, former Santanista governor of Oaxaca and now serving as Maximilian's minister of war, and with José María Lacunza of the Treasury Ministry revealed that no more men or money could be sent to Oaxaca. García told Franco's agent that all but 800 troops were to be moved from Oaxaca. Larrainzar countered, in shock, that the imperial visitor could not fulfill his mission unless he had 1,900 men plus the Austrians in Oaxaca City and 950 men in Tehuantepec. Lacunza informed the agent that not a single centavo more would be sent to Oaxaca. When Larrainzar argued that the campaign against Díaz could not be undertaken unless there was money to pay the troops, that Franco could not improvise money, and that if Oaxaca were lost it would take 6,000 men and a million pesos to recover it, the bureaucrat shrugged his shoulders and replied, "That makes no difference; I cannot send anything to the imperial visitor."[47]

The only solution really workable—and it proved a happy one as far as mollifying Franco was concerned—was that offered by the visitor to Maximilian in May: the creation of a Ninth Military District with headquarters at Oaxaca City, under the command of Mexican General Carlos Oronoz. Within a month of this change, however, it was evident to Marshal Bazaine that Oaxaca was lost. He wrote: "They [Thun and Oronoz] have not followed my advice and have been the cause of the loss of Oaxaca, which cost me so much work to take. The Austrians have allowed Porfirio Díaz to escape from prison."[48]

THE RECONQUEST

Díaz had remained in prison in Puebla from late February 1865, to the following September 20, when he escaped. Two days later, he had joined a small guerrilla band operating near Puebla City. As far as Díaz was concerned, the campaign for the reconquest of his native state began the moment he dropped down from the rope he used to escape from his convent cell. Some did not take him seriously: Franco, when Bazaine informed him of the flight, replied, "This even has been considered of little importance here, since as you know Porfirio is generally not held in very high regard [*está . . . desconceptuado*]."[49]

In October, Díaz headed into Guerrero State to seek help from the political boss there, the old Liberal Juan Alvarez. He received only token support, but enough to enable him to begin operations on a small scale in the western and southwestern corners of Oaxaca. As news of his escape spread, scattered, small guerrilla bands sought him out to join his crusade. He even resorted to impressing captured soldiers into his ranks. Gradually his army grew in strength. Yet after six months he had no more than seven hundred men under his command. Failing to get aid from Alvarez, he begged money and arms from Matías Romero, his fellow Oaxacan who was serving as minister of the Juárez government to Washington, and even from Juárez himself, who, in the winter of 1865–66, was in Paso del Norte on the Rio Grande. "You may imagine how much I need resources," Porfiro wrote the president, "and the great good I could do if I had them; but, if your situation in that particular is as bad as mine, I ask no help, only I must let you know that I need it, and will do what I can with my ragged men and their old muskets."[50]

Throughout the spring of 1866, Díaz continued to operate around Tlaxiaco and Jamiltepec, while Luis Pérez Figueroa, another guerrilla leader, harassed the Austrians in the area near Tehuacán. By late summer they had become sufficiently strong to break out of their isolation and capture Huajuapan. Then on September 14, Díaz learned that his brother Félix was operating around Oaxaca City. This was the key he needed to open the door for the reconquest.[51]

Félix Díaz was foraging for supplies with his small cavalry detachment when Oaxaca City fell to the French in February 1865. He set out on what was to become an odyssey. Making his way to Tuxtepec, he put himself at the service of General Alejandro García, who had succeeded Porfirio as commander of the Line of the East. But Félix, trained in the military academy, was too dissatisfied with the unprofessional approach to the war taken by his fellow officers and the undisciplined manner in which García conducted the limited operations his strength allowed him to make. He decided to go to the United States and there offer his services to the Mexican government in exile. Arriving in the States, he stayed slightly longer than a month before he was on the move again, this time to Chihuahua, where he incorporated himself in the forces commanded by the governor, General Luis Terrazas, and participated in the attack on Chihuahua City under General Sóstenes Rocha. When news reached him of his brother's escape, Félix left for Tampico and from there made his way into Oaxaca. He organized a small band of guerrillas and began to harass the Austrians and Mexican imperialists to the north of Oaxaca City. In early September he wrote his brother that the city was weak, since Oronoz had left with most of the troops to pursue Porfirio. Félix, in their absence, had entered the capital with his men and gone as far as the marketplace, throwing the entire town into alarm.[52]

At this point, Franco was recalled from Tehuantepec, where he had been directing operations, to take over the prefecture of Oaxaca. He had too few men to prevent the department from falling back into the hands of Díaz. In the capital there were 30 officers and 533 men, of the infantry, artillery, and cavalry, with 191 horses; in Tehuantepec there were 33 officers, 303 artillerymen and cavalrymen, and 47 horses; and in Nochixtlán there were 10 officers, 174 men, and 125 horses—a grand total of 73 officers, 1,010 men, and 363 horses for the entire department.[53]

Porfirio Díaz devised a plan that would put maximum strain on the small forces of the enemy while giving the even smaller republican army the greatest advantage. Félix Díaz would station himself behind the village of San Felipe del Agua, a few miles north of the state capital. Porfirio, with his larger force, would move into the area south of Oaxaca City. If Oronoz came out to strike at Félix, Porfirio would hit the city from the south; if, however, Oronoz moved to attack Porfirio, Félix would make a thrust from the north. Oronoz followed the latter course of action, and sent out a large column to seek out and attack Porfirio. The battle took place at Miahuatlán on October 3. Díaz was triumphant, and Oronoz retreated back to Oaxaca City with the remnant of his column, only to find that Félix had drawn a siege line around the northern edge of the capital. The battle of Miahuatlán, though of short duration and on a small scale, was nevertheless important. In later years, when writing his memoirs, Porfirio Díaz recorded: "I consider the victory of Miahuatlán the most strategic battle that I fought during the war of the Intervention and the most fruitful in its results, since it opened to me the doors of the cities of Oaxaca, Puebla, and Mexico."[54]

The republican chief had injected into his campaigns a new note of terror. In the late summer of 1866, he held up the mail stage from Oaxaca City and found a letter from Francisco Sáenz de Enciso to Manuel Dublán, President Juárez's brother-in-law, who was in Mexico City at the time, having been recently appointed procurator of the Empire. Sáenz expressed fear for his life should Díaz capture Oaxaca

City, since he had been collaborating with the imperialists by serving as administrator of the sales tax office. This letter inspired Díaz to adopt in his correspondence and in his behavior a threatening tone against all traitors. After the battle of Miahuatlán, he ordered twenty-two Mexican officers whom he had captured shot by a firing squad. In looking over the prisoners taken in battle, Díaz, on horseback, came upon Captain Manual Alvarez, who had served as the general's adjutant during the seige of Oaxaca City twenty months previously and who had deserted in the last days to go over to the French. Upon seeing him, so much anger welled up in Díaz that he drew his saber and struck the captain. The escort accompanying the general took this as signal for execution and finished off the officer by hacking him to pieces with their lances and swords.[55]

So afraid was Franco for his life that he fled Oaxaca, heading for Mexico City, as soon as he heard the news of the defeat at Miahuatlán, thereby leaving General Oronoz in complete control. Bishop Covarrubias, also somewhat anxious as to what he could expect and ever playing the politician, wrote Díaz a note of inquiry regarding the considerations the general would give him if Oaxaca City should fall. Díaz answered that he would be stood against a wall in his grand bishop's garb and shot. So Covarrubias also fled, leaving his flock to the mercy of the hated Liberal.[56]

After the victory at Miahuatlán, Díaz reached Oaxaca City on October 8, and learned that his brother had forced the Austro-Mexican army to take refuge in the fortified monasteries of Santo Domingo and Carmen Alto and the nunnery of Santa Catarina. The enemy also still controlled the principal fort on the hill overlooking the city. This news prompted Porfirio to complete the siege line on the south and to make no further moves for a week.

Then Díaz intercepted a messenger to Oronoz bearing news that a relief column was on the way. He decided to defeat this column before it could reach the capital and, accordingly, on the night of the 17th, led his forces southward toward La Carbonera where he calculated he would meet the enemy troops. His estimate was correct—contact was made there the next day and Díaz won the second major battle of the reconquest. On October 20, he returned to occupy the siege line once more. Preparations were made to dislodge the enemy from the hill fort, but Oronoz asked for a parley in which he offered to surrender on certain terms. Díaz refused. He was in no mood to compromise because he knew he had the upper hand; only an unconditional surrender was acceptable. Hours passed. A second parley was held in the theater in the city on October 31. Oronoz could do nothing but accept the terms, so he surrendered unconditionally. The prisoners were guaranteed their lives and were allowed to keep their personal equipage, their own horses, and their rifles. To be included among the prisoners were all civil employees and other private Mexican citizens who had collaborated during the siege. Later that day, the capitulation was signed, the supplies were delivered, and the soldiers laid down their arms—753 Mexican Conservative troops, 18 Austrian officers, 13 French officers, and 199 Franco-Austrian soldiers, plus the civilians, among them Francisco Sáenz de Enciso, whose letter Díaz had intercepted from the mail stage; Juan B. Santaella, the sometime prefect and cohort of Franco; Juan N. Cerqueda, a rojo Liberal of earlier days; and José Inés Sandoval, one of the old Liberals whom Santa Anna had sent into exile along with Juárez over a decade earlier.[57]

The escape of Porfirio Díaz from his Puebla prison marked the beginning of the end of the French regime in Oaxaca; the surrender of the state capital signaled the downfall of the Mexican Empire. A decade of intermittent warfare in and around the Central District had at last terminated. Now plans could be laid for the future, a future, one hoped, no longer so uncertain as in years past. Crops could be planted in the secure knowledge that a harvest would follow. Families would be reunited, property repaired, losses recuperated, and the wounds of the nation healed. The coming year, 1867, promised to be one of peace and joy.

But developments proved otherwise. The moderate-radical split during the decade of reform had left deep scars, which some politicians, particularly Félix Díaz, wished to keep festered in order to forward their own careers. The mixed moods of Oaxacans—lust for revenge and ambitious self-seeking to advance personal interests balanced against a general desire for stability, harmony, and the establishment of a secure future—would take time to work themselves out. Old scores would have to be settled before the unhappy past could be swept from memory. And some Reform measures still had to be implemented.

CHAPTER 5

THE POST-REFORM ERA, 1867–76

AT THE BEGINNING OF 1867, Maximilian still ruled, although his empire was shrinking almost daily. Napoleon III had found the Mexican experiment too expensive. This, coupled with growing opposition in France to the adventure as well as pressure from the United States, caused the heir to Bonaparte to order withdrawal. So the evacuation began. In the early months of 1867, some French troops remained on Mexican soil, but they too would soon be gone and Maximilian would ultimately have to rely on the Conservative Mexican army. Juárez was still in the north but would soon begin a series of moves, each time bringing his republican government ever closer to the national capital. Porfirio Díaz, the intrepid general, now that Oaxaca had fallen to him, was planning to push his reconquest from the south on toward Mexico City. In April, Puebla would fall to him after a month's siege, the third in five years. In June, the great metropolis of the national capital would be his. A month after that, Maximilian and two of his generals would stand before a firing squad in Querétaro. Mexico once again would be in the hands of Mexicans.

As these developments unfolded, an overwhelming desire for peace manifested itself in the areas liberated from the French; by midsummer it consumed the whole population—a peace in which the acrimonious debates of politicians would cease, a peace in which the Constitution of 1857 could be put into effect in all its vigor and glory, a peace in which the brotherhood of all Mexicans would assert itself to erase the scars of the terrible decade of civil strife.[1]

But as in all great military conflicts of a prolonged nature, once the general conflagration is extinguished, brush fires blaze up. Toward the end of the year, in Oaxaca the political struggle became

110

dominant as ambitious men captured factions that battled for control of the administrative machinery of the state. Hand in hand with this political vying for power were two other trends, contradictory in nature and so intertwined with politics that the issues raised frequently became blurred and would not be settled within 1867 but would remain persistent in the state throughout the decade of the Restored Republic. On the one hand, there was the desire to bring about a fulfillment of the Reform and to punish those who had given allegiance to Maximilian; on the other hand, there was the desire for conciliation, a wish to forgive and forget all indiscretions of the past.

REVENGE AND CONCILIATION

In a state in which nearly all leaders had cooperated with the Empire, it would have been impossible to reconstruct a government without using the collaborators. As it developed, many of those Oaxacans who lent their support to the Intervention saw their treason publicized and suffered the threat of economic sanctions against them; a few actually experienced reprisals; and one lost his life.

Juan Pablo Franco, the imperial visitor, who had been considered by Maximilian for the cabinet post of minister of the interior, left his family in Oaxaca City when he fled following the defeat at Miahuatlán in early October 1866. He traveled as far as Mexico City and immediately began making plans to bring his wife and children to him. There he met Manuel Dublán the imperial procurator, who also had left his family in Oaxaca City. Together they schemed to have their families leave the southern state and met them in Tehuacán; all would then return to Mexico City. Franco and Dublán traveled together to Puebla, where the latter had second thoughts, deciding that the trip involved too many risks and that Porfirio Díaz was too formidable and dangerous an enemy to tempt him by their proximity to his headquarters. Probably Bishop Covarrubias had spread the word that Díaz threatened to shoot the prelate if he were caught. Franco, however, was determined to rescue his wife and children and decided to go to Tehuacán. He got as far as Tlacotepec where he was apprehended by one of Díaz's patrols under the command of Colonel Ignacio Sánchez Gamboa. That afternoon he was taken to Acatlán, where Sánchez offered to free him if Franco would pay the colonel 5,000 pesos. The former imperial visitor managed to arrange for the money, but that evening, another officer, Espinosa Gorostiza, arrived in Actlán, learned of the events, and insisted that Franco be taken to Oaxaca City as a prisoner.

He remained a prisoner during most of January 1867, spending sixteen days of that period in solitary confinement. On the 26th, he was brought to trial before a military tribunal, which found him guilty of treason and sentenced him to be executed by a firing squad on the 30th. In addition, his property was to be confiscated. Many citizens were shocked by the harshness of the penalty, for Franco had committed no excess in office save that of destroying the villages of Cotahuixtla, Nacaltepec, Atatlanca, and Jayacatlán because of the aid they gave to the republican guerrilla bands. Indeed, he had frequently used his office to protect many who might otherwise have suffered at the hands of the French and Austrians.

Only three days were to pass between sentencing and execution, hardly enough time to muster any sort of support in his behalf. A petition for clemency, nevertheless, was circulated and signed by many leaders of the city. Many women of the upper level of society, friends of Señora Inés Larrainzar de Franco, who were moved by the prospect of a family left without a head, appealed to the authorities that the penalty be lessened. One private and influential citizen, Gabriel Esperón, wrote to his friend Matías Romero in order to get him to intercede with Juárez. But all efforts were fruitless: Franco was executed on the ball field near the old Belem convent at the appointed hour, January 30, 1867.[2]

The execution seemed to satiate the military regime controlling Oaxaca, which presumably felt the need for finding a victim and a scapegoat. There are indications, however, that other collaborators suffered property confiscations or had their property pillaged. Luis María Carbó, the rojo Liberal and former pharmacist who had served Franco as co-editor of the official gazette and as local agent in charge of nationalized real estate in Oaxaca during the Intervention, was one of those whose property was violated. He escaped Oaxaca City before it fell to Díaz but was among the prisoners taken in Puebla five months later. Luis María's son Guillermo, one of Díaz's most loyal officers, wrote to the general asking that he intercede to protect his father's property. Díaz replied from Acatlán on February 6 that he could do nothing except try to prevent Luis's house from being entered and looted, and that he doubted if he could even keep this promise.[3]

By midsummer, after Maximilian's execution, the desire for revenge had run its course and the opposite trend began to manifest itself. On August 16, 1863, Juárez had decreed a law confiscating the property of all those who accepted emoluments or honors from the Empire. On August 12, 1867, this decree was modified: the confiscatory articles were eliminated and fines substituted in their place. By Article 3, all those subject to the 1863 law were required to report within fifteen days either in person or through commissioned agents, to the local officials of the Treasury Ministry so that a registry might be formed of their names and fines levied against them. In Oaxaca City, 249 men appeared before the chief of the Treasury bureau between August 12 and September 21 to have their names put on the register. Among them were thirty-four lawyers and four doctors.[4]

By late that autumn, conciliation and clemency had become the order of the day. The list of collaborators was submitted to the Treasury Ministry and studied by Juárez himself. The president resolved that all men on the list would go free of the proposed punishments except Dr. Domingo Cházari, who was fined 5,000 pesos, and the lawyer José Inés Sandoval, who was to pay a 1,000-peso fine.[5]

Treatment of the military prisoners of war was likewise lenient. On April 15, Félix Díaz, at the time serving as military commandant of the state and acting on orders from his brother Porfirio, decreed that the captives were free. Apparently, before this declaration, the prisoners had remained under house arrest. The following day, the secretariat of the commandancy issued orders that all former imperialist soldiers should declare where they wished to reside in order that they might take advantage of the grace conceded them by General Díaz.[6]

After the recapture of Oaxaca on October 31, 1866, Porfirio Díaz retained in his hands both military and political control of the state. But this proved to be too great a task for one man, since he also was still serving as chief of the Army of the East and formulating plans for the attack upon Puebla. On December 11, 1866, he therefore relinquished the control of the state government and appointed General Alejandro García as governor and commandant of Oaxaca. García, who was second-in-command of the Line of the East, remained in these offices only slightly longer than two months. He was removed because of a certain degree of hostility toward him since he was not a native Oaxacan and also because Félix Díaz, consumed by ambition, was anxious to gain control of the southern state. On February 23, 1867, Porfirio Díaz designated his brother military commandant and Juan María Maldonado civil governor.[7] Once more, the two branches of government were separated and given to different men, a practice

Juárez had recognized over a decade earlier as the root cause of so much turbulence. Given the political aspirations of Félix Díaz, his Jacobinism, and his popularity among a large group who wished him to have full control, trouble was not long in coming. The issue that gave him the opportunity to attack the policies of Maldonado was that of the fulfillment of the Reform program.

AGAIN THE NUNNERIES

On April 18, Félix Díaz addressed a note to Governor Maldonado. "With true concern," he began, "I have noted that some of the reform laws have not been put into effect in the state, notwithstanding the spirit of our institutions, the orders of the supreme government, and the blood spilled to make these laws prevail." He demanded that the nummeries be closed as soon as possible.[8]

It will be recalled that the monasteries were suppressed in August 1859, in consonance with the Law of Nationalization of Ecclesiastical Properties. That same law had restricted the affairs of the nunneries, but the latter remained open until a presidential decree of February 26, 1863, had ordered their closure. It was this 1863 Reform law that had never been implemented in Oaxaca.

The move on the part of Félix Díaz seemingly took Maldonado completely by surprise. On April 24, the civil governor wrote the military commandant a long letter in which he acknowledged receipt of Díaz's note of the 18th. Then he reviewed the history of the implementation of the Reform laws within Oaxaca and pointed out that their state was in the first rank in scrupulously adhering to the program of the national government and in defending that program. Thinking that Díaz was basing his demand for closing the nunneries on the law of July 12, 1859 (the Law of Nationalization of Ecclesiastical Properties), Maldonado proceeded to point out in detail, article by article, that that law only restricted the nunneries by limiting their income, regulating their expenses, and stipulating that individual nuns could recover their dowries if they wished to do so. Then he reviewed the steps taken in 1862 by the state officials to get the nuns to accept their dowries, how the women had refused to do so, and enclosed documents setting forth these events of five years previously. The only knowledge Maldonado professed to have of any suppression of nunneries was a decree of the state of Puebla issued on April 4, 1867, just after the capture of the city by Porfirio Díaz, which made mention of a law of February 26, 1863, but Maldonado had seen neither decree nor law and supposed that they were state measures that Puebla alone was taking. He reported to Félix Díaz that a search in the Oaxacan archives, in newspapers, and in private libraries in the city had revealed no national law requiring the closing of the nunneries. But perhaps, he reasoned, if there was a national law, it never arrived in Oaxaca; or if it arrived, it was never promulgated. In this manner, Maldonado excused himself from taking any action to close the convents.

Then he turned the discussion to the necessity of doing what Félix Díaz demanded. He pointed out that even when General Porfirio Díaz was fortifying the city to protect it from the French, and in so doing occupied the nunneries, or that even during the subsequent bombardment, the nuns were not driven from their convents. If General Díaz did not deem it necessary or convenient in those critical days of 1864–65 to close the nunneries, why should the government today, in 1867, have reason to do so?

He ended his long exposition to Félix Díaz by writing: "Despite what I have said, if you believe that the cloistered nature of the nuns ought to be suppressed and also believe that such a measure is included in the attributes of your office, you can do whatever you like, in the knowledge that this government will not put any difficulties in your way."[9]

This was an astute reply to the commandant's demand, for it placed the burden of proof and the responsibility for action on Félix Díaz; the commandant, however, was not to be outdone. Several days passed before he made his next move. On May 4, he wrote to José Esperón inquiring if the February 1863 decree had been received officially in the state during the period in which the leader of the borlado faction had served as head of Governor Ramón Cajiga's secretariat. Esperón replied in the affirmative that same day, but added that its promulgation was not "judged convenient for reasons of high politics that would take too long to enumerate." The law had been deposited in the state archives by superior order "until the opportune occasion was presented for its fulfillment," Esperón wrote.[10] Armed with this information, Félix Díaz played his trump card and in one stroke discredited the borlado party, placed himself before the public as the only true defender of the Reform in the state, maligned the lawyers who traditionally controlled state affairs, and set the stage for his eventual power grab in the style of the demagogue that he was. No matter that in the process he alienated his elder brother, Porfirio, whose radicalism had not the same firebrand quality as did Félix's.

The move came on May 9. In *La Victoria*, the official newspaper of the state government, Félix Díaz published letters from his brother Porfirio to Maldonado and Maldonado's reply, both of which revealed that the civil governor indeed had knowledge of the law ordering the closure of the nunneries prior to Félix's calling it to his attention and that Maldonado had done nothing to implement the law. In the same issue of the paper, Félix published a long personal statement, which he entitled "The Law and the Nuns." The military commandant asked in a sarcastic tone why the law closing the nunneries had not been put into effect, once promulgated, if the men in control of the government were truly such honored and well-educated lawyers as they claimed to be. He closed his statement by assuring all Oaxacans that he, as military commander of the state, uneducated in law but always resolute in its fulfillment and in the development of progressive principles, would never abdicate his position as a firm republican.[11]

In the same issue of *La Victoria*, the law of February 26, 1863, its regulatory statute of February 27, and the special provisions regarding the closing of the nunneries promulgated by Juárez on March 13, 1863, were all three printed.[12] In this year of peace, 1867, the nine reasons given for suppressing the convents seemed, in the main, not very pertinent. The gist of the reasoning was that the nunneries were a source of wealth, which the national treasury needed in order to meet the expenditures forced upon the nation by the Intervention. The conventual buildings also could be used as hospitals for soldiers and orphanages for children of men killed in the coming battles. Furthermore, religious vows and measures used to enforce them were alien to a popular, republican government; by removing the nuns from communal establishments, one more segment of the population was being withdrawn from the pernicious influence of priests.

The law of February 26 provided that inventories were to be made of all articles in the nunneries and that treasury officials would take control of the buildings. The nuns would be allowed to keep their personal belongings and their dowries would be returned to them. Churches attached to the convents would remain open for public worship if so designated by state governors. Excepted from these provisions were the Sisters of Charity since they did not follow a common rule and were consecrated to the service of suffering humanity.

The real details for carrying out the law were contained in Juárez's amplifying decree of March 13, 1863. Nuns, once no longer cloistered, were required to live with their parents; or, if their parents were dead, they could choose where they wished to reside, except that no more than two could stay together and none could live in the homes of priests. If they wised, they could manage their own personal affairs henceforth, but should they feel unable to cope with these problems, having spent their lives closed off from society, they were free to appoint agents to look after their affairs. No agent could serve more than one nun. Should nuns elect not to handle their own concerns and yet refuse to name agents, the local political authority was empowered to appoint such agents. Since the heart of the problem was the fear that the nun might be defrauded of her returned dowry money, these provisions essentially were taken by the government to insure that the women were not made victims of unscrupulous persons. If anyone tried to keep the nuns from returning to their homes or attempted to hide them or employed any means to keep them recluse, he could receive the death penalty. If nuns chose to reside in private homes, these houses could not be closed at any time during the day and were subject to visits by local political authorities, by the agents, and by the local committee of women to be appointed to look after their welfare. But should the nuns choose to live with their parents, then only their agents could visit them, unless there was evidence that the parents were trying to force their daughters to observe their vows in the privacy of their homes. A group of women would be named in any locality where the nuns took up residence, charged with looking after their welfare and seeing that they enjoyed perfect freedom. The nuns could not wear religious habits in public, nor could they leave Mexico without the permission of the government.[13]

The day following the promulgation of these decrees, Governor Maldonado designated the churches attached to Soledad and Los Príncipes as the two conventual chapels that would remain open for public worship.[14] Although the discredited Maldonado continued to carry out the letter of the decrees regarding the nunneries, gradually implementing the provisions preliminary to their closure, his days as govenor were numbered. On April 24, he had presented his resignation. General Porfirio Díaz accepted it on May 6 and appointed Miguel Castro to replace him. This change became effective a week later. Félix Díaz was removed from the commandancy at the same time; both military and civil control were to rest in Castro's hands.[15] Three days later, Félix left Oaxaca to go to the theater of operations around Mexico City.

Miguel Castro was a poor substitute for Maldonado. If the latter had been negligent in carrying out his duties, the former was tainted with treason, for Castro, the wealthy miner, lawyer, proprietor, and political boss of the Sierra de Ixtlán, had served the imperial regime in Oaxaca as counselor of government. Because of this activity, at the time of his appointment as governor he was still subject to punishment and his extensive holdings were liable to be confiscated.

It was Castro, therefore, who was given the task of presiding over the suppression of the nunneries in Oaxaca City. At seven o'clock on the evening of May 16, 1867, when the streets of the town had become quiet after the day's activities, the nuns were ejected from their convents. There were no demonstrations to mar the transfer and the official newspaper reported that the women seemed to be content and resigned to their removal. It is impossible to determine the exact number of nuns who were ousted, but there were approximately seventy-eight all told, including the Augustinian Recollets, Spanish and Indian Capuchinesses, Dominican Sisters, and Conceptionists from the convents of La Soledad, Los Príncipes, San José, and La Concepción.[16]

The sight of these women being conducted from their cloisters was undoubtedly one that aroused a certain amount of pity among the few silent spectators. Most of the nuns had entered the convents in their early years and any other way of life was but a vague memory to them. In guarding their isolation jealously, they had maintained little contact with the world outside the convent walls.[17] When they had entered the nunneries the church held an exalted position in the lives of nearly everyone; now they were coming out into a world in which the church counted for little, a hostile world in which they could be nothing other than misfits. The church at that moment was powerless to aid them; moreover, it had accepted them as faithful daughters, the brides of Christ, and now that their vows were no longer to be enforced, the church had little use for them. The nuns themselves looked upon their vows as holy promises that must be observed no matter how adverse the circumstances. They were untrained in making any livelihood, having spent their lives in contemplation or in begging alms for the work of God. Except for a select few who had developed managerial skills as mothers superior, they knew little about looking after their own affairs, for chaplains, majordomos, and lawyers had always controlled the business matters of the convents. Their dilemma was one that beggared solution. Perplexed, they did only what they knew how to do—they lived secluded in the midst of society.

Remarks written by Archbishop Eulogio Gillow in the late 1880s suggest that thirty of the nuns were still living at that time. They stayed in private homes and would not venture outside even to hear Mass because they still considered themselves cloistered. In order to minister to their needs, Gillow appointed a nuns' vicar, moved them together to live in groups of three, and designated certain priests to say Mass for them on Sundays and days of obligation. This was the only way in which the archbishop could get them to attend Mass, for the nuns considered their rule of cloister of such force that it excused them from the obligation of going to services in a parish church. Gillow added that when the convents were suppressed, the chancellor of the diocese would not allow the nuns to accept their dowries, as the government stipulated they should do, with the result that the capital represented was lost to the nuns; the diocese, ever since it had become disposed to look after the women, was forced to provide for their welfare and had spent an enormous sum over the years for this purpose.[18]

The records become sparse after the late 1880s. In 1889, the two of three surviving Recollets from La Soledad came together to hold their last election of officers, and the first since 1865. Poignantly, this handful of nuns maintained the tradition of recording the results of the election:

> In this present year of 1889 in July, still outside the Convent, the election of Prioress of the Community was held with the result that Most Reverend Mother María Encarnación del Señor San Gabriel was chosen unanimously, whose election the Chancellor Don Ignacio Merlín, Dean of this Holy Church, by [the authority of] the Monsignor Archbishop of this Holy Church of Antequera, approved and signed, and by order of the Chancellor I sign.—Sister María Encarnación de Sr. Sn. Gabriel.

And then, almost as an afterthought, the good sister, sixty-eight years old, added: "Being this the last election which the community of Recollets of Nuestra Madre de la Soledad will hold." By 1905, Sister María Encarnación was not only the prioress but the community, for all other Recollets had died and she alone survived, eighty-four years of age. In 1908, only four of the seventy-eight formerly cloistered nuns were still alive. After that, the records fall silent.[19]

THE RISE AND FALL OF FÉLIX DÍAZ

After the nunneries in Oaxaca were closed and Governor Maldonado was discredited, Félix Díaz returned to the battlefield to support his brother's military operations to liberate Puebla and Mexico City. Once the war was over, however, the Díaz brothers were not absent from politics for long. When Juárez announced in August 1867, that elections would be held in the autumn, Porfirio launched his campaign for the presidency. In the October balloting, he lost his bid and Juárez won by a large margin. At the same time that the elder brother was conducting his national campaign, Félix ran as a candidate for the governorship of Oaxaca. Porfirio had a double stake in his brother's race. If Félix showed strong in his own campaign, it might increase the groundswell for Porfirio's candidacy. And if Félix won, even if Porfirio were defeated, it could enhance the latter's chances for a second attempt at winning the presidency four years hence by insuring that the Oaxaca electorate would vote for Porfirio Díaz. It was well known that whoever sat as governor in effect counted the votes. Félix's November victory over his opponent, Miguel Castro, was overwhelming by a three-to-one margin.

But Porfirio's assumption of his brother's cooperation was false—he failed to take into account Félix's independence and stubborness and the borlados' determination to destroy any support Porfirio might otherwise have in Oaxaca. Throughout 1867, the borlados had been cooperating with Juárez and his local agent, acting-governor Castro, even though they had great distaste for the radicalism displayed by the president throughout the Reform and Intervention. But principle had always given way to expediency in the borlado camp; it was more expedient now for them to neutralize their bitter enemy, Porfirio Díaz, and this momentarily threw them into the Juárez fold. The borlados had much to fear from Félix, also, for he had already displayed his enmity to them, and his scorn, by his stand on the nunnery issue earlier in the year and his successful move to discredit the moderate Maldonado. They calculated that in all likelihood he would serve his brother unless that relationship could be destroyed. If a wedge could be driven between the two, then Félix's strength as governor undoubtedly could be limited. Consequently, the Oaxacan moderates, always the shrewd politicans, devised a strategy for the 1867 gubernatorial elections that concentrated on winning control of the state legislature and making no attempt to put forward a strong candidate for the governorship. Félix as governor could do little without the cooperation of the state assembly. As this strategy became known, Félix Díaz saw it as an opportunity to work an accord with his borlado rivals, to win them over to his cause, and so he refused to accept direction from his brother in the conduct of the campaign and suggestions of candidates to run with him for other state offices. Porfirio wanted Félix to support Juan de Mata Vázquez as regent of the state supreme court, an elective post, but Félix instead supported Félix Romero, an ardent Juarista who was now parading as a moderate in order to gain an entry into the borlado ranks to hold that group in their allegiance to President Juárez. The strategy worked. Félix's refusal to accept the Mata Vázquez candidacy brought about the hoped-for rupture between the two brothers—a relationship already damaged by Félix's demand for closing the nunneries; signaled that Félix would operate independently of Porfirio's influence; and gave hope to the borlados that they could so mold the policies of the new governor as to deny Porfirio any widespread, enthusiastic support in his native state. The strategy was also successful in that the borlados gained a majority in the state legislature.[20]

Thirty-four years old when he became governor, Félix Díaz, popularly known by the nickname Chato (Pugnose), was the youngest of the seven Díaz children, born a few months after his father's death. Raised in poverty, like Porfirio he managed to obtain an education, first in the diocesan seminary and then in the local Institute. He spent some time in the national Military College, which provided him a commission as an officer. Throughout his career he consistently displayed an independent streak, which led him to support Santa Anna against the Ayutla Revolution, and the Conservatives throughout most of the War of the Reform. He did not join the Liberal army until March 1860. Once the transfer of allegiance was made, however, he had given enthusiastic support to the republican cause, serving in his brother's Army of the East much of the time. His support in the recapture of Oaxaca City in 1866 was crucial.[21] In addition to his independence, there was also a measure of severity, of demagoguery in his thought and manner. And there were contradictions in his personality: he could at times be noble and rise above partisan politics to conciliate rival groups but at other times he could resort to brutality against those who failed to accept his leadership. He could be a fearful enemy and a dangerous friend, one always to be handled with care. To deal with him was not easy; to control him was practically impossible. He would govern with a strong will and his ambition would be limitless. In short, he was a despot, sometimes enlightened but more frequently not.

During his four-year term, he proved to be a master of men. The borlados found themselves more manipulated than manipulating; before long he had won their support, largely accomplished by a shrewd, calculated use of his wide patronage powers. He was careful to appoint a number of borlados to posts dependent on him, particularly in the important and lucrative political chieftaincies of the districts. He also placed some former supporters of the Empire in high-level positions within his administration. Especially did he rely on Félix Romero, whom he appointed to the directorship of the Institute of Sciences and Arts and then made secretary of state. Finally, in time he worked a rapprochement with Porfirio and appointed some of his brother's adherents district political chiefs.[22] Thus he made an appeal to all parties to cooperate in governing the state.

At the same time, he went through the motions of expressing concern about the economic situation and isolation of Oaxaca. Some attempts were made at road improvement and construction and there was much talk about the need for revitalizing primary education, but little was accomplished in this regard.[23] Political issues continued to receive the major emphasis, and in the game of politics Félix Díaz displayed a facileness that some came to admire and many came to despise. The U.S. consular and commercial agent in Oaxaca, L. L. Lawrence, wrote a report to Hamilton Fish, the secretary of state, after Díaz's governorship had fallen apart in 1872, in which he described in some detail the repressive conditions imposed on Oaxaca by Félix—forced loans, confiscations of property, heavy taxes, imprisonments—that went on during his four years in office but that became particularly burdensome in the last months.

> From the 8th of November [1871] until the 5th of January [1872] all laws were suspended by a decree of the State Congress and absolute authority vested in the Governor. This was however *in fact* virtually exercised by him for the last four years and I doubt if any Ruler in the World has controlled more personal power. The Court and Judges were his most servile tools. The Federal and State Members of Congress of this State were of his own selection and have been for the past four years

with the exception of the Members of the present Federal Congress from this State; these were selected by his Brother Porfirio Díaz, who received this privilege as a part of the bargain made with the Governor when he withdrew his name from the canvas for Governor.[24]

Within the authoritarian framework, however, and from the very beginning of his administration, the tone was set for conciliation of all groups and for harmony. He saw to it that the borlado-dominated legislature honored his brother Porfirio with a gift of a small farmstead called La Noria on the outskirts of Oaxaca City, purchased from Manuel Dublán, as a mark of appreciation for services rendered to the nation. The same legislature honored Juárez with the gift of an engraved sword. But very clearly harmony and conciliation, peace and prosperity were more talked about than achieved, and what accomplishments there were in these directions were not done for any altruistic motive but rather for the single purpose of strengthening Félix's hold over men and his command of the state.

In the elections of 1869 for representatives to the state assembly, the governor further consolidated his power base by gaining control of a majority of the legislative seats. As his dominance increased, the influence of President Juárez diminished. The borlados saw the advantages to be gained from the patronage of Félix Díaz and thus were more and more attracted to follow him, which made them less than fervent in their allegiance to the president. At the same time they were unaware of the newly cordial relations between the two Díaz brothers, so they did not realize that their acceptance of Félix as caudillo was indirectly making it easier for their enemy Porfirio to count on Oaxaca in any future bid for the presidency.

In two regions of the state, the governor's power was challenged. In the Isthmus of Tehuantepec, many citizens of one of the larger towns, Juchitán, had been engaging in contraband trade and circumventing the payment of state sales taxes. The Juchitecans were also resentful of the designation of a political chief for their region who was not a native of the Isthmus and they had driven out the appointee. Governor Díaz led a contingent of the National Guard into the region to crush the smugglers, after which he turned against all the Juchitecans, attacked the town, executed prisoners, robbed the municipal treasury, and, giving the most affront, carried off the image of their patron saint, Saint Vicente Ferrer, from the major church. Thus there was a deep reservoir of ill-will against Félix Díaz in the Isthmus of Tehuantepec.[25]

In the mountainous region of the northern part of the state, Félix was likewise distrusted. That was Juárez territory, the birthplace of the president, and that area, largely given over to small-scale mining operations and subsistence farming based on tiny, individually owned plots of land, was loyal to former governor Miguel Castro, Juárez's good friend and agent, the wealthiest miner of the region. Castro used two younger men who worked for him, Fidencio Hernández and Francisco Meixueiro, as his lieutenants in controlling the politics of the mountain towns. The mountaineers had adhered to the Reform programs enthusiastically and had fought valiantly in the many campaigns either to keep invading armies out of the state or to eject them once they had entered. With deep loyalties to their own kind and deep antipathies to outsiders, the serranos were an independent lot whose aid or enmity could be crucial, as was proved in the period of the second Cobos invasion in the War of the Reform, when the village of Ixtlán gave sanctuary to the refugee Liberal government. The towns were small, the population sparse, and the terrain rough, but in the decade of the 1870s, the mountaineers emerged as the dominant force in Oaxacan politics. In July and August 1871, in Ixtlán and nearby villages, Fidencio Hernández staged a "disturbance" against the governor, who had authorized an Austrian miner to make a survey of the mineral resources of the sierra, at the same time ordering an already unpopular political chief, an outsider, to support the survey. Castro, who had been defeated by Díaz for the governorship in the 1867 elections, resented Félix's interference in the mining economy of the mountains. Another provocation for the disturbance was an order issued by the governor for the mountain district to send 800 soldiers of its famous Juárez Battalion of the National Guard to the state capital for muster and review. As in the case of Juchitán, Díaz acted swiftly in putting down this local demonstration.[26]

A sign of Félix Díaz's power in the state by 1871 was the fact that he was unchallenged in the summer elections in his bid for a second term. His brother's concurrent national campaign for the presidency was again unsuccessful, although with Félix's support he carried Oaxaca and received all 228 of the electoral votes in his native state. As the tallies from the other states came in, it became clear that the only way Porfirio was going to gain the presidency was through military rebellion. Plans had been developing for months, in case the Porfiristas had to resort to such a measure. The plans included the summoning of the dispersed National Guard battalions to Oaxaca

City, one of the causes for the intervention in serrano affairs mentioned above. Oaxaca, the staging ground, had been made into an armory at the disposal of the Díaz cause. Félix was fully supportive in the key post of governor and could command the state's National Guard units to aid the rebellion. He could also channel state funds to aid the power grab.[27]

Throughout the fall, pro-Díaz movements broke out in widely scattered areas of the Republic: Tampico, Guaymas, Nuevo León, Sinaloa, Chiapas, even in Mexico City where antigovernment troops seized the Ciudadela fortification. But in all areas the Juárez government moved rapidly to contain these isolated outbreaks of violence. Juárez's victory was validated on October 12, 1871. A month later, on November 8, from his farmstead at La Noria on the edge of Oaxaca City, Porfirio Díaz issued his call for revolution to overthrow the Juárez regime.

Since Félix controlled the state legislature, it was easy enough to swing that body behind the rebellion. On the same day the Plan of La Noria was proclaimed, the legislators issued a decree declaring their support of Porfirio and taking Oaxaca out of the union until the war was won: in the phrase used so frequently in past crises, Oaxaca "reassumed its sovereignty."[28]

President Juárez was not caught off guard. His agents in Oaxaca had kept him informed of the drift toward rebellion in the late summer and early fall. Now with the Noria proclamation, he acted decisively to contain the disturbance within Oaxaca. Generals Ignacio Alatorre and Sóstenes Rocha were ordered to move toward the state with large contingents. Castro and his lieutenants refused to lend their support to the rebels and held the sierra for the federal government. In the Isthmus of Tehuantepec, the Juchitecans, with their memories of Félix Díaz's brutality of a few months back, also remained loyal to the nation.

Félix Romero, who had been playing a double role as regent of the state supreme court and good friend of the governor, while secretly remaining loyal to Juárez, was prepared to act quickly. On the night of November 10, he fled to Castro's ore reduction plant at Cinco Señores in the Ixtlán Mountains to issue a proclamation, already prepared and dated a day earlier, which stated that he was assuming the governorship of the state, since he was next in line to succeed. He sent a message to the minister of gobernación in Mexico City to inform the national government of his actions.[29]

Generals Alatorre and Rocha moved into the western area of the state and began to maneuver into a favorable position to strike at the rebel army, commanded by General Luis Mier y Terán. Attention was focused on the Mixteca Alta. Alatorre defeated the army of La Noria first at Chilapilla and then in a crushing victory at San Mateo Xindihuí in Nochixtlán District on December 22–23. Losses were high on both sides, but it was clearly a federal triumph over the centrifugal forces of rebellion and secession. The rebel general Mier was seriously wounded at Xindihuí. The remnants of his army retreated toward the state capital, but Governor Félix Díaz no longer had the manpower to defend Oaxaca City against the combined strength of Alatorre and Rocha, whose armies were approaching. Just as Alatorre's division occupied the capital, on January 4, 1872, without firing a shot, the governor fled southward with a small escort and a few friends, whom he ordered to return to their homes so they would not be endangered by his presence. For all practical purposes, the rebellion had ended, although Porfirio Díaz still tried to spread it and gain adherents in central Mexico, with little success.[30]

Félix Romero relinquished all political control to General Alatorre on January 8. Four days later, the federal commander designated Miguel Castro the governor, with civil powers only, military command being retained by Alatorre.[31] Gradually order was restored, not a difficult task given the absence of the brothers Díaz. Castro scheduled elections for the late spring, in which he was chosen governor. He was installed in the office on July 18, 1872, the same day on which Juárez died of a heart attack in Mexico City.

Porfirio's army was defeated in the state of Zacatecas in February 1872. After making a halfhearted thrust toward Mexico City, Díaz then turned westward toward Jalisco and sought asylum with the feared cacique of Tepic, Manuel Lozada. In other areas where there had been support for Díaz and armed conflict—Yucatan, Durango, Sinaloa—the Noria rebels were defeated by the late spring of 1872. By the time of Juárez's death, the rebellion was virtually stifled.

The fate of Félix Díaz, after his flight from Oaxaca City, took on the dimensions of a Greek tragedy. He intended to make his way to the Pacific Coast to secure passage on a ship by which he could escape. But the ship he intended boarding left before Díaz arrived at the port. In order to elude his enemies, he disguised himself as a ranchero and hid out in the woods near Pochutla. But someone learned of his whereabouts and betrayed him. A group of angry Juchitecans, bent on revenge for the rough treatment meted out to their town and fellow citizens by Díaz in 1870, went in pursuit, found him, and lynched the governor after first subjecting him to a beating and stabbing him with bayonets. Then cutting off his genitalia and sticking them into his mouth, they sent the corpse into the district seat of Pochutla at five o'clock on the morning of January 23, where it was identified by local authorities.[32]

Once more Oaxaca had been plunged into war, resulting from extreme political factionalism fed by the personal ambitions of prominent men. The long build-up to the the Noria rebellion and the fighting that resulted received most of the attention of the people of the state and made it impossible to bring about the economic progress and social stability promised by the Reform.

TOWARD TUXTEPEC

The lack of progress and absence of stability were everywhere noticeable in Oaxaca following the Noria rebellion. The backwardness and isolation of the region, which stood out in even starker relief because of all the talk about progress indulged in by the Reformers, was attested by the American ambassador to Mexico, John W. Foster, who traveled to the southern state in the summer of 1875, in company with his wife, the Italian minister, and a doctor from New Orleans and his wife. From Mexico City, the party journeyed by train as far as they could and then by stagecoach to the end of the line. The last leg of the journey, 100 miles, was covered on horseback and took three days. Appalled by the accommodations available to travelers along the route, Foster described one night spent in an inn, a cabin catering to muleteers, all guests sleeping on beds of corn leaves, which the travelers had to cut in a neighboring field.[33]

The state was rich in minerals but the triumph of liberalism with its hope of economic development failed to create an ambience favorable to the exploitation of Oaxaca's mineral wealth. Most attention focused on the northern Sierra de Ixtlán, but there the mines were small, and operated in starts and stops. They were controlled by a few local entrepreneurs, such as Miguel Castro, who had little vision and not much capital and who were at the mercy of their isolated location with no good roads by which to move machinery to the mining sites or to move large quantities of ore to reduction plants. There was frequent and enthusiastic talk of linking Oaxaca City to the Veracruz–

Mexico City railway, but little came of this. In May 1875, Governor José Esperón was granted a concession by the Lerdo government for the construction of the link, but surveying of the route had barely begun when another rebellion forced the concessionaires to abandon the project for the time being. In agriculture, no progress was made, largely because the markets failed to develop but remained small, low-key affairs. For the development of markets, there had to be first the construction of roads. Some effort had been made in this regard, but the results, the roads radiating out from Oaxaca City to Ixtlán, to Puerto Angel, and to Tehuacán, all built while Félix Díaz was governor, were only a beginning, a fraction of what was needed. For such an enterprise as roadbuilding on a large scale, there were few funds available, since the state expenditures went primarily to maintain a military establishment, at first to support the Díaz brothers' attempt to seize the presidency and then, afterwards, to insure that Porfirio Díaz made no other attempt to use the state as a springboard to national control. In 1872, the total industrial output was only 119,821 pesos, and most of the items produced came from the land—milled flour (84,108 pesos), refined and brown sugar (14,139 pesos), mezcal and aguardiente (7,142 pesos), soap (8,352 pesos), and ginned cotton (5,600 pesos), plus a few other products of inconsequential value. Taxes originating in the Reform era or earlier were heavy. An unjust tax, but one that was highly productive in terms of revenue for the state, was the capitation (head) tax, applied equally in the same amount to rich and poor alike. With few exceptions, every male from age 16 to 60 was required to pay 12½ centavos a month, later raised to 19 centavos. The increase was added in order to support primary education, but little of the revenue derived was actually used for this purpose. The capitation tax was particularly burdensome to the large and economically deprived Indian population.[34]

There were dreamers who designed schemes that would stimulate progress, but little if anything came of their plans. A group of businessmen in 1868 wished to import machinery costing 200,000 pesos to start a textile mill producing cloth and thread. Another group planned to establish an iron foundry and a carpentry works. A Frenchman planned to settle colonies of European immigrants in the state to cultivate cotton and indigo. Matías Romero, a native son who had risen high in the national government, tried to stimulate the movement of goods and people by coastal shipping, which would benefit other states as well as Oaxaca. But the Oaxaca coast was unchartered and this was a major obstacle to his grandiose scheme.[35]

In addition to the poverty perpetuated by isolation, there was additional misery resulting from natural disaster. Throughout the late 1860s and the 1870s there were frequent hurricanes devastating the coastal areas, bringing in their wake deluges that caused flooding. And always there were the earthquakes, some of which in this period were intense and caused widespread damage to property. Foster noted the earthquake scars evident in Oaxaca City. These recurrent catastrophes could only intensify the ruined appearance of property that originated in the warfare of the 1850s and 1860s.[36]

The politicians, in their scramble for power and in their constant bickering, paid little attention to the problems of the economy. When they did, their analysis was marked by the kind of verbosity that comes from fools who think that wishing something makes it come true. Typical of the rhetoric was the statement of Governor José Esperón in his 1875 report to the state legislature. "In a word, as the paralytic of the Bible draws near the pool so that he might be healed at the magic words of 'rise up and walk,' the state emerges from illness [*marasmo*] and walks steadily along the path of progress to arrive at the height of its destinies."[37]

As far as stability was concerned, it, too, like economic strength, was elusive, the result of bitter political infighting among the liberal heirs of the Reform. In the wake of the Noria rebellion, scattered violence and banditry persisted for some time, particularly in the more isolated parts of the state. In the political realm, there was a lack of continuity as successive governors dismantled the administrative bureaucracy constructed by their predecessors, only to build their own power bases through the use of patronage. Thus the jefes políticos appointed by Félix Díaz were dismissed by Miguel Castro, who effectively purged all the government agencies of Díaz's supporters.[38] When Castro was hounded from office two and a half years later by borlado politicians supported by President Lerdo, another purge took place. As each year passed, the rivalry acquired ever increasing tones of antagonism and rancor so that the state was always poised on the brink of anarchy.

Now that their major enemy, Félix Díaz, had been eliminated and the feared and hated Porfirio was out of the state, supposedly following agricultural pursuits in the state of Veracruz after the fiasco of his

La Noria revolt, the borlados once more had an opportunity to seek to control the state's affairs. Miguel Castro, governor since the defeat of the rebellion, was basically a borlado, although his moderation in the Liberal program within the state never caused him to lose the friendship of the radical Juárez. He used many borlado leaders in the upper levels of his administration, among them José Esperón, the chief of the party, who served as Castro's secretary of state, and the former priest, Bernardino Carvajal, who served as the chief clerk of that office. But Castro was not totally committed to the borlado principles and at times could express independent views and take independent actions. On occasion, there was an indecisiveness about him in the conduct of state affairs that angered many of his associates. Consequently, a rift developed with the borlados in late 1873, when Esperón and Carvajal resigned their posts. As the borlado strategy evolved over the next few months, Castro would be discredited and the moderates would capture control of the state legislature, making way for the election of Esperón as the new governor and thereby returning the state to the full control of the die-hard borlados.

In the elections for the state legislature in 1874, the borlados captured nine seats whereas Castro saw elected only seven of his supporters, including Hernández and Meixueiro, his two serrano lieutenants. Rumor spread that soon after the installation of the new assembly, the borlado majority would bring charges against the governor for alleged violations of the law. To forestall this, Castro tried to postpone the scheduled mid-September installation of the legislature. The national congress, the supreme court, and finally President Lerdo became involved in this local dispute. The federal congress decreed that Governor Castro must allow the state legislature to assemble and Lerdo sent General Alatorre with an escort of one hundred soldiers to Oaxaca to enforce the mandate. Governor Castro was given three days to publish the decree locally. At first he balked, resolving to stand fast against the national government, to uphold the principle of state sovereignty. His inclination was to lead a rebellion against the national government, but at the last minute he yielded and ordered the publication of the decree.[39]

For the next few weeks Castro attempted to remain in office, but his fate was sealed. Many of his partisans became so disillusioned that they deserted his camp because of his vacillation. The national government was not friendly; the borlados at best were uncooperative, at worst conspiratorial. There was no alternative to presenting his resignation, which he did on November 4. Three days later, José Esperón received appointment as acting governor and in the following year was elected to the office.

As usual, this change brought about dismissal of the Castro bureaucracy. More important, there were other shifts in the political spectrum, which would have far-reaching consequences for the state and the nation. The death of Juárez had left two major contenders for the presidency, one of whom, Sebastián Lerdo de Tejada, had stepped into the office by virtue of his presidency of the supreme court. Anxious for another term, he was, by 1874, insolently attempting to manipulate state and regional political groups and individuals as well as national figures to create a machine that would assure him a prolonged tenure. He had the reputation of being a radical, a hardline purist, as far as the ideology and program of the Reform were concerned. Thus it was logical that he should not look with favor on the traditionally temporizing borlados of Oaxaca. But logic and principle always seemed to give way to expediency, and it was now convenient for Lerdo and Esperón to cooperate. What brought them together was their shared hatred, and perhaps fear, of Porfirio Díaz, the other major contender. After the defeat of his La Noria rebellion in 1872, Díaz had finally settled in Veracruz state where he was engaged in farming. But agriculture was not the chief thought on his mind. He still coveted the presidency, while enthusiastic supporters throughout the Republic kept his candidacy before the people. Now he lacked the official backing of the political regime of his native state, which he needed if he were to realize his goal. How was he to find support among the Oaxacans if his old enemies, the borlados, controlled state politics? The only way was to cultivate the dissident elements in Oaxaca. The main dissidents were Díaz's former enemies, Miguel Castro and those who had remained loyal to him, especially Fidencio Hernández and Francisco Meixueiro. From his headquarters in the Ixtlán Mountains, Castro tried, without much success, to make life uncomfortable for Governor Esperón, using his two protégés who served in the state legislature. Now it was convenient for Díaz and the Ixtlán dissidents to make common cause against Esperón. If they were successful, both parties would benefit: Castro would reclaim Oaxaca if Esperón were ousted, and Díaz would be aided in Oaxaca in his struggle with Lerdo.

The growing centralism that occupied such a prominent place in Lerdo's policies required cultivation and control of the state governors, many of whom he transformed into "obedient agents of central authority," as a biographer of Lerdo describes them.[40] Esperón was willing to cooperate with the president and in doing so, went to great lengths to insure that no support for Díaz developed. But the governor was sitting on a powder keg in Oaxaca. For one thing, there was widespread complaint about Lerdo's policies and methods. The opposition stridently and bitterly harped on dishonest electoral practices, the vanishing autonomy of the municipalities, corruption in high government circles, abusive taxes, the selling of the nation's resources to foreigners through railroad concessions, the suspension of civil liberties, the subjugation of the judiciary to political considerations. Their list of grievances was seemingly endless.[41] Since Esperón was Lerdo's minion, local dissatisfaction with the drift of national affairs focused on the governor.

For another thing, many citizens of Oaxaca were armed, having been distributed rifles and ammunition on past occasions when the state was threatened by the Conservatives during the War of the Reform, by the French during the Intervention, by the federal forces during La Noria rebellion. By 1875, there was virtually a network of small armories dispersed in the towns and villages. When rumor spread that the people were to be disarmed, Esperón thought it prudent to assure them, through his jefes políticos, that this was not true—as long as the people continued to obey the laws and the orders of the government. He required his district agents to send in monthly reports of the amount of ammunition and number of rifles in each locality and to see that the war material was guarded adequately.[42]

From his headquarters in Tlacotalpan, Veracruz, Porfirio Díaz had worked effectively between 1873 and 1875 to bring about a reconciliation with the serrano chieftains, particularly Fidencio Hernández, who was by now the leading man of affairs of the region. In his early forties, Hernández had branched out from mining operations under the auspices of his mentor, Miguel Castro, to become involved in such diverse enterprises as experimentation with growing coffee trees, road construction, commerce, the manufacture of candles for use in the mines, a bakery, and the production of hams for local consumption. In his commercial dealings, he made frequent trips into the state of Veracruz, where he had opportunity to consult with Díaz, to keep him informed of events in Oaxaca, and to air their mutual concerns over national political questions. Through these contacts Hernández became converted into the principal Díaz agent operating in Oaxaca and the man most responsible for the propulsion towards the Tuxtepec Revolution.[43]

Díaz sanctioned that rebellion as the 1876 elections approached. The idea originated in Veracruz, but the action began in Oaxaca, when, from Tuxtepec District in the northern part of the state, a revolutionary proclamation was issued on January 10. After listing the grievances against President Lerdo, the plan called for all states to withdraw recognition from the national government in support of uprising. Porfirio Díaz was proclaimed the commander-in-chief of the rebel army. Those state governors who did not adhere to the plan would be removed and replaced by interim governors named by Díaz. The program also called for constitutional reforms, which would guarantee the principles of no reelection and municipal autonomy. The aim was the removal of Lerdo and the installation of Díaz.[44]

Despite the close watch that Esperón maintained on the various districts through his agents, the Tuxtepec pronunciamento caught him by surprise. The governor was visiting pueblos outside the Central District at the time. He rushed back to the state capital to marshal support and to oversee the crushing of the rebellion. Then word reached him on January 22 that on the previous day a few of the leading citizens among the serranos plus some of the officers of the National Guard unit in Ixtlán District had seconded the Tuxtepec plan, withdrawing their recognition of the state government and the political chief of the district and recognizing instead the administration of Miguel Castro, which had ceased with his resignation from the governorship in early November 1874. One of the eight signers of the Ixtlán statement was Fidencio Hernández.[45]

Governor Esperón quickly mustered an infantry detachment of 500 men to march into the mountains to suppress the rebellion. Hernández likewise summoned the National Guard regiment, 200 strong, of Ixtlán District, which began moving toward the largest of the mountain towns, Ixtepeji. When scouts brought him word of the Esperón column, Hernández turned to intercept it and struck on January 23. Though inferior in size, the small Hernández army had the advantage of surprise and after only a short engagement dispersed the governor's army, forcing it to retreat. Desirous of having more information of what was happening in the central valley and the state capital, Hernández then moved his troops to the foothill towns of San Felipe del Agua, Tlalixtac, and Huayapan, which were occupied on the 26th and 27th. In the late afternoon of January 27,

Esperón sent out a column of 400 soldiers to attack Hernández in San Felipe. By now, the serrano commanded 1,200 infantry, so rapidly had his ranks swelled after the Tuxtepec and Ixtlán statements had circulated. Hernández struck at the approaching column and forced it to retreat the few miles back to Oaxaca City. The rebel army followed in close pursuit, and, owing to ineffective resistance in the state capital, by eight o'clock that night the mountaineers and their allies were in control of the city. The more than 300 prisoners captured accepted Hernández's leaderhsip and were incorporated into his ranks. The major part of the governor's artillery and supply of ammunition was captured. Esperón fled.

The next day, Hernández issued two proclamations, one declaring that he came as a liberator and inviting the support of the people, and the other praising his soldiers for their courage. Two days later, he assumed all executive power until elections could be held. Until mid-February, Hernández devoted his attention to the civil affairs of the state and to preparation for the anticipated invasion by a federal army. He justified his seizure of power by pointing out that Esperón was unpopular, vicious, and immoral, and that the governor worked hand-in-hand with President Lerdo. To allow these two men to stay in office would only perpetuate the evils of corruption and the misery imposed by their illegal methods on the people of the nation and the citizens of Oaxaca. Hernández insisted that he had rebelled not to attack the people but rather to defend them, not to destroy their rights but rather to restore them. He urged the Oaxacans to support enthusiastically the Tuxtepec Revolution and to give their allegiance to Porfirio Díaz, in whose name the rebellion was staged. Finally, on February 11, shortly before leaving Oaxaca City to command the Tuxtepec army in defense of the state's territory, Hernández named his fellow serrano and co-worker, Francisco Meixueiro, governor and military commander. Hernández's command no longer rested in the authority of the Ixtlán revolution within the state against Governor Esperón but in the greater and wider authority of the national Tuxtepec Revolution against President Lerdo.[46]

The federal army sent to put down the revolt in Oaxaca was once more commanded by Division General Ignacio Alatorre, who had been sent to the southern state on two previous occasions in recent years—in 1871 to contain the Noria insurrection, which he had accomplished with the support of the serrano militia under Hernández; and in 1874 to enforce the congressional orders that forced Governor

Castro to allow the disputed state legislature to assemble. From mid-February to mid-July 1876, both the rebel militia and Alatorre's Second Division of the federal army played a cat-and-mouse game, clashing here and there in the western part of the state, across the border into Puebla, and on into Veracruz—Suchixtlahuaca, Yanhuitlán, Epatlán, where one of the better Porfirian generals, Luis Mier y Terán, was taken prisoner, and Monte Blanco, where Hernández himself fell captive to General Alatorre.

In this earlier and unsuccessful phase of the southern warfare, Porfirio Díaz was elsewhere, trying to spread the Tuxtepec Revolution in the northern reaches of the nation, with mixed results. Defeated at Icamole in Coahuila on May 20, he escaped across the international boundary to make his way to New Orleans, thence by steamship to Veracruz and from there overland, eluding his pursuers, to the safe haven of his native state. After nine months of maneuvering and fighting, the revolution generally had failed and now was centered again in the Porfirian stronghold of Oaxaca. Alatorre invaded in September, but Díaz was able to accomplish what his lieutenant, Hernández, had failed to do; to defeat the federal forces in a large-scale, hard-fought, definitive action at Tecoac in the state of Puebla on November 16. The federal troops suffered 1,900 dead and 800 wounded, while the Porfirian army lost 875 dead and 475 wounded. This overwhelming victory for the Textepec rebels forced President Lerdo to resign four days later. On November 26, the Díaz army entered Mexico City in triumph; Porfirio had captured the presidency.[47]

The war had lasted eleven months. Again Oaxaca had served as the recruiting ground, the source of men, as it had in the Reform, the Intervention, and La Noria revolt. Again there was economic upset, the necessity for sacrifice, the levy of taxes, the wasting of human and natural resources to forward the ambitions of the politicans. The state had experienced two decades of continual crises arising from the Liberal-Conservative clash over the establishment of the Reform program, from the moderate-radical debate within the Liberal ranks to define the exact nature of that program, and from the rivalry for leadership of the Reform.

Although the long struggle to impose the Reform on Mexico had resulted in curbing ecclesiastical power and influence and in virtually destroying conservatism as a political force, it had not eliminated two other tendencies, militarism and unbridled personal ambition, which the Liberals clearly had recognized from the beginning as major and endemic threats to the achievement of their goals. To the contrary, these two traits were further stimulated, and the contradiction, which was to bode ill for Mexico during the post-Reform decade, was manifested at every level of political organization, municipal, district, state, and national.

Oaxaca was no exception. Indeed, perhaps there more than anywhere else in Mexico the unleashing of militarism and the failure to subordinate personal aspirations to national order were the most prominent features of state politics during the ten years following the triumph of the Reform. The titanic struggle between Díaz and Juárez for the presidency, which quickly developed after the defeat of Maximilian, had a major impact upon Oaxaca simply because both men were native sons of the state and each had his own local following. This was reflected not only in realignments in political groupings in Oaxaca but also to a certain extent in regional tensions within the state. The combat between Díaz and Juárez climaxed in 1871–72 with the Noria rebellion, of Oaxacan origin, and the death of Juárez. Díaz lost this first attempt to seize power, only to become more determined. He then disputed the presidency of Lerdo de Tejada, who had succeeded Juárez. His third bid for the executive office likewise brought about an armed struggle, the Revolution of Tuxtepec, also of Oaxacan origin, which merged with the regional Ixtlán rebellion aimed at ousting the unpopular Esperón from the governorship. Díaz's attempts to become the leader of the nation thus not only brought about the renewal of warfare in the state on two occasions, but also resulted in constant political friction. His supporters and opponents maneuvered to control the machinery of state and local government; this in turn involved discontent in the Sierra of Ixtlán and the eruption of violence in the Isthmus of Tehuantepec.

Despite the slightly improved situation of Oaxaca through completion of the telegraph line and the opening of the road to Tehuacán, giving quicker and better access to Mexico City and the central core of the nation, the political and military turbulence stemming from Díaz's aspirations harmed the economy of the state. No real progress chould be measured in improved living standards, agricultural production, manufacturing, education, or any other aspect relating to social or economic betterment, the cornerstone of the Reform edifice. In effect, Oaxaca was held back by the power struggle, which diverted attention away from fostering progress and nurturing stable governmental institutions and practices. Instead, the contest consumed the state's income and capital resources and occupied its citizens, directly or indirectly, as the case may be.

In a very real sense, much of what the Liberal Reform had attempted to achieve was sacrificed in Oaxaca to the personal rivalries and aspirations of the politicians and to an intensification of the role of military force in realizing those ambitions.

CHAPTER 6

THE DISENTAILMENT AND ALIENATION OF PROPERTY, 1856–76

MUCH OF THE CONTROVERSY of the years following 1856, when the Lerdo Law was issued, swirled around the attempt by the Liberals to deprive civil and ecclesiastical corporations, especially the latter, of their property and to put it into circulation; that is, to take real estate out of mortmain and place it in the hands of private citizens. This question has been discussed in part in the foregoing chapters but it seems appropriate to devote a separate chapter to an analysis of the question—the type of property affected, the procedures used to accomplish the goals, the people who purchased the real estate, the problem of the Indian lands, and other related aspects. Such an analysis reveals that some of the myth that has grown around the Reform, specifically concerning the great economic issue of property, has little factual basis when considered in the context of developments in the state of Oaxaca.

PROBLEMS

To trace the disposal of the corporate real estate holdings, describe the procedures, and analyze the results of this movement present many difficulties. Surrounding the property question there is much confusion, the roots of which are diverse. In the first place, the political turmoil in Mexico from 1856 through 1867 produced ambiguity and uncertainty in matters of governmental policies. During much of this time, there were two governments, each with fundamentally different philosophies and therefore diametrically opposed to the other on important issues, and each claiming to speak for the nation. From such political duality came deep hostilities, which frequently resulted in prolonged periods of warfare. This meant that the Liberal program of disentailment and then nationalization of corporate properties had to be implemented under conditions that proved difficult if not impossible.

A second source of perplexity, and a direct outgrowth of the political rivalry, was the lack of care in maintaining the records of sales and transfers of titles. Property tax rolls, the records of the Ministry of the Treasury, lists of disentailed properties, transcripts of proceedings of auctions, and notary books recording transfers were moved about frequently, resulting in the loss of some important files, and many of the records were deliberately destroyed by the Conservatives. Consequently, in some locales where warfare or political dispute was particularly prevalent, insufficient records have survived from the Reform era to allow a thorough analysis of the property question. For the area outside the Central District in the state of Oaxaca, the lack of records presents many problems that have to be approached indirectly. For the Central District itself, including the capital city, although many records were destroyed at the time or have been lost since, enough information survives to give a rather complete view of the problem of disentailment. Of those notary books recording property transfers between 1856 and 1867 in the Central District and kept in the state capital, approximately 75 per cent have been preserved. Few notaries were active in the state outside the capital during the Reform period, and fewer of their books have been preserved. But even in the books not lost or destroyed, one cannot help forming the impression that officials were imprecise in the language and terms used in recording the sales and title transfers. Often the notaries were overworked and perhaps this accounts for their frequent inattention to details. At times properties are not clearly defined as to location; previous owners are not always mentioned; the financial transactions arranging for methods of payment, even the valuations of the properties and their selling prices, are not as clearly described as one would wish. Despite the deficiencies, the notary records give an abundance of important and necessary information.[1]

A third source of confusion lies in the realm of the Reform statutes themselves. Indeed, perhaps the laws issued by the Liberals are the primary reason that disentailment was carried out in such a seemingly haphazard way. The process by which the Reform laws were written and debated in cabinet circles before issuance remains almost completely unknown. In some cases even the identity of the authors is difficult to determine. One gains the impression that little systematic thought lay behind the writing. This conclusion is reinforced by comments made by Melchor Ocampo, member of the Reform cabinets, who lamented the timing, wording, and procedures stipulated in the 1859 Law of Nationalization of Ecclesiastical Property, and who attributed the defects to the hurry in which the measure was formulated, discussed, and written. In the various laws concerning real estate held in mortmain, the language was frequently too vague and the general rules laid down were not sufficiently detailed to cover all kinds of property, all forms of holdings or ownership, or all situations that might arise. The lack of precision and detail meant that a large amount of correspondence had to pass among officials on all levels of government, that a great number of petitions from private citizens were sent to government agencies, and that many disputes developed, all arising from the need for clarification on diverse points.[2]

The difficulties centering around the need for clarification were heightened, furthermore, by the structure and situation of the Liberal government. In those regions under republican control that could maintain contact with the national government as it shifted its headquarters from Mexico City to Veracruz and later to San Luis Potosí, Chihuahua, and Paso del Norte, every inquiry, every confused point seemingly had to be referred to President Juárez for resolution. This tended to cause frequent and prolonged delays between the time a specific controversy arose and the time a decision was rendered by the national government to resolve the problem. In addition, it meant that high officials of the national government had to spend much time with the minutiae of the property question. The heavy demands placed upon all levels of the government involved in the property decisions were immediately evident following the issuance of the Lerdo Law in the summer of 1856, and the burden of paper work grew heavier as the months passed.[3] Simply to follow the thread of the question as interpreted and modified in subsequent circulars, decrees, and correspondence is an almost insurmountable task.

One of the most severe deficiencies of the law of 1856 was its failure to define adequately the administrative machinery for handling the properties to be disentailed. As stipulated by the law, the chief political authority in each district was placed in charge of the procedures and given responsibility for receiving and registering denunciations, conducting auctions, appointing appraisers, and delivering titles to purchasers. He was assisted by the judge of the first instance in some tasks, such as holding auctions and delivering titles, and the judge was also charged with hearing and settling disputes that might arise from the denunciations and sales.

In Oaxaca, the highest district official was the district governor, later called the district political chief, an appointee of the governor of the state. Thus the process of disentailment was kept in the realm of the executive branch and would necessarily have political overtones. The judicial branch of the government was cast in a supportive role. It is readily seen that disentailment was not made strictly a fiscal matter overseen by local agents of the national Ministry of the Treasury. The only role to be played by the treasury agents was passive: each week they were to receive lists, sent to them by the notaries, of all disentailment transactions that had taken place during the preceding seven days.

The administrative organization outlined above suggests that an additional burden was placed on government officials already overworked. The district chiefs had countless administrative and political functions to perform and could not easily devote the necessary attention to disentailment proceedings without neglecting their other duties. Despite weaknesses, the organization remained fixed until mid-1859, when the Law of Nationalization was issued. Even under the new statute, the district chiefs still retained some responsibility, primarily in appointing commissions to appraise and inventory nationalized properties and goods and in overseeing the general confiscatory operations. But the 1859 law charged the local offices of the national Treasury Ministery with the conduct of the auctions and sales. In Oaxaca, this office was headed by José Maza, brother-in-law of President Juárez.

The main goal of the 1859 law was confiscation without indemnification of all real estate previously owned by ecclesiastical institutions. While overall jurisdiction was retained locally by Maza's office, the bureaucratic agencies involved multiplied and record keeping became particularly complex. On July 26, 1859, immediately following the promulgation of the law in Oaxaca, an Office for the Liquidation of Ecclesiastical Properties was established in the state capital. Another office was created in September, with the former priest Bernardino Carvajal at its head, which was charged with administering the income and expenditures of the nunneries and their attached churches. A third operation concerned the collection of rents from properties previously owned by the church and disentailed in 1856 but not yet sold to private citizens. Subsequently, two state agencies, the Fund for Public Instruction and the Fund for Public Beneficence, became involved in handling properties, conducting sales, and maintaining records because these offices were given endowments consisting of unsold confiscated properties and also mortgages.[4]

Finally, another change was brought about in 1864, when the state revenue department took charge of the sales. The reason for this is not clear. Perhaps the change came about as a result of increasing difficulties in maintaining communcations with the central government as it moved about in the north, fleeing the army of the Intervention. And in time, after General Porfirio Díaz established his headquarters in Oaxaca City, the administration of the nationalization procedures became largely a function of the republican Army of the East.[5]

While these state and national agencies were becoming involved, another level of government also participated in the redistribution of real estate. The ayuntamiento of the city and the councils of the Indian towns were concerned with divesting their corporate entities of properties they owned. Not much attention was given to the civil properties in the Central District, except in the case of lands held by Indian villages, probably because they constituted only a small percentage of the real estate involved in disentailment and because the municipal government in the state capital was controlled by Liberals who could be trusted to do their duty. On the other hand, outside the Central District the civil properties received more emphasis than the church properties. But information had to be exchanged with the other agencies, lists of properties alienated had to be sent back and forth, all adding to the paper work involved and thereby creating a situation of potential confusion.

The array of municipal, state, and national agencies, including the executive and judicial branches, the military, the treasury, and the charitable and educational funds, tended to compound the difficulties involved, first in determining what properties were to be disentailed, and second in making arrangements for and keeping records of the ultimate disposal of the real estate. Thus, much of the muddle that has long perplexed the historian interested in the Reform is only partially the result of the lack of care of later generations in preserving the records of the era. A major share of the confusion surrounding the property question rests squarely on the shoulders of the Reformers themselves and their poorly written laws and hastily or ill-conceived bureaucratic methods and structures that resulted in overlapping authority.

THE CENTRAL DISTRICT

As best as can be determined from existing records, 1,436 pieces of property were disentailed in the Central District in the years under study. Such a statistic has no intrinsic meaning, however, unless it is compared with the total number of parcels of real estate existing in the district at the time of the Reform. This figure can be determined only partially, and then only in Oaxaca City. By far the greatest portion of the disentailed property in the district was located within the boundaries of the state capital. An 1848, block-by-block count of houses within the city gave a total of 1,526 dwellings.[6] It would probably not be inaccurate to assume roughly the same number of dwellings in 1856, given the unsettled political conditions of the era, the depression following the Mexican War, and the civil war of Ayutla, all occurring in the intervening eight years falling between the termination of the hostilities with the United States and the beginning of the Reform. Such conditions undoubtedly discouraged construction of new dwellings to any significant degree. Of this number of houses, at least 1,102, or approximately 72.2 per cent, were owned by the various ecclesiastical institutions. The preponderance of church-owned property in the state capital becomes even more pronounced when it is compared with the total amount of real estate disentailed in the entire Central District during the two decades following the promulgation of the Lerdo Law. These 1,102 dwellings constituted almost 77 per cent of the 1,436 pieces of property forced out of mortmain, which indicates immediately that disentailment in the Central District was primarily urban in nature, that is, centered in Oaxaca City, and was preponderantly concerned with former ecclesiastical properties.[7] In addition, at least 647 properties were disentailed within the state boundaries but outside the Central District by 1876, giving a grand total of 2,083 properties. The 1,102 houses owned by ecclesiastical institutions within the city of Oaxaca represent almost 53 per cent, just over half, of the disentailed civil and ecclesiastical properties in the state. At the same time, the population of the district represented only approximately 14 per cent of the total population of Oaxaca.

Although it has been impossible to determine values, it can be said with assurance that the properties in the capital city represented well over half the value of the total disentailment operations within the state.

Given the compactness of the area and its broken terrain, there were no vast stretches of land available for the establishment of latifundia so characteristic of other regions of Mexico, particularly the north. Although the soil of the district was rich enough for the production of a variety of crops and the grazing of herds, land was not available for the creation of numerous large haciendas, and the church therefore was not a great landowner in the rural area by the middle part of the nineteenth century. This perhaps accounts for the reason the church had concentrated its attention through the decades on urban real estate. Despite the heavily urban character disentailment assumed in the state, the few rural lands the church owned and was forced to sell received primary attention during the months immediately following the promulgation of the Lerdo Law, and even in later years sporadically continued to cause some controversy.

Of the eighteen haciendas listed as part of the Central District when the districts were created in March 1858, apparently only seven were in the hands of the church. Of these seven, three were owned by the Dominicans, one by the Carmelites, one by the Augustinian Recollets, and one by the Dominican Sisters. Another hacienda, frequently referred to in the records as a *labor*, or "small farm," belonged to a pious fund. In addition to these seven tracts, the Indian Capuchinesses held four small pieces of rural land totaling approximately six acres near the village of Tlalixtac; the parish church of Cuilapan owned a rancho; and two confraternities each owned a rancho.

The Lerdo Law provided a period of three months following its local promulgation during which time the only sales that could be made were to the tenants of civil or ecclesiastically owned properties. In other words, those who rented or leased these properties were being given an opportunity to buy them without having to compete with other prospective purchasers. If the tenants decided not to buy, then the real estate was to be put up for auction at the end of the three-month period. Only two other types of movement of corporate properties could take place in this initial period before the auctions began: the corporations could sell their holdings privately or in conventional sales (as opposed to auctions) with the government's permission; or, for those properties not rented or leased at the time of the promulgation of the law, auctions were authorized.

Within the three months following July 3, when the law was published in Oaxaca, five of the seven haciendas were sold in auction. That none of the purchasers was a tenant of these properties at the time of sale means that roughly one-third of the church's rural holdings in the district were being farmed with day or resident labor, were not being worked at all, or were being farmed only minimally. Either of the last two cases would provide telling evidence of the diminished income of the church. The pertinent facts regarding the sales of the seven haciendas are given in Table 1.

The five haciendas sold during the three-month waiting period were almost the only properties that received any attention in the days immediately following the promulgation of the law. Their auctions were reported in the newspaper, and the bidding was keen in some cases, forcing the sale price for one, San Luis, to go above the official valuation. The bidding for Carmen Hacienda started at only 39,000 pesos, far below the official valuation, but was significantly increased to 80,000 pesos, which represented two-thirds of the official value.

The purchasers were mostly professional men. José María Díaz Ordaz and Ramón Cajiga, both lawyers, were the only ones destined to play prominent roles in Oaxaca during the Reform. Juan María Carlios was a medical doctor and professor at the Institute; Manuel Sánchez Posada was also a lawyer and judge, and both he and his partner, Manuel Pardo, served on the town council during the Reform era; Gabriel, Esperón was a member of the wealthy and prominent family whose members were active in state politics. His brother, José, became one of the borlado leaders. Nothing is known of Justo Leyva. Ignacio Urda was a Conservative and devout Catholic; his purchase of Carmen Hacienda gave rise to a sensational scandal a few years later, to be discussed below.

The documentary evidence regarding these haciendas leaves many questions unanswered. For example, no indication of size is available except for Carmen. The records show that it contained approximately 1,603 acres, certainly not large for what is generally thought of as a hacienda. And it was the most expensive one in the Central District. If selling price is any indication of size and productivity, as undoubtedly it was, then it is readily seen that the other haciendas would be much smaller in extent or much less productive.[8]

The existing information regarding these sales also provides

Table 1*

Haciendas Sold in the Central District, 1856

Hacienda	Owners	Purchasers	Date of Purchase	Official Valuation (pesos)	Selling Price (pesos)
San Luis	Dominicans	Manuel Pardo and Manuel Sánchez Posada	8/13/56	16,109.75	16,500
Dolores	Dominicans	Juan María Carlios	7/29/56	14,501.25	11,002
El Rosario	Dominicans	José Ma. Díaz Ordaz	7/30/56	42,750.00	28,500
Sta. Rosa Panzacola	Dominican Sisters	Justo Leyva	8/12/56	?	1,450
Soledad or Crespo	Obra pía de J——— tepec	Ramón Cajiga	?	?	4,000 at least
Carmen	Carmelites	Ignacio Urda	8/1/56	120,000.00	80,000
Montoya	Augustinian Recollets	Gabriel Esperón	10/11/56	32,794.00	29,121

*Sources of information on the transactions involving the seven haciendas are: *El Constituyente, Suplemento de Actas*, July 17, 1856, 2nd page; July 31, 1856, 4th page; Aug. 3, 1856, 2nd and 3rd pages; Aug. 21, 1856, 2nd page; *Dem.*, 1:3:4, Oct. 9, 1856; 1:4:4, Oct. 12, 1856; 1:7:2, Oct. 23, 1856; AN, Protocolo de Juan Rey, 1856, Tomo 5, *hojas* 192 *vuelta*–207, 225 *vuelta*–40, 270 *vuelta*, 277–78 *vuelta*, 325, 326–27, 339–52, 354–55, 698–718, 719; Protocolo de Felipe Sandoval, 1861, Tomo 8, *hojas* 112–112 *vuelta*, 114–16 *vuelta*, 118–21.

hints of perplexing problems that early beset the Reformers in their efforts to dispose of church lands. The full stories do not emerge from the records, but there is enough evidence to indicate that the implementation of the Law of 1856 gave rise to much vexation.

In the case of Montoya Hacienda, there was an attempt to block the sale. Several men were interested in buying it, among them the Englishman Diego Innes of Ejutla, a cochineal merchant, and Agustín Aguirre, the Spanish vice-counsul in Oaxaca. The auction was first scheduled for August 17. But a few days before, Ignacio Goytia declared that the hacienda belonged not to the Augustinian Recollets of La Soledad convent but rather to Goytia's children and grandchildren. He stated that the hacienda had been given to the convent by one of his ancestors in the form of a *capellanía*, to be enjoyed in perpetuity by a member of the family of the donor or his descendants.[9] A clause in the donation provided that if the land was ever alienated from the nunnery, for whatever reason, it should revert to the descendants of the donor, of whom Goytia was one. When the auction was held, the Spanish Consul, Aguirre, appeared and claimed the hacienda for the heirs of Baltazar Montoya, the donor, on the supposition that they undoubtedly resided in Spain. José Esperón was also present, representing the interests of his client, the Duke of Monteleón, and claiming that whoever bought the hacienda would have to pay the Duke an annual fee for the use of the water in the streams. The claim indicates that the hacienda lands were once a part of the Cortés estate, for it was the Monteleón family who were the heirs of the conquistador. And finally, the municipal authorities of Santa María Oaxaca, or the Marquesado, entered a claim stating that some of the lands constituting the hacienda actually belonged to the municipality. These claims and counterclaims interrupted the bidding several times. Finally the judge decided to disregard all claims, and the hacienda went to Gabriel Esperón, who submitted the highest bid.

But the trouble was not over. Later that month, Esperón encountered difficulties when he attempted to obtain the title to the land and to inventory the property. The buyer claimed that the official valuation of 32,794 pesos was the value entered on the tres al millar tax rolls, and was based on land and cattle. The cattle Esperón estimated to be worth 2,365 pesos. When the inventory was attempted on October 31, it was discovered that the hacienda had been stripped of all seeds, implements, and animals by order of Padre Nicolás Vasconcelos, the administrator of La Soledad convent. At this point, the records become silent until July 1863, when Esperón petitioned the governor that he be granted relief from the taxes owed on his hacienda.[10]

The Hacienda of Carmen was valued at 120,000 pesos and purchased by Urda for two-thirds of that amount. Almost five years later, in February 1861, it was discovered that Urda had bought the property as a front man for the monastery of Carmen Alto in Oaxaca City, the original owner, so that the Carmelite friars could continue deriving an income from the operation of the estate. Through the years following the purchase, Urda's conscience apparently bothered him, and he confessed the simulated sale on his deathbed.[11] When this was revealed, the authorities decided to divide the hacienda into four farms, each of equal size, and to put them up for auction. The four together were appraised at the price Urda had paid for the land, and in March 1861, Colonel Cristóbal Salinas acquired all of them in auction, paying 55,846 pesos, an amount just over two-thirds of the new valuation and well under the original appraisal of 120,000 pesos.[12]

When Urda's malfeasance became known it was well publicized by the Liberal politicians who used it as a convenient propaganda piece to illustrate the perfidy of the church. This was the only case of a simulated sale that came to light in the period from 1856 to 1876, but there remains the possibility that other cases were exposed in the years following. The charge is frequently made that much of the property throughout Mexico was bought in simulated sales, as Urda had done, by persons who were devout Catholics, only to be returned to the church once the turbulence had subsided.[13] Such fraudulent sales would allow the church to continue enjoying the usufruct of the property while on the surface purchasers appeared to be upholding the Reform laws. The infrequency of this type of subterfuge in the state of Oaxaca thus makes it impossible to apply the generalization universally to the Reform movement throughout Mexico.

In regard to the other church-owned rural lands, they were in rather small parcels and little interest was generated in them. No records of sale exist for the four strips owned by the Indian Capuchinesses. The rancho known as El Carrizal, which was owned by the parish church of Cuilapan, was bought by the Spanish consul, Aguirre, in October 1856. Luis Gómez, who served as secretary of the Oaxaca City ayuntamiento at one period during the Reform, purchased a small rancho belonging to a confraternity. And the other rancho owned by a different confraternity was bought by a man about whom no information is available. Both of these confraternity ranchos probably were purchased sometime in late 1856, although the records are not clear on this point.[14]

After the three-month waiting period expired, during which the five haciendas were sold, the emphasis shifted to the urban properties within Oaxaca City. Few of these had been adjudicated by their tenants in the months set aside for such transactions.[15] The reasons for this failure are diverse. Most important, it may be another indication of the scarcity of capital and savings in Oaxaca, even though not much of a cash outlay was needed for adjudication. The former tenants who became owners were to continue making monthly payments to the corporations from which they had rented previously, the only difference being that the payments were no longer rent but were now interest on mortgages. No demands were made or schedules set for redeeming the mortgages, so that the owners could continue making the monthly interest payments indefinitely. The only requirement for cash derived from the stipulation that a 5 per cent transfer or sales tax had to be paid on the value of the property, which was fixed by capitalizing at 6 per cent the annual rent paid by the tenant before disentailment. The law gave advantages to those who adjudicated early in the three-month period: those who did so in the first month could pay half of the sales tax in bonds on the national debt; in the second month, one-third of the tax could be paid in bonds; and in the third month, one-fourth could be paid in bonds. After the three-month period had expired, all the tax had to be paid in cash.

Furthermore, among certain segments of the population the law was unpopular, and those tenants loyal to the church and the Conservative cause would hesitate or refuse to adjudicate. Perhaps many were at least waiting to see how intense the controversy would become that was beginning to rage around the law. Undoubtedly the Lerdo proposal had some shock effects on citizens, no matter how Liberal and anticlerical they were. Perhaps they needed some time to realize that they were being given a chance to acquire property that had been out of circulation for decades and not available to them for purchase.

Another important factor that might serve as a partial explanation for the failure of tenants to adjudicate lies in the procedures established by the law. There were definite financial advantages to be gained by those citizens who wished to purchase property who waited until the expiration of the three months. If a tenant adjudicated property during the stipulated time period, the price he had to pay eventually to redeem the mortgage was equal to the full valuation of the property as established by the decree—the annual rent capitalized at 6 per cent. If he waited until the three months expired, he might be able to acquire the property at two-thirds of that valuation, thereby saving a third. Of course, by waiting he also ran the risk that others might be interested in the same piece of real estate and would either denounce and claim it, a procedure allowed by the law if the tenant did not adjudicate within the three months, or would bid against the tenant in the auction, thereby forcing up the price and perhaps even causing the tenant to lose in the bidding. But this was a chance that apparently many in the state capital felt well worth taking. The possibility of saving money, of buying at a lower price, by waiting seems a much more reasonable explanation of the paucity of activity immediately following the promulgation of the law than the shock effect theory or the explanation that the populace was anti-Liberal, dismayed at the Reform law, hesitant to act under its protection, and wanted to wait and see what the church would do before venturing to acquire property that was being forced out of mortmain by a group of bold but wildly radical Liberals whom many feared or distrusted.

The law allowed ecclesiastical institutions eventually to receive the full purchase price, when mortgages were ultimately redeemed, if they cooperated in the proceedings by volunteering information concerning their real estate holdings. It was anticipated, however, that some of the clergy would attempt to hide evidence or otherwise destroy records showing the properties held by the church. To meet this contingency, the law provided that properties could be denounced by private citizens—that is, citizens were encouraged to appear before the civil authorities to inform them of properties held by the church. For this service the denouncers were to receive one-eighth of the selling price if the properties were later sold, and this would be deducted from the amount to be received by the church from the sale—that is, the mortgage to be held by the church would be for the value of the property reduced by one-eighth. Or, if the denouncer happened to buy the property, then he received, in effect, a discount of one-eighth of the selling price, thereby reducing his mortgage, and the church would receive the remainder in the form of the reduced mortgage. Financially, then, it was to the advantage of the church to disclose all real estate it held in mortmain so that it would receive the full purchase price.

The documents are frequently imprecise, ambiguous, or otherwise incomplete in the matter of denunciations. Existing information indicates that 233 pieces of real estate were denounced by at least 62 persons, most of the denunciations, 191 altogether, taking place on October 3, 1856, the day following the end of the three-month waiting period. Very few of the men who appeared before the civil authorities purchased the same properties they denounced. It was probably the intention of the law that whoever should denounce would also buy the same property, but the records for Oaxaca show that some few men had the idea of denouncing many properties without desiring to purchase them, thereby earning one-eighth of the selling prices as reward money and accumulating tidy sums. One man, Mariano Cruz, led the field in this endeavor, denouncing a total of thirty-eight pieces of property and buying none of them. His profits were not as substantial as he possibly anticipated, however, for only thirteen of the properties were eventually sold. Agustín Aguilar also engaged in this activity, denouncing ten pieces, two of which were sold but neither of which he bought. Francisco Ortiz y Quintas denounced thirteen pieces, none of which was sold, so he made nothing for his effort. On the other hand, Antonio Ramos denounced seven pieces and purchased all of them, which meant he received rather substantial discounts on his purchases. By far the great majority of the properties denounced were located in the city of Oaxaca as opposed to the rural area of the Central District.[16]

For those who waited until the three months had expired, there were two methods of purchasing disentailed properties, either by competitive bidding in public auction or by making an acceptable private offer to a designated government official. The offer, as stated previously, had to meet the minimum of two-thirds of the official valuation. The properties were to be put in auction over and over again until they were sold or until an acceptable private offer was received. The Law of 1856 provided for three successive auctions. If still not sold, the real estate would be withdrawn for a time and anyone could request that a revaluation be made. Appraisers would then be appointed, at the expense of the person making the request. In nearly every case the resulting revaluation was lower than the original valuation. Sometimes this process was repeated, the appraisal being lowered each time. This is not unusual or deserving of suspicion when one considers that properties quickly fell into states of disrepair as time passed, which would bring about lower valuations, and that, too, the financial needs of the government grew, which encouraged selling

at lower prices in order to move the properties. The corporative owners, knowing that their tenure would soon end, would have no interest
in keeping up their properties, and the government was uninterested
in getting involved in the property-repair business after the nationalization decree of 1859. So the values gradually and steadily declined.[17]

Clergymen who served as the administrators and majordomos of
church holdings were required by the law to deliver the titles of the
properties to the new owners. They were nearly all unanimous in
refusing to do this, to sign any documents, or to participate in the
sales in any way. The law, anticipating such attitudes, made provision
for their refusal by allowing the civil authorities to intervene and act
for the priests if they proved obstinate. Most of the clergymen were
firm but polite in voicing their refusals. But occasionally some of the
clerics seized the opportunity to lash out at the Liberal government.
There is one recorded case in early January 1857, where two priests
who served as treasurers of the cathedral, when notified of the sale of
a house that was part of the endowment of the treasury, used such
strong language in heaping insults on the government that they were
each fined fifty pesos for their insolence. On the other hand, one
occasionally can detect in a few of the priests' statements a note of
regret that they were not allowed to furnish the documents or sign the
transfers of title because they believed the law was just. Nevertheless,
they withheld their cooperation. Even those clerics of outright Liberal
sympathy who would later defect to the Liberal cause, such as the
prior of the Dominican monastery, Margarito Maldonado, refused to
cooperate. In a few cases, lay lawyers served as the administrators of
ecclesiastical properties. José Esperón, the moderate Liberal who
would in time emerge as one of the leaders of the borlado faction,
refused to cooperate in a sale of a piece of real estate belonging to the
Oratorians for whom he served as administrator, saying that the
bishop had forbidden cooperation. Since his unwillingness to participate could be circumvented by the law, which provided for the intervention of government agents, Esperón undoubtedly realized that he
could obey God in this case and that Caesar would still receive his
due.[18]

As the civil war intensified and the Liberal government's need for
cash increased, redemption of the mortgages provided one source for
governmental capital. The Law of Nationalization in 1859 called for
redemption of mortgages on properties acquired under the Lerdo
Law in 1856 and 1857 and stipulated the procedures by which this

was to be accomplished. The government began to sell unredeemed mortgages in order to find the funds it needed. The records on these mortgages were kept separately in *libros de hipotecas* by the Oaxacan notaries but few of these books are available today. Since information was so sparse, it was impossible to make an analysis of the mortgage transactions.[19]

After 1859 the government also found that it must deal in properties that had previously been disposed of but had subsequently been returned to it before they were completely paid for by the purchasers. Some buyers decided they did not want the real estate they had purchased while others failed to meet all the payments and taxes or in other ways lost their holdings. For example, at least 204 properties were returned to the nation under the law of February 5, 1861, a statute that designated who would lose their titles as a result of complying with the Zuloaga laws, decreed in 1858, by the Conservative president. The Zuloaga decrees required purchasers of ecclesiastical properties under the Lerdo Law to return them to the original owners. This measure of the Conservatives was implemented by General Cobos when he was in control of most of the central region of Oaxaca in 1859–60. The 1861 Reform statute stipulated that those who had returned such properties without protesting that they were being forced to do so had willingly given back their purchases to the church and had no claim to restoration of titles. The 204 properties in question in Oaxaca City had been bought by 153 individuals, some of whom were prominent Liberals—Marcos Pérez, Juan María Maldonado, Juan Nepomuceno Almogabar, Félix Romero. Some were hit hard by this measure. Lino Campos lost seven properties in this manner, and Pablo Moreno lost five. There were thirty women in this group, which may indicate that women more than men were particularly vulnerable to Conservative pressures. These devolutions were carried out from August 1862 through April 1863.

At least fourteen buyers lost their acquisitions through failure to make payments. Fifteen purchasers or their heirs lost their right to title for unspecified reasons. Nine purchasers or their heirs renounced their titles. And one purchaser, Ignacio Urda, lost his title because he confessed that he had acted as a front man for the monastery that originally owned the hacienda he bought. Existing records show that 243 properties, almost 17 per cent of the total number disentailed and nationalized in the Central District, were returned to the nation after they were sold the first time. Of the 809 properties sold in the Central District, the 243 pieces of real estate represent roughtly 30 per cent; or stated another way, approximately one-third of the properties that were sold had to be handled a second time by the state and federal officials, largely as a result of the confusion that existed during the Three Years' War when two national governments simultaneously claimed the right to legislate for the nation. In these second sales there was seldom a rise in selling price; to the contrary, the price either remained stable or was lowered as a result of reappraisal.[20]

There was a certain small amount of resale that went on privately by citizens who had bought disentailed real estate and then, for one reason or another, decided not to keep it. A variety of reasons might account for the decision on the part of the buyers to sell their recently acquired properties. Some undoubtedly found that the special property taxes levied to support the war effort or to make repairs to public facilities after the three sieges were too heavy a burden, thus cancelling any advantages the purchasers might have gained by buying the properties. Some probably had difficulties in meeting payments. Several simply decided they did not want or could not use the real estate they had acquired. And perhaps some decided they should sell in order to buy other pieces of disentailed properties. Statistics were not kept on this type of transaction (private resale) because the notaries did not always enter a statment that the property had belonged originally to an agency of the church or the civil government. When such notations were made, however, it is apparent that the second sale price was usually the same as the original sale price. Infrequently the second sale price was lowered in these private negotiations between individuals, probably because of the declining state of repair; never was the price raised for the second sale.

It is often stated that speculation in urban property or rural lands was one of the chief characteristics of the attempt by the Reformers to put real estate into circulation.[21] Although in some cases it is clear that speculation was taking place openly and on a large scale in certain areas, one should be extremely cautious in considering the problem of speculation in real estate in mid-nineteenth-century Mexico, for major problems are involved that, all too frequently, are not taken into account. Basic to the issue is the definition of speculator. As Robert P. Swierenga has pointed out, American historians who have dealt with the subject, particularly in the frontier areas, have not been able to agree on a precise definition.[22] Certain elements are necessary, but the degree to which they are held important determines the direction or "slant" of the study undertaken. For example, someone could be considered a speculator if he bought more than he could use. But the problem then becomes one of determining how much land or property was basic to one's immediate needs and how much could then be considered excessive. Second, intended use of the land or property acquired must be defined. A purchaser might acquire much more land than he himself could use but with the intention of leasing a portion of it to tenants; or he might buy a large amount of land intending to use a part of it himself, lease another portion, and sell a third part if the value should rise. Or he might acquire a large amount, intending to sell when the inevitable price increase occurred. Intent is difficult to determine. At what point does one become a speculator—when he buys more than he needs, when he uses only a portion of what he has purchased, when he holds onto a part of what he has acquired in the hope that he can sell at a substantial profit, or when he actually sells at a profit?

For purposes of this study, land speculation is considered to have taken place when a purchaser bought cheaply and later sold the property he had acquired, or a portion of it, at a substantial profit. In this framework, speculation was not evident in the Central District of Oaxaca or in the state at large, as far as can be determined from available records. Otherwise there would have been frequent traffic in private resales of disentailed real estate with the prices raised for the second transaction. From the notarial records of the period, only one man emerges as a speculator, and he seldom dealt in alienated properties. Rather, he was constantly buying from private individuals small rural tracts, some of which he kept only briefly and then resold at prices somewhat higher than his purchase price. He may have been trying to mask an attempt to acquire a large block of land, although this is not clear because of the vagueness of boundary descriptions set forth in the *libros de protocolos*.[23]

If speculation is defined as buying cheaply in the hope or expectation that property values would rise markedly in a relatively brief period of time so that one's investment would reap high returns, then one must look for an increase in values during the Reform era. Such increases did not take place in Oaxaca in that period. Whether the real estate values increased over a longer range of time would require a detailed study of property value fluctuations during the Porfirian years, and this lay outside the scope of the present study. In a sense, though, speculation did take place, but in another form. This involved the use of national debt bonds as partial payments for purchases, transfer taxes, and mortgage redemptions. These bonds fluctuated in value but were generally worthless, purchaseable at approximately 10 per cent of face value. To the extent that these bonds were used in the property transactions, the charge of speculation does hold true—but this is not what is meant normally when using the term speculation.[24]

As stated previously, a total of 1,436 properties in the Central District were disentailed and nationalized during the Reform. Of this number, 809 pieces, or 56 per cent, were disposed of, that is, placed principally in private hands, by various methods by the end of 1867. If we add to the 809 pieces the 118 properties that passed hands twice by being bought, returned to the government, and sold a second time by the government, there was a total of 927 "actions of disposal," a phrase that is more accurate to use than terming the transactions sales, as will be explained shortly.

For a majority of these disposals, the exact method used cannot be determined, but most were sold either conventially or in auction. The great majority of notarial and newspaper listings either state specifically or imply sale as the method of disposal, but fail to specify whether the sale was in the form of private transaction between buyer and government or a public transaction in a government-sponsored auction. Despite the lack of information specifying type of transaction, an accurate analysis of the methods of disposal between 1856 and 1867 can be made, and is indicated in Table 2.

Some of the above types of transactions need to be explained. An indication of the poverty of the area during the Reform is the fact that the municipal government of Oaxaca City frequently was in arrears in paying the wages and salaries of municipal employees. A convenient device for providing these sums, or part of them, was the deeding of properties owned by the ayuntamiento to employees in partial or full compensation for their unpaid wages. In other words, instead of taking real estate out of mortmain by the usual method of adjudication or sale, the properties were put into private hands by ceding them to employees of the municipal government. For example, the city council owed Mariano Saavedra, a teacher in one of the city schools, back

TABLE 2

METHODS OF DISPOSAL OF DISENTAILED PROPERTIES, 1856–67

491	properties disposed of by unknown methods, probably by sales
232	properties sold in public auction
183	properties sold conventionally, that is, not in auction
13	properties ceded to individuals in lieu of back pay owed by government agencies
5	properties ceded to local government agencies by the national government for direct use in local government operations (excluding physical plants of the suppressed monasteries and nunneries)
1	property ceded to an individual in lieu of a military pension
1	property ceded to an individual to cover damage sustained to property during the siege of 1865
1	property sold privately by the church, probably with the government's permission
927	total transactions or actions of disposal

wages amounting to 1,072.75 pesos. On November 25, 1856, the ayuntamiento ceded a lot to him, valued at 276.50 pesos, as partial payment.[25]

In 1857, the convent of Santa Catarina found itself hard pressed to pay taxes on its property, which still had not been sold. It owed 200.50 pesos in taxes. The canon, Nicolás Vasconcelos, who served as administrator of the convent, sold one of the houses the establishment still possessed in order to have enough money to pay the taxes, undoubtedly having first obtained permission of the government to do so, although this is not stated. The purchaser, Doña Jacinta Manso, paid 600 pesos to the convent. This is the only case of such a nature—a private sale by the church—that is recorded during the period of the Reform.[26]

On January 28, 1862, the national government ceded five properties to the city of Oaxaca to be used for municipal purposes. These were in addition to the ecclesiastical real estate, such as the seminary, the bishop's residence, and most of the suppressed monasteries and closed nunneries, which had been given to the state and municipal governments at an earlier date. Included were four houses, formerly owned by agencies of the church, which were to be converted into primary schools. The fifth transaction involved the former municipal jail, which had been taken over by the national government at the same time that the city was given the former convent of Santa Catarina to use as a jail. Now the old jail was given back to the city to be turned into a municipal theater.[27]

One house was given by the national government to a private citizen to compensate for damages sustained to property during the siege of early 1865. The precedent had been established for this when President Juárez decreed in 1860 that owners of property damaged during the prolonged siege of Veracruz during the War of the Reform would be indemnified with real estate that had been taken over by the nation as a result of nationalization. Señora Simona Alvarez owned a house in Oaxaca City that was damaged in the siege of 1865. The headquarters of the Army of the East ordered the official in charge of nationalized real estate to cede to Señora Alvarez a house that had been owned previously by an agency of the church. The house she was given was valued at 635.25 pesos, but only 332.06 pesos of this amount was to be considered compensation and she was to give the difference back to the government. She did not pay cash, but gave the national government a mortgage at 6 per cent interest.[28]

Surprisingly, only one piece of real estate was given to an individual in lieu of a military pension. On November 17, 1864, just before the fall of Oaxaca to the Interventionist forces, the headquarters of the Army of the East ordered that Señora Dominga Castillo be given a house to cover a pension of 1,799.37 pesos, due her grandson and ward, the son of the late Battalion Commander Leandro Díaz.[29]

A similar case involving a mortgage was recorded. In 1857, Doña Luz Ibarra purchased a house, under provisions of the Lerdo Law, which was owned by the convent of La Soledad. The house was valued at 7,000 pesos and she paid 4,667 pesos for it; she offered nothing down and the convent was to hold a mortgage at 6 per cent interest on the property. The law of 1859 nationalized the unpaid portions of mortgages as well as unsold properties. On June 14, 1864, the mortgage was given to Señora Vicenta Díaz Ordaz Barriguete because her son, an officer in the army, was killed in action, and the transfer of the mortgage was intended to provide a pension for the mother.[30]

It is curious that more transactions of this nature—giving properties or mortgages as part of military pensions—were not in the notary books, just as it is equally enigmatic that, given the extensive damage to private dwellings and business properties in the siege of 1865, more real estate was not ceded to citizens as compensation for damages. These are only two of the many mysteries that arise from a study of property in Oaxaca during the Reform. Perhaps the various state and national agencies of the government during the Porfiriato used nationalized properties and mortgages still undisposed of and unredeemed as payments replacing or supplementing military pensions for veterans and their families.

In addition to the methods used to dispose of the disentailed and nationalized real estate, the question of how quickly the properties were disposed of becomes important, for the rate may conveniently serve as a gauge by which enthusiasm for the Reform program can be measured. Before analyzing the rate of sale, however, another problem must be considered: that of the factors that determined the selling prices of the corporate properties and the basic economic issue of supply and demand. There were several forces at work in Oaxaca, as throughout Mexico, each acting to determine the price of and demand for the disentailed real estate. To begin with, as a consequence of the Lerdo Law, the machinery of disposal—auctions, private sales, reappraisals, revaluations, and more auctions—tended to force downward the asking price of the properties. And when it is added that payments could be stretched out over long periods of time in low installments or mortgage payments, and that after 1859, part of the purchase price could be financed by offering bonds on the national debt, made nearly worthless by the unsettled conditions of the Reform and Intervention, it is seen that the disentailed properties could be acquired easily without assuming heavy financial burdens. In other words, the real estate was placed in the reach of the middle class citizens, the backbone of the Liberal party. The Reformers hoped these citizens would buy, thereby fulfilling the goal of creating a nation of small property owners and as a consequence forging a stronger bond between the party and the middle class.

But there were other, contrary forces at work to discourage people from purchasing the disentailed properties. One was the depressed economic situation of Oaxaca in the years just before the Reform era, a depression the decade of civil war and foreign intervention did not ameliorate. Factors contributing to this state of affairs were the poor roads, the economy of the region (which operated at a subsistence level of agriculture), an unfavorable balance of trade, the decline of cochineal production, and the slow pace of the mining activities in the state. As a result of this long and debilitating depression, there was little capital available in private hands to channel into the purchase of property when the Reform program caused so much real estate to be put on the market, despite the low values placed on the real estate. A second factor that made people disinclined to buy alienated property was the heavy taxes and forced contributions levied on real estate to support the war effort of the Juárez government. Who in his right mind would wish to invest scarce capital in fixed real estate, which might be taken away from him or destroyed by some unforeseen event, or thereby increase one's liability in making financial contributions to the war effort?

The interplay of these positive and negative forces, low cost of acquisition and easy payments versus the insecurity of the times, has a direct bearing on the amount of disentialed property absorbed into private hands and the rate at which this conversion was made. The negative forces in time became dominant. Whatever the reasons for not wishing to invest in real estate, two trends are evident. First, the market became glutted. Only just over half—56 per cent—of the Central District properties put on the market in the years 1856–67 were placed into private hands by the various actions of disposal discussed previously.

The graph in Table 3 shows the number of Central District properties put up for auction during each six-month period from mid-1856 through the end of 1867, in relation to the number of properties bought publicly in auction or privately in conventional sales or disposed of in some other manner. It should be noted that through 1862, more properties were auctioned than were bought, but between January 1863, and December 1865, the trend is reversed, more real estate being bought than was placed in auction. This of course meant that more property was being bought in private sales, where prospective buyers appeared before the officials and made acceptable offers. It should be noted also that for many months the volume of auctions and sales remained low, which suggests that there was little interest in acquiring the real estate.

The fluctuations in the graph can be partially explained. There is, for example, a lull in the market between January 1860, and July 1863. During the first eight months of that three-and-a-half-year period, the Cobos army was in control of the Central District. Undoubtedly it took some time after the August 1860, victory of the Liberals for the gov-

TABLE 3

RATE OF DISPOSAL OF DISENTAILED PROPERTIES
IN THE CENTRAL DISTRICT, 1856–67

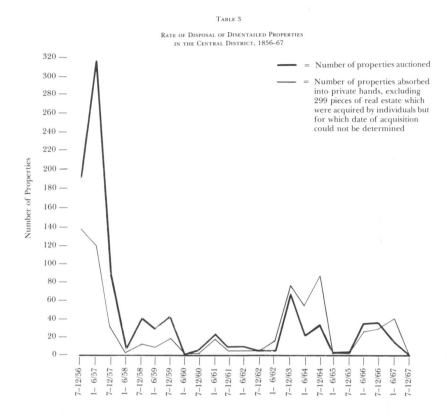

ernment officials to gather together and straighten records and begin the property operations anew. The people also probably had to undergo a period of mental adjustment before they could express once more an interest in real estate. There is a brief upsurge in the first half of 1861, the year of peace that fell between the end of the Three Years' War and the landing of the Interventionist army, and then a shift back into a rather inactive period as the civil war resumed, the experiment leading to monarchy began, and the nation again was thrust into turmoil.

The increased activity of the period from July 1863, through December 1864, is surprising and more difficult to explain. The Interventionists had captured Mexico City in May 1863, and it would seem more natural for this to be reflected by a diminution in activity rather than a relatively strong resurgence in the real estate market. But Oaxaca in this period remained relatively undisturbed by events farther to the north. The borlados were in control of the state during part of this time and perhaps their more moderate views and policies inspired the people and seemed to promise them permanence and stability. The precipitous drop in the market at the end of 1864 coincides with the siege and capture of the city by the Interventionists under the command of Marshal Bazaine. The increased activity of 1866 corresponds to the period of the Intervention in the state, but it must be remembered that Maximilian followed a policy of reviewing property transactions and allowing sales to continue. And the final year, 1867, is marked by the end of the war, a resurgence of the national aspirations of the Mexican people, and a return to comparatively tranquil conditions that held the promise of full security. The graph terminates with 1867, although disentailment proceedings continued sporadically in the period of the Restored Republic and even in the Porfirian years.

But there remained unsold at the end of 1867 almost half of the former church properties. Only conjectures can be made concerning the ultimate disposal of this body of real estate. The national government continued to administer some of the properties, collecting rents from those leased out and receiving mortgage payments on properties nationalized in 1859, bringing pieces of real estate to auction and receiving offers. The state Funds for Public Instruction and Public Beneficence were allowed to continue to use the income from a substantial portion of the real estate as endowments for the purpose of underwriting their operations in the fields of education and eleemosynary work. The cheaper properties were supposed to be given to widows and orphan children of soldiers killed in fighting to preserve the Liberal Republic.[31] But the rate of disposal was greatly reduced. From August 1, 1867, through July 31, 1870, some thirty-five houses in Oaxaca City were sold. In the next biennium, twenty-six houses were sold. In 1873–74, only two houses were disposed of, and in 1874–75, two more houses were placed in private hands. Governor Miguel Castro reported to the citizens of the state in 1872 that the operations were continuing smoothly and predicted that within a few years not a single piece of property nationalized by the Reformers would remain in the hands of the government. This was the goal. Whether it was reached can only be determined by a study of the district during the period following 1876. There are indications that disentailment proceedings were still going on in the 1890s and even in the early 1900s but the primary concern then was with communal lands, not disentailed urban real estate formerly owned by the church.[32]

The second trend that manifested itself during the era of the Reform was the low degree of participation. Only 742 persons, approximately 1.3 per cent of the total population of the district, took advantage of the Reform program to buy disentailed property. At first glance, this figure would seem to represent a negligible showing and might possibly lead one to conclude that the disentailment of real estate failed to accomplish, even to approach, the goal of creating a large body of owners of private property. To refute this conclusion, it would be necessary to take into consideration the amount of property owned by the purchasers before 1856 as well as the characteristics of the population of the district. This information cannot be determined from available data. Certainly not all 45,000 residents of the district could be considered prospective buyers of disentailed real estate. One must consider such factors as the middle-class origins, goals, and support of the Reform program as well as such intangibles as political persuasions, economic status, availability of money, education, health, attitudes toward the church, age, race, and social status. It is readily seen that the number of prospective buyers would shrink drastically when those segments of the population such as the youth, the Indians, the poor, the Conservatives, and others are subtracted from the number of residents. And at the same time, the ratio of actual purchasers to prospective buyers would rise.

The identification of the 742 purchasers is important, as is the determination of their economic status or lack of it and their place in society. Two-hundred thirty-three were residents of the Indian villages of Cuilapan and Jalpan. Of the remaining 509 purchasers, some information was turned up on 229, or roughly 45 per cent. In breaking down this block of buyers into categories, there are some surprising revelations. For example, there were ninety-two women who acquired disentailed property. Some few of them were married to or related to important Liberals in the Central District. This phenomenon is not unique to Oaxaca. Another historian, Walter Scholes, has expressed some curiosity regarding the "large number of *señoras* who bought land."[33]

The next big bloc of purchasers can be identified by their connection with the ayuntamiento of the state capital. There were sixty-five men in this category who had held in prior years or who held during the Reform era seventy-seven different positions on the town council. Forty-eight of these sixty-five men at one time or another served as regidores, eight held the position of president, thirteen served as alcaldes, six held the post of sindic, and two were secretaries. Whereas a few of these men so connected with the ayuntamiento were Liberals of national prominence, by far the great majority played only minor, insignificant roles at the local level of government.

Sixty-eight of the 509 purchasers are identified with politics on a level above that of the town council. Of these, thirty-five served as delegates or alternates to the unicameral state legislatures of the era and nine were national congressmen or senators. Nine were appointed as political chiefs of the districts of the state, and twelve served as state governors during or after the Reform. Three held cabinet posts in the Juárez government, and one, Benito Juárez, the first citizen of Oaxaca, was the president of Mexico.

Professional men and women account for a large group of the purchasers. There were forty-eight lawyers, seven medical doctors, four elementary school teachers, two brokers, seventeen soldiers, sixteen judges, four men who at one time or another had been journalists, two notaries, four pharmacists, and sixteen professors at the Insititute of Sciences and Arts.

There were twenty-eight bureaucrats who bought property. This term is used to describe appointees to state offices and national government agencies with offices in Oaxaca.

There were one Frenchman who purchased property, at least two Spaniards, and two whose names indicate they were either Englishmen or Americans, all residents of the Central District. Jan Bazant, in his recent study of the alienation of ecclesiastical properties throughout central Mexico, found that a considerable number of wealthy foreigners acquired disentailed real estate.[34] In this regard, as in others, the disentailment in Oaxaca does not follow the pattern. It was impossible to determine with any accuracy if any of the purchasers in the Central District were from outside the state, that is, based in other regions or areas of Mexico, but if there were such purchasers they were no doubt few in number. The bulk of the property disentailed in the Central District went to citizens of the state if not of the District itself. This may serve as another indication of the isolation of the state, not only geographic but economic and social, from the rest of the nation.

Of the 509 buyers, only twelve were identifiable as merchants. One would normally think that this class of people would be the one group with money available to invest in real estate and with the desire to acquire property. Yet commerce was carried on at such a slow pace in Oaxaca that the merchants were not of the wealthier segment of society. There were two Conservatives who bought three pieces of disentailed property, and another Conservative who tried to buy but failed. Two of these three men were leaders in their party. And there were four priests, all of them of Liberal persuasion, who purchased real estate. One of the priests, Bernardino Carvajal, a close friend of Juárez, bought twenty pieces of property in Oaxaca City valued at 30,696 pesos, as well as one piece outside the district for 4,100 pesos.[35]

What of the 280 purchasers on whom it was impossible to find any information? It is easier to describe who they were not than to describe who they were. Since their names did not appear in the newspapers during the twelve years of the Reform nor appeared in any of the accounts or archival records available to the researcher, is it not reasonable to assume that they were not prominent citizens? Rather it would appear that 55 per cent of the non-Indian purchasers were the Señores Fulano de Tal, the John Does of the region, a group of men and women who were probably not wealthy or involved in politics, who had perhaps previously rented the properties they now had the opportunity to buy. This impression is buttressed by an examination of the purchasers from another viewpoint, that of the values of the property they acquired. Table 4 gives a breakdown of this information.

In other words, only 64 persons out of a total of 742 bought property worth more than 5,000 pesos. The value of the acquisitions of 47 individuals could not be determined. The remainder, or 631 men and women, approximately 85 per cent of the total number of buyers, bought properties valued at less than 5,000 pesos, and 379 of these, including the citizens of the Indian towns, made acquisitions worth less than 500 pesos apiece.[36]

It is seen, then, that the great majority of those who bought invested very little money in acquiring their properties. Although only a fraction of the total population became involved in acquiring the disentailed real estate, indications are that there was a wide social distribution among the purchasers. In the foregoing analysis of the 742 purchasers, roughly one-third (233) were Indians; another third (229) were preponderantly of the middle class—the lawyers, doctors,

TABLE 4

VALUE OF PROPERTIES ACQUIRED IN THE CENTRAL DISTRICT, 1856–67

Number of Purchasers	Value of Property Acquired
1	More than 100,000 pesos
1	50,001–100,000 pesos
4	25,001–50,000 pesos
4	20,001–25,000 pesos
6	15,001–20,000 pesos
13	10,001–15,000 pesos
35	5,001–10,000 pesos
252	500–5,000 pesos
379	Less than 500 pesos

merchants, schoolteachers and professors, soldiers, bureaucrats, members of the town council; and the final third, the 280 unknowns, probably ranged somewhere in between, from the middle class to the lower class.

The developments in the Central District do not support the general theories that the disentailed property got chiefly into the hands of those wealthy few who already possessed valuable real estate.[37] Naturally, some of the rich did manage to increase their wealth by buying alienated property but this is far from being the whole story. There were undoubtedly men and women in the Central District who became property owners for the first time as a result of the process of disentailment.

DISENTAILMENT DURING THE INTERVENTION

When the French army inherited the Intervention and attempted to consolidate its support, it had to take into consideration the Conservative attitude toward the Reform program if the proposed empire was to succeed. That it failed to do so provides one of the keys to the lack of success in the experiment in monarchy. The Interventionists were in a difficult position. Their principal Mexican support came from the Conservative camp, which was, of course, opposed to the whole Reform program. This Conservative opposition had been most cogently expressed in a group of laws, issued during the presidency of

Félix Zuloaga in 1858, which had the effect of nullifying the Reform statutes and forcing the buyers of disentailed properties to return their purchases to the ecclesiastical organizations that owned them prior to June 1856. The French imperial policy in Mexico attempted the impossible task of trying to harmonize Conservative and Liberal interests, and thus was forced into a middle-of-the-road position in regard to the property question. The policy adopted by Maximilian in this matter evolved over a period of several months but was based solidly on positions assumed by the French commanders acting on instructions from Louis Napoleon before the emperor's arrival, instructions that in turn embodied the desire to create harmonious relations among the warring factions in Mexico so that the prospects for the establishment of the empire would be propitious.

The French attitude was expressed first in 1862 in a letter from Napoleon III to his commanding general in Mexico. General Elie Frédéric Forey received instruction to "show great deference to religion but at the same time reassure those who had acquired nationalized property." A year later, the same instructions were repeated to General Bazaine when he took command of the imperial armies: "Do not become reactionary; do not retract the sale of clerical property . . . ."[38]

In the year intervening between this change of command, Forey had followed a policy of recognizing the legal acquistion of property under the Liberals' statutes of 1856 and 1859. Only fraudulent sales were to be cancelled and the property returned. But this policy was not made official until the early summer of 1863, just before the change of command. The principal delaying factor was the military campaign to move from the coast, attack and capture Puebla, and enter Mexico City, developments that began in the early summer of 1862 and took a full year to materialize. Once these military objectives had been reached—and this was not apparent until May 1863, when Puebla fell—Forey began to turn his attention to consolidating his gains, eliciting wide support from Mexicans of all political persuasions, and carrying out the program regarding property that Napoleon had outlined for him a year earlier. Puebla served as the testing ground for the policies pertaining to the ticklish property question, just as it had served as the testing ground for the Reformers' attempt at disentailment during Comonfort's presidency in 1856.

In Puebla a functionary of the Intervention named Budin, who had been appointed the receiver general of income, came to the conclusion that the municipal government of the city had suffered a drastic reduction of income as a result of having to divest itself of its real estate holdings under the Reform statutes. Income from the real estate had been used to meet "expenses of public utility of the first necessity," expenses the civil corporation could no longer meet. Budin stressed—and perhaps this was the chief factor motivating his proposal—that the property had been sold to persons who now refused to support the Intervention. This situation led the receiver general to suggest to Forey that a review of all sales under the Reform laws should be undertaken. In fact, Budin reported to the general that he had issued a decree in Puebla that brought all the transactions of disentailed property under review. If it were determined that the purchase price had been extraordinarily low in relation to the value of the property, the buyer would have a choice of paying a just price or of returning the property and receiving a refund.[39]

The French commander eagerly grasped this solution as a means of implementing Napoleon III's instructions. Immediately upon receipt of Budin's letter, Forey issued a decree that established a committee of five in the city of Puebla, which was to serve as a review board to determine fair valuations. Budin was placed in charge. A month later, following the seizure of Mexico City by the Interventionist army, and after a national provisional governing council had been designated, steps were taken by the interim government to apply the Puebla formula to all the areas under its control.[40]

The basis for imperial policy, review of all transactions under the Reform laws and recognition of those sales not found to be fraudulent, had therefore been established by the time Maximilian arrived in June 1864. Eight months after his arrival, the emperor issued the definitive decree of his reign regarding the nationalized property.[41] To the anger of the church hierarchy, he recognized in principle the right of the government to take over such properties. But he also incorporated into his measure the procedure of review adopted first in Puebla by Budin and Forey. This review of previous sales was to be pursued systematically by an office called the Adminstration of Nationalized Properties, established in Mexico City, of which Juan Suárez Navarro was appointed director. By March 20, 1865, the office was ready to begin operations.

None of the measures of Forey or the governing junta had had any effect in Oaxaca since that area still remained under the Juárez government. But the imperial decree issued in February 1865, coincided with the fall of the state capital to the Interventionist forces and was therefore put into effect in the Central District. It is difficult to determine how these policies were implemented because the records of the imperial administration there are either lost or in private hands. Apparently a local committee of five members was appointed to conduct the review of the transactions that had taken place since the promulgation of the disentailment law of 1856. Juan Pablo Franco and Manuel María de Fagoaga, the political and municipal prefects respectively, probably headed the committee, if the pattern of Puebla and Mexico City was adopted in Oaxaca. Luis María Carbó, who had taken an active part in the disentailment and nationalization procedures of the Liberals, but who now had joined the imperialists, served as the local official of the Administration of Nationalized Properties. Presumably the revisory committee carried out the policies under the auspices of the national office directed by Suárez Navarro. It would be of great historical value to have the records of the local committee and the national office available to the researcher. Since they are not, one must use the sparse documents available to piece together the story and surmise what the process entailed.

The imperial gazette, the *Diario del Imperio,* published in Mexico City, began to announce the auctions of nationalized properties in late October 1865, indicating that by that date the sales had been reviewed by the various local committees. The first time real estate in the Central District of Oaxaca was announced for sale in the national newspaper was on November 29. And the notices continued sporadically until August 13, 1866, at which time Porfirio Díaz was beginning to tighten the circle around Oaxaca City. In that period of eight months, the auctions of a total of sixty-eight properties were announced. The great majority were listed as houses, but there were a few scattered miscellaneous pieces—rooms, lots, and so forth. Of these properties brought under review and auctioned, thirty were sold. Records of the transactions no longer exist in the public archives.

Information available in scattered documents suggests that some few of the purchasers of nationalized properties reviewed by the national office or the local committee were confirmed in their titles. One can infer, then, that the committees did make an attempt to recognize as valid those transactions that had not violated the Reform laws in some way or another.

RURAL PROPERTIES

For the alienation of real estate within the Central District, including the capital city, the notarial records serve as the major source of information, supplemented by announcements of sales and other details of the disentailment process taken from the newspapers published in Oaxaca City. For alienation outside the Central District, notarial records are generally no longer preserved or are otherwise unavailable. Therefore, greater reliance had to be placed upon the reports that appeared in the newspapers. Such reports are not complete and provide few details, usually nothing more than buyer or adjudicator, former owner, location, type of property, value, and date of acquisition by the purchasers. Throughout the following discussion, the figures given must be interpreted as minimum. Nevertheless, while the record is incomplete the information seems sufficient to give some insight into the processes, problems, trends, and results.

The church possessed few properties outside the boundaries of the Central District.[42] Notices appeared mentioning the disentailment of only forty-two pieces of property held by the various ecclesiastical institutions. These forty-two pieces consisted of ten haciendas, eleven houses, one sugar mill, three grain mills, four ranches, two metal foundries, and eleven small plots of land designated in various ways as *sitio, solar, finca,* and *terreno.* They were scattered throughout the state in the following districts:

Teposcolula	13	properties
Tlacolula	8	"
Zimatlán	7	"
Ocotlán	4	"
Ixtlán	4	"
Villa-Alta	1	property
Jamiltepec	1	"
Tlaxiaco	1	"
Precise location unknown	3	properties

Although there may have been more ecclesiastical properties outside the Central District, notices of which were not found, it is probably safe to assume that there were not many more than the number indicated above. The newspapers of the era were prone to publicize consistently the disentailment of church properties and it is doubtful that many would have been alienated without maximum publicity. The paucity of ecclesiastical real estate is noteworthy and becomes even more pronounced when one considers the activities of the religious orders, especially the Dominicans, in the region during the colonial era. No religious order other than the Dominicans had established monasteries or convents in the state outside the Central District, but the Dominicans had built fourteen such monasteries in their remarkable history of evangelization in that southern area. Six of these, however, had been virtually abandoned since the time of independence.[43] This suggests the decline of the church in Oaxaca and the loss of wealth that had taken place in the years before the Reform.

Of major interest are the ten haciendas owned by ecclesiastical institutions. Table 5 gives the pertinent information. For three, there is no record of sale. Of the remaining seven, one (Dolores, in Teposcolula) was apparently sold in two tracts, one by auction and one by unknown method. The tract sold in auction for 17,000 pesos included a grist mill and was bought by four residents of the village of Chindúa. The unnamed hacienda in Teposcolula district purchased by Mariano Zavala for 83,333.33 pesos was the second most expensive piece of real estate disentailed in the entire state, but no record of it was found in state archival sources. The information available was derived from the Lerdo de Tejada report of early 1857, mentioned earlier, which is so full of errors that one should use it with the greatest hesitancy and caution. It may be that this particular listing in the report is in error. The other Teposcolula hacienda, purchased for 16,829 pesos, involves one of the very few cases in the state where a company purchased property. Bazant has found that in central Mexico corporations were formed with considerable frequency to buy disentailed real estate, but this did not happen in Oaxaca on any noteworthy scale.[44] That it was specifically stated that the Hacienda of Tocuela (designated as Tornel in the 1857 Lerdo report) was bought without the cattle may mean that the hacienda was purposely stripped of its livestock, implements, and seed by the ecclesiastical overseers. Toro, who purchased San Antonio Hacienda in Tlacolula District, found after the sale that his hacienda had also been stripped and he threatened to reduce his payments by the value of the cattle that had been carried off. Of the seven haciendas for which there was notice of sale, the method of disposal was unknown for two and a part of the one sold in two tracts. The other four plus the other tract of Dolores were sold by auction. One of these, Compañía, bought by Parada, was auctioned first on October 22, 1856, at which time there was no sale. Then it was revalued to 68,256.82 pesos, which was probably lower than the original valuation—although this is not specifically stated in the notices—and bought in a second auction a month later in which Parada was the only bidder. Only one purchaser, Toro, has been identified, and he was a bureaucrat, a local official of the Ministry of the Treasury, and a supporter of the Liberal party.

Of the thirty-two ecclesiastical properties other than the ten haciendas, no notice of sale exists for five, at least four of which were put up for auction, some more than once and two as late as January and February 1861. Another five pieces of real estate sold in auction, all in October 1856. Three pieces were adjudicated to tenants in August, September, and November 1856. One of these three, a plot of land, was valued at only 12 pesos. The remaining nineteen pieces were sold but the method of sale, whether adjudication, auction, or conventional, is not revealed in the records.

It is possible to establish an approximate value for these forty-two pieces of real estate by using either the selling price or the official valuation, one or the other of which is given for all but three haciendas. The haciendas were worth 229,878.46 pesos, the other thirty-two pieces of varying types—mills, plots of land, houses, and so on—were worth 60,852.91 pesos, for a total of 290,731.37 pesos.

Seemingly the most perplexing problem facing the Reformers in regard to the redistribution of property was the effect of the Lerdo Law on the lands owned by Indian communities. These lands fell under the category of real estate belonging to civil corporations. It must be emphasized that the Reformers were no more concerned with the Indians than had been any political groups prior to the mid-nineteenth century. The Reform was a middle-class, mestizo movement, led by men from the bourgeoisie who thought in terms of their own self-interests, and these interests gave little consideration to the political, economic, or social welfare or needs of the Indian. Even the commander-in-chief of the Reformers, Benito Juárez, the full-blooded Zapotec, once he had reached the heights of national power, forgot his Indianness and assumed a bourgeois outlook. While he had been a struggling lawyer in Oaxaca, even as state governor, he had concerned himself with the welfare of the Indian, but once he became president and was preoccupied with the greater issues of the preservation of the Liberal Republic and national sovereignty, his concern with the Indian problem vanished. Indeed, it is improper to speak of "the Indian problem" during the Reform, for the Indians took little part in developments and were for the most part passive. Not until

Table 5*
Haciendas Outside the Central District Sold in 1856

Location and Hacienda	Owners	Purchasers	Date of Purchase	Official Valuation (pesos)	Selling Price (pesos)
Teposcolula District: Dolores	Dominicans of Yanhuitlán	Juan M. García	late 1856	?	11,002.00
"	"	4 residents of Chindúa	10/20/56	?	17,000.00
Unnamed	"	Secundino Pérez and Company	late 1856	?	16,829.00
Unnamed	"	Mariano Zavala	late 1856	?	83,333.33
Ixtlán District: Cinco Señores	Hospicio de Oaxaca	No record of sale	—	?	—
San José	"	No record of sale	—	?	—
Tlacolula District: San Antonio	Dominican Sisters	Manuel Toro	8/4/56	15,806.63	10,000.00
Compañía	Augustinian Recollets	Rafael Ursulino Parada	11/28/56	68,256.82	45,504.54
Zimatlán District: San Juan Bautista	Carmelites	No record of sale	—	?	—
Matagallinas	Dominican Sisters	Severiano Canseco	11/7/56	20,000.00 (approximately)	13,150.68
Ocotlán District: Tocuela	Dominicans of Ocotlán	Santiago Salmón	8/21/56	?	4,500.00 (without cattle)

*Sources of information on the transactions involving these haciendas are: *Dem.*, 1:5:4, Oct. 16, 1856; 1:13:2, Nov. 13, 1856; 1:14:2, Nov. 16, 1856; 1:15:6, Nov. 20, 1856; 1:19:1, Dec. 4, 1856; *El Constituyente, Suplemento de Actas y Decretos Oficiales,* July 31, 1856, 4th page; Aug. 10, 1856, 2nd page; and Sept. 4, 1856, 4th page; *Mem.-LdeT,* pp. 426-428, 432, 434, and 438.

Porfiriato did the plight of the Indian begin to receive attention, and the problem was not recognized as such until the great Revolution of 1910.[45] Nevertheless, the Reformers had to approach the problem of the Indian lands, the only source of livelihood for a great, silent mass of their fellow Mexicans, simply because of the Law of 1856 stated that no civil corporation could own property other than that which was necessary for the operation of the government.

Lands owned by the Indian towns and villages were essentially of four types. There was the so-called *fundo legal*, or the townsite itself. On the edge of the village was the ejido, land belonging to the municipality and used in common by the villagers for water, pasture, fuel, and building material. In other words, the ejido primarily consisted of woodland and pasture and was not otherwise farmed. There were the *propios*, lands belonging to the municipality and used in various ways to defray the expenses of the town or village. These lands could be cultivated in common, with the products used to defray the public expenses of the municipal government. Or the *propios* could be rented to tenants, either citizens of the village or outsiders, the income so derived being used for the same purposes. Many plots of land of this type were loosely designated as *cofradía* ("confraternity") lands, a type that should not be confused with lands held by confraternities canonically established and recognized by the church. Noncanonical confraternity plots could either be leased out or farmed by the Indians of the community and whatever income derived from the usufruct was reserved for the support of the religious festivals held in honor of the town's patron saints. Finally there were the *tierras de repartimiento*, lands belonging to the municipality but divided among families and worked by them on a semipermanent basis with ownership and title resting in the municipality. This term is used interchangeably to mean inclusively the ejidos and *propios*, or exclusively to mean a separate type of holding other than the confraternal, ejidal, or municipal lands. As far as a legal definition of these *terrenos* is concerned, as it applied to Oaxaca the term was used to mean all types of lands, even confraternal, held by the Indian communities. There are a few examples where some portions of *tierras de repartimiento* were used to support the priest of the municipio, and in this regard they could be considered a kind of endowment or benefice provided by the village.[46]

Oaxaca's population was heavily Indian, and one would normally assume that there would be an abundance of communal lands within the state. But this is not necessarily the case. Recent studies of central Oaxaca in the colonial period have emphasized that much of the land was held privately by Indian landlords. This situation derived from the peaceful nature of the Spanish conquest of the region. The Indian nobility cooperated with the conquistadors, who allowed the caciques to retain much of their land. The Indian nobles-landlords quickly adapted themselves to the Spanish system, learning the language and the law, passing their lands on through succeeding generations of their families, and dividing them among heirs according to Spanish law. In the late colonial era these Indian families lost some of their lands through sale, encroachment and occupation by their Indian subjects, or debts and foreclosures, but the loss was not necessarily to the whites or to Indian communities but in many cases to other individual Indians. The implication of this process is that by the nineteenth century there was a substantial body of private Indian landowners in central Oaxaca who were tenacious and aware of the legal intricacies of land ownership. William Taylor, in his *Landlord and Peasant in Colonial Oaxaca,* concludes that Helen Phipps was correct in her study written in the 1920s, to the effect that in the colonial period there was a "gradual acceptance of private ownership by individual natives." This has largely been ignored by most writers, who portray the Indians as constantly preyed upon by greedy Spanish or creole landowners or placed in a perpetual state of tutelage by the Spanish colonial government and having access only to their communal lands. Brian Hamnett in his studies of cochineal and agricultural production reaches generally the same conclusions as Taylor. He describes the Indians as independent, resistant to white encroachment, able and ready to protect their rights, and practiced in the defense of their land titles.[47]

What emerges, then, is a picture of mixed landownership among Indians: communal properties and private holdings, with the Indians aware of their rights, rather fiercely independent of pressures exerted by creole and Spanish politicians, businessmen, and landowners, and successful in defending their holdings. But Taylor and Hamnett were almost exclusively concerned with the Valley of Oaxaca, that fertile area that had at its center the Central District and the capital city. In the more remote parts of the state it may be that the mixed pattern of landownership prevailed but with perhaps the scale tipped toward communal holdings. Even in the more remote areas, however, it would seem that the Indians were equally resistant to alien pressures whether they came from churchmen, politicians, or land-owners.

In the Central District there was little communal land to be dis-entailed. Of what there was, the *cofradía* plots were most readily dis-posed of. Although in time there proved to be some resistance on the part of Indians in the central area of the state to alienation of their lands, such resistance was much less common here than in other areas of Oaxaca. This may be explained by the fact that in the territory near the capital, racial mixture was more advanced than in the more re-mote regions, and that the Indian element had become more inte-grated into the political affairs and economic life of the state and was therefore more aware of and willing to accept the Reform program and its ideals and goals. The notary records contain several cases in which Indian villages in the Central District eagerly sold the con-fraternity lands to outsiders or divided the lands up among them-selves, each recipient paying the treasury of the municipality a small sum in return for the small parcel he thus obtained. For example, in early October 1856, the village of San Bartolomé Coyotepec resolved to sell four tracts to *cofradía* lands to four outsiders for the total sum of 1,000 pesos. A communal meeting was held on October 2 at which time the prospective buyers proposed their transfer. The purchasers pointed out at the meeting that the tracts in question were not strictly *cofradía* lands because they had never been formally established as such according to canon law. Therefore, the community had the right to sell them, since the tracts were communal lands that the municipal-ity had always administered, traditionally investing the rent paid by those who worked them in offsetting the expenses of the village festi-vals. After hearing the prospective buyers, the citizens resolved to sell the lands in question. The four purchasers promised to let the in-habitants of the village continue pasturing their cattle on the upland portion and taking charcoal from the woodland. Five days later, four officials from San Bartolomé traveled to Oaxaca City and asked that a notary register the sale.[48]

On October 30, 1856, the entire village council of San Bar-tolomé—the alcalde, seven commissioners, and the sindic—went into the city to register the sale of another *cofradía* tract to two men who paid 180 pesos for the land. The village leaders stated that they pos-sessed no paper showing title but they assured the notary that the village "had always been in the tranquil and peaceful possession [of the tract] . . ." and, furthermore, as an extra precaution, this time the village had received permission from the district political chief to alienate the land.[49]

It is clear, then, that some of the villages of the Central District willingly and quickly complied with the Lerdo Law in regard to municipal and confraternal lands.[50] It is frequently stated that Indian communities were forced by the Reform laws to give up their communal and municipal lands and the citizens of these communities were left destitute as a result. In the Central District this is not true. Nor is it true in a wide stretch of territory surrounding the state capital, but it is a valid statement for the hundreds of villages more remote from the center of Liberal control. In the Central District, there was only one complaint issued from a community that it had been defrauded of its lands, and this complaint was leveled more at the buyers whom the Indians charged with practicing deceit in convincing the village authorities to sell at a low price rather than at the spirit or purpose of the Lerdo Law.[51] Most of the remaining Central Valley villages possessing land apparently willingly and freely decided to comply with the law by selling their real estate. The representatives of the communities would come into Oaxaca City and the delegation of leaders would appear before the authorities to state that in a village meeting a decision had been reached to sell the lands as required by the law. In the notarial transfers the records indicate that sometimes the lands were bought by individual citizens of the village, sometimes by outsiders. Many of the Indian lands were thereby converted into private properties, bought in small parcels, perhaps too small to provide sustenance to the new owners.

Reports sent to Oaxaca City from the more distant areas by district political chiefs in the autumn of 1856 indicate an initial suspicion on the part of the Indians in their reception of the Lerdo Law. But the administrators, perhaps too enthusiastic in their desire to paint a glowing picture in the districts of a zealous and loyal population attuned to Liberal principles and programs—which, of course, would reflect on the thorough job being done by the district chiefs—go on to point out that once the law had been explained to the Indians, the suspicions disappeared and many were ready, indeed anxious, to divide the lands among themselves through purchase.[52] These reports do not present an accurate analysis of the process of disentailment in corners of the state far removed from the center. Here was truly Indian Mexico, and the Indians, uneducated, traditionalists if not Conservatives, desirous of perpetuating their ancient ways and patterns of life, and largely ignorant of the political questions raging throughout the Republic, having contact with the Liberal programs only occasionally through infrequent visits by the district political chiefs constantly subverted the letter of the law, in two contrary ways: either by being overzealous in seeking to divide their lands in severalty, hoping thereby to avoid alienation; or by obstructing the division. Records are generally lacking in these matters, but one may approach the problem indirectly through the decrees and circulars issued to deal with the situation.

In the days immediately following the promulgation of the Lerdo Law, Governor Juárez directed two inquiries to President Comonfort, on July 30 and August 18, 1856, both asking if the residents of Indian villages could divide among themselves and purchase their communal lands instead of allowing the lands to be bought by tenants. The latter inquiry was sent in behalf of the residents of Pinotepa in the northeastern portion of the state, across the sierra from the capital. In both cases, Miguel Lerdo de Tejada, the treasury minister and author of the law, replied that to allow this to take place would destroy the intent of the statute. Preference had to be given to tenants; only if they renounced their right to adjudicate would it be acceptable for the Indians to purchase the lands in severalty. This policy was further clarified on December 20, 1856, in a letter from the treasury minister to the minister of development.[53]

Three years elapsed and the question was raised again, this time the inquiry coming from Tehuantepec near the eastern boundary of the state. The date indicates that probably many Indian villages had not made attempts to implement the law of 1856 and now were feeling new pressures to comply as a result of the promulgation of the Law of Nationalization of 1859. In response to the inquiry, the treasury minister wrote that President Juárez had agreed that *cofradía* and communally owned lands and cattle should be divided among the Indians and reduced to private property.[54] Although this at first seems to be a reverse of the earlier policy forbidding division in severalty, it was not, in effect, a radical change, for in the three years that had passed, probably such lands leased out had been acquired by those tenants who wished to acquire them and the government's decision now pertained to those lands still in the hands of the communities. Indeed, the circular of December 20, 1856, is cited to show that policy had not changed. On September 7, 1859, Melchor Ocampo, interior minister, sent all state governors a circular calling upon them to aid the treasury agents in any way possible in the matter of transferring communal lands into private hands.[55]

To carry out the intent of these resolutions, the governor of Oaxaca, Miguel Castro, issued a decree on October 20, which detailed the methods to be used in seeing to it that the Indian lands and cattle were divided and transferred from communal ownership to private holdings.[56] The heads of the villages were given fifteen days to form censuses of the citizens of the communities and notices of the amount of cattle and lands held. Then the political chiefs were to issue titles to each person who received land or cattle, and the fee was to be minimal for these titles. If anyone disagreed with the divisions or had any complaints concerning the procedures to be followed, he was to file his complaint within fifteen days following the division to the district chief, who would rely on impartial residents for advice and then render his judgment, beyond which there was no appeal.

Castro's decree came to embody the basic state policy regarding Indian properties, and thereafter the officials of Oaxaca were concerned with implementing it. But compliance apparently proved to be very slow, if the amount of supplementary legislation can be taken as an indication. One of the primary reasons for delay was undoubtedly the invasion of the state late in 1859 by the Cobos army, which was not finally expelled until August of the following year. On February 13, 1861, José Esperón, borlado secretary to Governor Ramón Cajiga, issued a circular to all district chiefs in which he pointed out that Castro's 1859 decree still had not been executed.[57] Now that peace and order had been restored, he stated, it was necessary to carry out the provisions of the decree and he called on each district chief to act accordingly. The fifteen-day period originally set by Castro was extended to begin on the day of receipt of the present circular in each district.

Exactly three months later, on May 13, 1861, Esperón was compelled to issue a second circular on the same subject.[58] He wrote to the district chiefs at length about what had been taking place in the state in regard to Indian lands. There had been repeated complaints that several pueblos in different districts had seized lands that had never belonged to them, taking the properties from private citizens. If this practice were allowed to continue, society would be disrupted and the present administration would be discredited.

The reasons for such seizures were of diverse origins. Some Indian towns, acting in good faith, had misinterpreted the decrees to mean that the governor was ordering the division of private estates as well as communal and confraternity lands. Other towns believed that, since they had suffered severely during Cobos's invasion, they ought to be compensated, and compensation to them meant the right to seize whatever private property they coveted. Thus some towns had raised a loud cry against private ownership of land and in some cases had seized estates. Some towns had listened to "false prophets," who told them that if they seized private lands they would have the protection of the state government. When the government failed to sanction or support "such bastard pretensions," as Esperón phrased it, the towns so misled rose up in rebellion.

Then Esperón forcefully reiterated the government's position: the pueblos cannot possess lands in common. The district chiefs were ordered to inform each town of this policy and to make it clear, on the one hand, that communal lands had to be divided in severalty and that towns could not seize private property, on the other hand. Apparently some of the private estates that had been seized were lands formerly held in common by the Indians, which were sold to lessees and tenants under the provisions of the Lerdo Law. Esperón promised to use armed force if necessary to halt these seizures and to punish malefactors.

The emphasis in this circular was placed on stopping illegal seizures, which suggests that they must have been taking place on a wide scale. Indirectly, Esperón was also insisting on the division of communal lands still intact. Apparently the illegal seizures were stopped or at least significantly diminished, but division in severalty still lagged, for on January 27, 1862, Esperón sent out still another communication urging the district chiefs to see to it that lands were divided.[59] As an extra measure, the secretary stated that if the lands remained undivided after two months following receipt of his letter, private citizens could then denounce and acquire the properties as if the Lerdo Law were still in operation. This threat was sufficient to bring about implementation in many areas.

An indication of the slowness of disentailment, which in turn must show the unwillingness of municipios to comply with the laws, can be derived from reports of district political chiefs that appeared in the Oaxaca City newspaper in 1861–62. For example, the political chief of Teposcolula District reported in March 1861, that the town of Teposcolula still owned a store from which it derived rent. Tejupan and Chilapa still received income from the leasing of pastures and common lands. In the same month, the district chief from Tehuantepec reported that disentailment in his area had been suspended since 1857. The chief from Yanhuitlán reported that adjudications were at a standstill. The official from Villa Alta wrote that a sugar mill was still to be disentailed. Other district chiefs were reporting only sporadic activity or that there was no civil property to be alienated in their jurisdictions.[60]

The problem of the Indian lands continued to perplex the Oaxacan Reformers. After Porfirio Díaz took over political and military control of the state as commander of the Army of the East in 1863, one of his first acts was to call on the district chiefs to continue dividing communal lands.[61] The problem persisted after 1876 and well into the presidency of Porfirio Díaz. Communal lands were still being divided and placed into private hands in the closing years of the century. Governor Miguel Bolaños Cacho, in the report he submitted to the state legislature in 1902, summarized disentailment operations for the past six years as follows:[62]

Year	Hectares Disentailed	Value (pesos)
1897	34,932	34,101.28
1898	79,758	62,349.08
1899	51,114	47,619.50
1900	59,140	55,423.11
1901	17,431	12,637.36
1902	4,970	4,388.70

Perhaps one would conclude that the dramatic decline in 1901–1902 suggests that at last the program of disentailment was approaching successful termination, but this might be a false assumption.[63]

Thus the efforts of the Liberals to convert communal lands into private holdings met with resistance in some areas, partial success in others, and complete success in still others, the degree of accomplishment being in direct ratio to the proximity of the Indian communities to the seats of Liberal control. The Central District presented few problems to the Reformers: there the Indian pueblos observed the provisions of the law with little delay. This can probably be best explained by the fact that the Central District was compact in size and had an adequate network of roads connecting the Indian towns with the district seat and state capital, the Liberal stronghold, thereby making it an easy matter for the politicians to insure compliance with the laws. Another explanation is that few of the twenty-eight Indian villages in the district still held communal lands by the middle years of the nineteenth century, for records reveal that lands belonging to only nine villages, including the suburb of the Marquesado, were sold into private hands. It is hardly conceivable that the Liberals would have allowed any nearby villages to retain lands of the types the laws required to be placed in the hands of individual citizens, for this would be a blot on the record of the uncompromising Reformers in one of the very fortresses of the Reform movement.

Whatever the problems involved, records reveal that a total of 604 pieces of real estate owned by civil corporations, that is, municipalities, were disentailed in the state, excluding the Central District, during the Reform to 1867. As stated previously, because of the nature of surviving records, this must be understood as only a minimum figure. The bulk of this property consisted of lands, described variously as *tierras, terrenos, solares, sitios, fincas,* and *parajes.* An analysis of types gives the following breakdown:

     22 grist mills
      1 orchard
     40 ranches
      8 sugar mills (*ingenios* or *trapiches*)
      1 herd of cattle
      1 corral
      1 lake
     23 houses
     10 stores
   497 plots of land
   604 total pieces of property

The location of these 604 properties shows that the major disentailment operations took place in those districts adjacent to or within easy reach of the Central District, especially in the areas lying in the Valley of Oaxaca, which fact supports the idea that in these areas the Indian populations were more receptive to the Liberal program. Table 6 gives an analysis of disentailment by districts. There were no recorded actions of disentailment in the peripheral districts of Juchitán, which borders on Chiapas; Silacayoapan, which borders on Guerrero and Puebla states; and Tuxtepec, bordering on Veracruz; or the district of Nochixtlán.

Although no records of sale or adjudication could be found on

TABLE 6

DISENTAILMENT OF CIVIL PROPERTIES OUTSIDE THE CENTRAL DISTRICT

District	Number of Properties Disentailed from Civil Corporations
Zimatlán	180
Ocotlán	94
Teposcolula	83
Jamiltepec	61
Miahuatlán	30
Villa Alta	28
Ixtlán	27
Etla	22
Ejutla	19
Tlaxiaco	15
Yautepec	14
Teotitlán	10
Tlacolula	10
Unknown Location	3
Huajuapan	2
Choapan	1
Tehuantepec	1
Pochutla	1
Cuicatlán	1
Coixtlahuaca	1
Juquila	1
TOTAL	604

104 pieces, it seems likely they were eventually taken over by individuals. Of the remaining 500 pieces for which notice of sale was found, the time period and method by which they were disposed of is indicated in Table 7.

It can be seen that as far as the civil properties were concerned, the impact of the Lerdo Law was felt immediately after its promulgation, and that after December 1856, there was little activity. This contrasts markedly with the ecclesiastical and civil properties alienated in the Central District, where disentailment operations continued apace through 1866–67. As has already been pointed out, however, these 500 pieces of real estate were located primarily in territories where the Liberals' influence was strongest and that in other areas there was delay and resistance to the Reform measures, causing pro-

TABLE 7

DATE AND METHOD OF DISPOSAL OF CIVIL PROPERTIES
OUTSIDE THE CENTRAL DISTRICT

Method:	Auction	Adjudication	Conventional	Unknown	Month
	15	3			Aug., 1856
	12	38			Sept., 1856
	60	76	9	166*	Oct., 1856
	11	99			Nov., 1856
	1				Dec., 1856
		2			Feb., 1861
				1	Apr., 1861
	1	1			Nov., 1862
	1				Jan., 1863
		1			Feb., 1863
	1			1	Mar., 1863
		1			Apr., 1863

*These 166 properties were placed into private hands in late 1856, that is, sometime from August through December, but the exact date is not known, nor whether they were adjudicated to tenants, sold conventionally, or sold in auction.

longation of disentailment, which resumed after the expulsion of the French and continued into the early 1900s.

Another characteristic of the disentailment process outside the Central District is the small amounts individuals invested in properties, or, stated another way, the low value of the properties alienated, which consisted primarily of small plots of land. Taking the civil and ecclesiastical properties together, there were 535 pieces of real estate that were either adjudicated or sold to private citizens. In the notices from which these statistics were derived, the valuation figure or purchase price was given for all but six of the properties, which provides us with a total of 529 properties that can be analyzed. These properties ranged in value from 75 centavos to over 80,000 pesos. Some individuals joined together to purchase one piece of property, and some few individuals purchased more than one piece, so the figures given in Table 8 do not represent either the number of purchasers or number of properties but rather reflect the number of investments made by individuals or groups.

TABLE 8

VALUE OF INVESTMENTS IN DISENTAILED PROPERTIES OUTSIDE THE
CENTRAL DISTRICT, 1856–67

Number of persons or groups	Money invested (pesos)
2	50,000.00–100,000.00
0	25,000.00–49,999.99
0	20,000.00–24,999.99
1	15,000.00–19,999.99
4	10,000.00–14,999.99
7	5,000.00–9,999.99
48	1,000.00–4,999.99
41	500.00–999.99
136	100.00–499.99
208	Less than 99.99

Many of the less expensive properties, primarily small plots of land costing less than 100 pesos, were sold to groups, some of which were large in number. For example, 108 residents of two municipios in Octolán District bought the lands and cattle of one of the pueblos, and 135 residents of Tlapacoya in Zimatlán District adjudicated lands belonging to their municipio. Although the sale price is unknown in either of the transactions, it seems reasonable to assume that on the average no one in the combined group of 243 citizens would have invested more than 25 pesos. In another example, 72 people divided in severalty and paid for, or took mortgages on, one piece of land valued at 276 pesos, which averaged out to approximately 3.83 pesos per person. Thirty-five individuals divided a plot of land valued at 112 pesos, which averaged out to an investment of 3.20 pesos per person. All in all, out of a total of at least 872 persons who received disentailed ecclesiastical and civil properties, 513 people invested less than 25 pesos each.[64]

It has been impossible to determine who the vast majority of these purchasers were. A few, twenty-two to be exact, who purchased property in the Central district were involved in disentailment outside the district. These included such prominent Liberals as Juan N. Almogabar, Bernardino Caravajal, Miguel Castro, Ignacio Mejía, and Manuel J. Toro, soldiers, bureaucrats, politicans. Several other of these twenty-two could be identified as lawyers or as connected with the Liberal regime in some way, but the overwhelming majority of the 872 purchasers were the anonymous citizens of the Indian communities of the state.

It was in keeping with tradition that the members of the middle class in Oaxaca City who figured prominently in the disentailment in the state capital should express little interest in rural properties. Taylor found that even in the colonial era few of the wealthier members of society in Oaxaca City invested in rural lands, except in the area immediately adjacent to the town, where small plots held by these men and women allowed them to consider themselves "country squires." This does not necessarily contradict the view of Hispanic "gentlemen" that land ownership carried a social value; it merely indicates that in Oaxaca this was not a primary motive for purchase of rural land. Nor do we find the converse true, as Jan Bazant seemed to see in his analysis of the Lerdo de Tejada report of 1857—that rural-based landholders strengthened themselves by increasing their holdings while they also purchased urban properties on a large scale, thus creating bases of operation in both town and country.[65] In other words, the example of Oaxaca would seem to indicate that the Reform did not bring about any major shift of interests—that instead rural-based persons brought property in the countryside, and that city residents generally concentrated their property holdings within the urban setting.

Although disentailment outside the Central District was largely a hesitant and delayed operation, the effects were soon noticeable on the Indian communities. In many cases, the funds and steady income from rents upon which the municipalities depended declined markedly. Governor Juárez, in his report to the state legislature in 1852, four years before the Reform began, included a list of the communities in the state that had at their disposal community funds, showing their annual amounts and sources from which such income was derived. Governor Ramón Cajiga included the same information in his report issued in 1861. A comparison of these two documents reveals some significant differences. The earlier list is much longer, taking six pages and including 285 municipios, whereas Cajiga's summary takes only three pages and includes only 120 municipios. San Bernardo Mixtepec in 1852 had municipal funds of 30 pesos; in 1861, it is not listed. In Yanhuitlán District, Tiltepec's fund for 1852 amounted to 12 pesos; in 1861, 1.72 pesos. In Tlaxiaco District, the municipio of Santiago Yozondúa had an annual fund of 136 pesos in 1852; nine years later this had dwindled to 50 pesos. San Juan Teposcolula in Teposcolula District saw its annual funds decline from 170.00 pesos in 1852 to 74.40 pesos in 1861. These pueblos and others had some if not all their properties disentailed in 1856.[66]

The municipalities lost their incomes and savings in other ways. Sometimes the district political chiefs appropriated municipal funds for their personal use, as happened in 1858 in the towns of Teotitlán del Camino and San Antonio Elozochitlán, both in Teotitlán District; and what was not stolen in this manner was taken by Cobos's army during its operations in the area in the following year.[67]

It is apparent that the process of disentailment in the State of Oaxaca unfolded on different levels with few if any connections among the various levels. In the Central District, it was an urban operation; in the state at large, it was a rural operation. By far the greater value of property and greater number of pieces of real estate centered in Oaxaca City. In the Central District, disentailment primarily involved properties owned previously by various institutions and agencies of the church, while beyond the district's boundaries, plots of land owned by the Indian municipalities constituted the major portion of disentailed properties. Considering the purchasers, those in the Central District were on the whole unidentifiable, but with a significant number from the politically active, well-educated, professional middle class. Outside the district, the adjudicators and buyers were probably overwhelmingly from the lower class. Rural-based persons did not seize the opportunities provided by disentailment and nationalization to acquire properties and only a handful of citizens in Oaxaca City showed interest in rural properties outside the Central District. There were significant delays in enforcing the laws effectively in the state at large, due to resistance on the part of Indians outside the orbit of control of the Liberals, so that rural—or civil—disentailment took many years before any great headway was made. Probably it was never totally accomplished. In the Central District, delay was not so much of a problem but lack of interest or inability to buy the properties because of a general absence of capital caused the Laws of Disentailment and Nationalization to fail of total and effective implementation. Much of the problem resulted from the turbulence and chaotic conditions that existed both at the time the measures were promulgated and afterwards during attempts at implementation. Nevertheless, if one considers the difficulties facing the Reformers and the obstacles they had to overcome, it would appear rather re-markable that in the disentailment of corporate properties their re-cord was as substantial as it was. Although only a small percentage of the populace of the state became involved, certainly the participants represented a wide social spectrum. The middle class in Oaxaca City probably benefited the most and their degree of involvement un-doubtedly strengthened the Liberal party in the state. But outside the Central District in the more remote regions the Liberals probably saw their constituency constrict as the Indians resisted alienation of their lands and undoubtedly blamed the Liberals for the attempt to take away their communal properties. This had the overall effect of limit-ing the Liberal party from becoming anything other than a party of the middle class—the stamp of the bourgeoisie was sealed onto it as a result of the Reform and any intention to widen the party to include the lower class was thus made impossible to bring about. Thus griev-ances would accumulate against the dominant political group over the next several decades and would provide fertile ground on which the Revolution of 1910 would find rich nourishment.

Does the Oaxaca pattern of the alienation of church wealth differ from that prevailing in Central Mexico, the wide belt of area from Jalisco in the west to Veracruz in the east, which has been analyzed by Jan Bazant? It must be emphasized that he dealt exclusively with church real estate, whereas this study considers both ecclesiastical and civil disentailment. To compare his findings with those of the present study requires consideration of only a part of the Oaxacan disentail-ment, that pertaining to the church.

In Central Mexico, Bazant found that buyers of clerical real es-tate were to a large extent from the merchant class, that many foreigners participated, and that speculation took place on a large scale. As has been pointed out, none of this happened in Oaxaca to any noteworthy or appreciable degree. We have seen that, in the first place, merchants had little capital accumulation in Oaxaca which would allow them to invest in clerical or civil urban properties and that traditionally they were uninterested in rural property. This con-dition is due in large measure to the location and economic activity of Oaxaca, which was not closely integrated into the comparatively more commercially, economically progressive center of the nation. In Oa-xaca, after the decline of cochineal production in the late eighteenth century, the region's economy lapsed into a recession that could not encourage substantial mercantile activity. Few foreigners lived in

Oaxaca and few were therefore involved in the alienation of real estate. And, seemingly, foreigners were not attracted to the area to purchase disentailed properties.

Speculation was not a prominent feature of the alienation process in Oaxaca. Perhaps the value of disentailed properties did increase in later years, but without significant economic advancement this is not likely. And certainly Oaxaca did not experience any great economic upsurge in the late nineteenth century that would raise dramatically the values of urban or rural properties. Sugar production was encouraged in the last quarter of the century, some coffee production developed, gradually extractive industries revived, and with the construction of the railroads and the telegraph lines the state was less isolated than in the era of the Reform, but still there was little noteworthy increase in economic activity that would raise substantially the values of property. So speculators, if they were present, did not see their hopes fulfilled. Thus the Reform in Oaxaca did not greatly facilitate or encourage industrial capitalism or stimulate economic growth in the southern region during the Díaz years, as Bazant concludes happened in Central Mexico.

As to change within the social system, this probably did come about but the degree cannot be measured with any accuracy. The middle class perhaps was slightly enlarged as a result of ecclesiastical disentailment. Given the fact, however, that so many of the properties went unpurchased or were returned to the state for various reasons, it must be concluded that many citizens were unable to acquire the properties put on the market by the Lerdo Law. Many of the houses were rather inexpensive, probably in large part because they were in varying states of disrepair, and these were acquired by members of the poorer class. Nevertheless, some people became property owners for the first time. What seems to have happened in Oaxaca, then, is that the middle-class urban citizens strengthened their position in society and some lower-class elements moved into the middle class or at least moved into positions from which the step upward could be taken, perhaps not immediately but in the next generation.

Since clerical properties were so heavily concentrated in Oaxaca City and its immediate environs, the disentailment in the area outside the city and its suburbs hardly provides a basis for making definitive statements. The haciendas were acquired by apparently rather wealthy men, but there were so few haciendas, and these so small in acreage, that it seems irrelevant to speak of the concentration of wealth in the hands of a few men or the smallness of the middle class that came to possess these glorified farms. Ecclesiastical disentailment in Oaxaca did not hold out the prospect of creating a rural middle class simply because not that much church real estate in the form of rural tracts existed to be placed into private hands. What did offer this prospect for Oaxacans was the disentailment of civil property. It has been seen that this was a prolonged process in the south and that some people did take advantage of the opportunities offered to them to become private landowners. Again, given the poverty of the area, a "rural middle class" could not be created. On the other hand, a substantial group of private landowners, small though the plots they held were, was enlarged, although to what degree cannot be determined.

One area of activity that Bazant fails to consider but that loomed large, at least in Oaxaca, was the aid given to education by the alienation of ecclesiastical wealth through endowment of the educational establishments with mortgages and properties; the gift of buildings, such as the former convents and monasteries, and some houses, which were converted into educational facilities; and the expansion of school libraries by the confiscation of monastic and seminary book collections. This again would serve in a sense to strengthen the middle class, the members of which would be the primary beneficiaries. But it would also hold the prospect of bringing to the lower classes some eventual benefit.

The disentailment of real estate did not accomplish all it set out to do. Both the Central Mexican and Oaxacan patterns prove this. And the reasons for falling short of the goals established were, in part, the same in both areas—the chaos brought about by the civil war and the Intervention, which in turn made disentailment haphazard. But it can be argued that while disentailment was not a total success, neither was it a total failure, for significant steps were made in the direction of fulfilling the goals established by the Reformers.

What one must conclude ultimately is that definitive statements cannot be made until more information becomes available and more studies are made of this crucial period in Mexican history. So much of the work of the Reformers depended upon later implementation that consequently the Porfirian years become the true testing ground of the Reform. Did the values of property increase markedly in the last quarter of the nineteenth century, or did they remain stable? To what use did the purchasers of urban properties put their profits, if any were made? At what rate were mortgages reduced? How much alienated property was resold during the later period? Was there a notice-able increase in school population in provincial towns and capitals during the late nineteenth century? In urban centers outside Mexico City was there a continuing consolidation of middle-class strength or any significant movement into the middle sector from the lower class? Such questions as these naturally are in the thoughts of anyone who undertakes a socioeconomic study of the Reform era and con-sequently beckon one to a consideration of provincial Mexico during the years of Porfirian rule.

CHAPTER 7

CONCLUSIONS

THE PRINCIPLES AND GOALS of the Reformers as enunciated in their executive orders and legislative decrees, refined in the editorials of their newspapers, and manifested in their actions are well known: they aimed to remake Mexico into a liberal republic of democratic procedures in which privilege would no longer be a determining factor in the dispensing of justice, in which freedom would be enjoyed by all, in which the economy would be revitalized through the strengthening and broadening of the property-owning class, in which civilian government would replace military anarchy, and in which religion would play no role in the economic, political, or social spheres. But these goals, in their pure state, in their pristine ideological form, could not be fully implemented given conditions already existing when the Reform began and situations arising as a consequence of attempting realization.

In other words, the Liberals' goals were necessarily bent or deflected in the process of passing through the prism of preexisting and developing circumstances. The prism was partially shaped by the historical evolution of the Mexican nation up to the beginning of the Reform era. Mexico was not an integrated nation but rather consisted of several Mexicos—the economically dominant center and the underdeveloped, largely isolated and backward periphery; the widely separated, numerically unequal social groupings with their sharp distinctions defined by race, education, occupation, political philosophy, and living conditions. It would be impossible for the Liberal program to be equally and evenly applied to or implemented in all parts of the Republic. In thinking that this could be done, the Reformers were idealists and not at all pragmatic in the conceptualization of their revolution.

Furthermore, their ideals were not universally shared by all Mexicans, some of whom opposed them vigorously for over a decade. This opposition also served to shape the prism. Given the Three Years' War, followed almost immediately by the Intervention, situations were created that accentuated already existing conditions and made it still more impossible for the Reform program to be put into effect in its pure form, either philosophically or practically. Oaxaca, the Liberal stronghold, serves as a case in point. It suffered three invasions between 1857 and 1866, and two of the invading armies managed to take control of parts of the state for a total period of almost three years. This caused great confusion in the implementation of the Reform program and consequently had the effect of slowing down and in some respects perverting it.

Not only were there these circumstances that diminished the thrust of the Reform in Oaxaca but there was also the factional struggle within the state's Liberal group, evident everywhere in the Republic at all levels of government and society but particularly bitter in the southern state. The moderates were more pragmatic and less idealistic than the purists or radicals. It was the borlado faction that tried to discover some way by which the Reform could be applied without upsetting the social, institutional, political, and economic balance of the neocolonial society upon which it was imposed. The factional disagreements over the rate and method of implementation also served to shape the prism.

Thus the results provided a variety of colors or shadings, or displayed varying degrees of effectiveness. This is the most notable feature of the Reform in Oaxaca, and presumably elsewhere in Mexico. In theory there was the one Reform; in practice, there were multiple Reforms, each of which must be evaluated individually. Historians have generally treated the movement as if it were singular in form and in application and have judged it, mistakenly, by the sole yardstick of the aims of the Reformers. In truth there was no single Reform, as the analysis of the Liberal revolution in Oaxaca clearly indicates, because there was no integrated nation in any sense, whether speaking in terms of geography, politics, society, institutions, the economy, or shared goals. Instead of one Reform implemented evenly and equally effectively, there evolved a multifaceted program activated unevenly and with disparate effects in different communities and at various levels of the social structure.

As far as the alienation, nationalization, and redistribution of property were concerned, there was the urban Reform in Oaxaca City and its immediate environs, and the rural Reform in the state at large, touching the other twenty-odd districts with their hundreds of small towns and Indian villages outside the immediate influence of the Liberal stronghold of the state capital. In Oaxaca City and the Central District, the program primarily affected the real estate or fixed assets of the Roman Catholic Church. Here, in the capital, this reform was largely accomplished or fulfilled, with the result that the church in Oaxaca was greatly weakened, not only in the economic sense but also in the social context. Certainly the political power previously enjoyed by the church was effectively broken. On the other hand, in the rural areas the church was largely unaffected by the property laws because it held little real estate outside the central valley. The church had not been strong in rural Oaxaca for a long time; instead there prevailed among the peasants a residual social influence and religious sentiment, highly tempered by syncretistic practices and customs, and this was never effectively changed by the Liberal program.

The rural areas were subjected to a different Reform, the one directed at the alienation and redistribution of corporate civil properties, the communal lands held by the Indian villages. This reform met with stiff resistance, especially in those areas least accessible to the Liberals in control of the machinery of government in the state capital. The reform of the ownership of civil properties was never fully implemented, even as late as the early years of this century, that is, on the eve of the Revolution of 1910. As William Taylor has already pointed out, this led some Mexicans to contend that there was no need for a revolution since much of the land in Oaxaca was still held in communal fashion, which gave the lie to the myth of despoilment of Indian lands.

Likewise, there was the Reform directed by the borlado faction of the Liberal party within Oaxaca and the Reform carried out by the purist Liberals when they controlled the state government. When the moderates were in power, the Reform program was less intensively applied, whereas the Reform directed by the radicals was always more drastic. This resulted in considerable resentment against such purists as Marcos Pérez, José María Díaz Ordaz, and Porfirio Díaz. The borlado leaders, such men as Ramón Cajiga, Miguel Castro, and José Esperón, seemed to demand less of a commitment to programs of change. Their approach offered a greater degree of peace and less turmoil in the lives of the citizens than did that of the purist leaders, and for this reason the moderates were able to stay in office for considerable stretches of time. The temporizing of the borlados may be seen at every turn, whether it meant lack of interest in supporting the war effort of the Veracruz government of Juárez in the late 1850s, dilatory application of the Reform laws, as in the case of ignoring the order to close the nunneries, or the widespread acceptance of the imperial regime of Maximilian by individual moderates.

Similarly there was the Reform that affected principally the white and mestizo middle class, the politically aware citizens of the central valley, and the Reform that left practically untouched the lives of the great majority of Oaxacans, the peasant folk who lived in the isolated towns and villages of the state. The urban dwellers of the capital city were constantly caught up in the movement and suffered—or prospered—from its consequences. Their property was destroyed in the various sieges; their high taxes and the money demanded from them in forced loans helped the Liberal defenders or the Conservative-Imperialist invaders by supporting the war effort of one side or the other; their businesses suffered at times and thrived at others in direct ratio to the victories or defeats of the side they supported; their markets were disrupted in times of siege and were intensively active when garrisoning armies swelled the population and had to be supplied; their menfolk were the ones most likely to join the armies active in the field; their children were denied an uninterrupted education; their careers in the military or the political forum were forwarded or set back; their fortunes increased or diminished; their hopes were raised or lowered. In other words, it was the men and women of the middle class or group who developed a real stake in the outcome of the Reform program.

On the other hand, the peasants, in the majority Indians, were seldom involved in the Liberal revolution in a consistent fashion. At times they were impressed into work gangs or into the armies of the contending factions. In some areas their communal landholding pattern was broken. But even when discussing the Reform as it affected the peasantry, distinctions must be made. Those rural folk who lived within the reach of the politicians of the state capital were more frequently touched by the efforts of the Reformers than those living farther away. Most of the latter were only occasionally involved, with some important exceptions. The serranos of the northern mountains frequently played an active role as partisans of the Liberals, first supporting the radicals, then switching their allegiance to the moderates, and finally enlisting in the second and last Porfirian revolution. Their role was always crucial in the shaping of events, attested by the sanctuary they gave to the radical administration of Governor Díaz Ordaz in the dark days of the Cobos invasion, their support of the federal army sent to put down La Noria rebellion, and their overthrow of Governor Esperón as an aid to Porfirio Díaz in his triumph of 1876. The country folk living in the western approaches of the state toward Puebla, that is in the Mixteca, were sometimes forced into activity because the invading armies always approached through their territory. More oriented toward the Conservative stronghold of Puebla than the Liberal center of Oaxaca City, the Mixtecs resented the highhanded manner in which they were treated by their defenders and the excessive demands placed on them by the Liberals; they were, contrariwise, more enthusiastic in their support of the Imperialists and the Conservatives. In the Isthmus of Tehuantepec there seems to have been less involvement, or at least it was more sporadic. In that region, what activity there was seemed colored by rivalries between the two largest towns, Juchitán and Tehuantepec, with the former more prone to be pro-Liberal. But in these rural areas, involvement on the whole was only occasional. The majority of the time, the great mass of citizens living outside the central valley had only tenuous and brief contact with the Reform, and then largely through the agents of the Reformers, the district political chiefs who had vast areas of difficult terrain to oversee and whose supervision consequently left much to be desired. These factors, shaped by local interests and historical evolution, tend to emphasize once more the chief characteristics of the Liberal revolution: it was, in large part—at least in those facets in which success was a tangible result—a middle-class, urban, rather elitist movement, which had little concern of a positive nature for the lower classes, the peasantry, the Indian, the masses.

It is difficult, then, to describe and evaluate concisely the Reform in Oaxaca and to summarize succinctly or precisely the results of the movement there because of its uneven implementation, its varying impact on distinct social classes and geographical regions, and the differing degrees by which it was resisted or accepted. Taking an overall view of the state over a period of two decades, certain factors were present in 1876 that did not exist in 1856, and certain other factors that existed earlier were, by the later date, more intensely present than ever before. This indicates that the Reform undoubtedly wrought some changes. The Catholic Church was no longer a force to be reckoned with. As a political philosophy, conservatism with its overtones of monarchism virtually had been eliminated. The base of property ownership had been broadened—not as much as had been intended originally, but a noticeable change had been brought about in this regard. The educational establishment was better endowed and had a more secure prospect than previously. One may well ponder if such changes were truly significant and if the prolonged disruption had made the cost of effecting these changes worthwhile. The exhaustion of resources, the destruction of life and property, the stagnation of agricultural production, the setback to economic progress, the unsettling of individuals' lives, and the bitterness and deep cleavages generated by the civil wars were, by any standard of measurement, high prices to pay for the changes that were made.

In their drive towards modernity, however, the Liberals had failed to break completely with the past. Most notably evident in the realm of the human spirit their program fell short of enunciated goals because their vision of the perfectability of man's estate was flawed. They failed to tame the beast of militarism, as evidenced by the turbulence of the post-Reform decade. To the contrary, the martial spirit was further elevated and stimulated by more than a decade of fighting, first against the enemies of the revolution and then among the victors. The success of the Reform to a large extent depended on the ability to subordinate the military; failure in this endeavor meant a greatly weakened thrust toward change.

The struggle to impose the Reform had similarly fanned the burning ambitions of many who rose to prominence as the result of military exploits or political effectiveness. Furthermore, the large portion of the population that had thrown itself into the struggle to save the Constitution of 1857 and the Republic expected, in traditional fashion, to be paid for loyalty, perseverance, and sacrifice. Payment usually was defined in terms of spoils. Such widely held expectations would make it exceedingly difficult to control personal aspirations as Mexico faced the transition to peace, tranquility, and stability, desired by all, but highly elusive because of the very nature of the problem.

Thus the Reform of Oaxaca, and presumably elsewhere, was a truncated affair. It went only part of the way toward solving the problems of the past that had kept Mexico in such chaos since independence was won from Spain. That it was a bourgeois movement and thus failed to right social imbalance beyond acquiring for the middle class a greater share of the wealth and a monopoly over the affairs of state; that it failed to control the militaristic spirit and curb immoderate ambitions; and that it failed to insure democratic procedures made it a lopsided revolution that had brought significant changes at a high cost but not enough changes in a sufficiently balanced fashion to complete the task the Reformers set for themselves. Eventually an attempt would have to be made to correct the defects that the Reformers were unable, or unwilling, to eliminate.

APPENDIX A

1. Oaxaca City

Andrés Portillo, *Oaxaca en el centenario de la independencia nacional,* p. 145, gives the following estimates of the population of the state capital:

1774 — 14,000		1828 — 17,306	
1792 — 22,113		1843 — 18,118	
1797 — 19,062		1863 — 24,433	
1808 — 17,599		1865 — 24,907	
1815 — 15,702			

Other estimates vary considerably from those given above. E.g., José María Murguía y Galardi, "Extracto general que abraza la estadística toda en su 1a y 2a parte del estado de Guaxaca" (1827), 1:20, gives 18,118 as the population of the city in 1827. Juan Bautista Carriedo, *Ensayo histórico-estadístico del Departamento de Oaxaca . . . Año de 1843,* uses this figure for 1832, saying he is sure the city has more inhabitants than this but that it is the official figure; and Portillo uses the same figure for 1843, taking it from Carriedo. General José María García, governor of the state in 1855, estimated the population for the city as 25,000, in the "Apéndice" to Murguía y Galardi's "Estadística antigua y moderna de la provincia, hoy estado libre, soberano e independiente de Guaxaca," *Boletín de la Sociedad Mexicana de Geografía y Estadística* 7 (1859):273. This figure is repeated by Eugenio Maillefert, comp., *Directorio de comercio del Imperio Mexicano para el año de 1867,* p. 40. Francisco Vasconcelos, secretary of the ayuntamiento during the French Intervention, compiled statistics showing the city with a population of 14,907 as of May 25, 1865, in AMO, Libro de Tesorería Municipal, 1859 a 1867, Tomo 8, expediente: "Curiosas Noticias del

Año de 1865, 'Censo de la capital en 1865.' " In light of the exodus from the city in December 1864–January 1865, this low figure may be accurate, and the 1865 figure of 24,907 given by Portillo above may be a misprint. John Chance, *Race and Class in Colonial Oaxaca,* p. 73, provides a set of population figures for various years, 1529–1970, with sources listed.

2. The Central District

The figure of 45,000 inhabitants of the Central District is arrived at by using a manuscript statistical survey made in 1857, entitled: "1857. Estadística del Estado de Oaxaca formada por el Sor. Dn. Enrique de Nassos [?] de Lafond comisionado al efecto por el Supror Gobo de la Nación," legajo 760, expediente 2, Antigua Colección, Archivo Histórico, Biblioteca del Museo de Antropología e Historia, Mexico City. Lafond's figures yield a total of 38,087, but he does not give the population for some places. For those entities he failed to include, figures were obtained and interpolated from *Mem.*-MC, document 6; and Murguía y Galardi, "Extracto general," 2:32–55. *Mem.*-RC, document 12, gives the population in 1861 as 41,148, and Manuel Dublán, *Memoria que sobre instrucción pública presenta el director del Instituto al gobierno del estado,* uses this figure in 1863. Considering that many men were out of the state and serving in the army in that period, it would seem that an estimate of 45,000 would not be far off.

3. The State

The following population statistics are taken from *Mem.*-RC, document 12, which contains no figures for the District of Tuxtepec. The Tuxtepec total is taken from Dublán, *Memoria,* p. 8. The Cajiga total is 533,733, but the Tuxtepec figure boosts the total population figure to 547,965.

POPULATION FIGURES FOR THE STATE OF OAXACA

District	Men	Women	Total
Central	19,404	21,744	41,148
Choapan	5,084	5,261	10,345
Coixtlahuaca	5,291	5,582	10,873

District	Men	Women	Total	
Cuicatlán	6,680	6,835	13,515	
Ejutla	6,757	6,637	13,394	
Etla	8,533	8,754	17,287	
Huajuapan	16,309	18,505	34,814	
Jamiltepec	11,863	12,759	24,622	
Juchitán	9,246	10,305	19,551	
Juquila	4,388	4,604	8,992	
Miahuatlán	14,194	14,026	28,220	
Nochixtlán	12,145	12,383	24,528	
Ocotlán	11,258	10,967	22,225	
Pochutla	4,580	4,758	9,338	
Silacayoapan	14,249	14,589	28,838	
Tehuantepec	9,836	10,193	20,029	
Teotitlán del Camino	9,463	11,069	20,532	
Teposcolula	9,742	10,863	20,605	
Tlacolula	13,653	13,818	27,471	
Tlaxiaco	16,252	17,700	33,952	
Tuxtepec			14,232	
Villa Alta	15,738	16,754	32,492	
Villa-Juárez				
(formerly Ixtlán)	9,525	9,820	19,345	
Yautepec	8,853	9,083	17,936	
Zimatlán	16,925	16,756	33,681	
Totals	259,968	273,765	547,965	(533,733)

Mem.-JMDO, document 11, gives the population of the state of Oaxaca in various years as follows:

1832 — 484,014		1845 — 521,187	
1834 — 457,330		1849 — 525,101	
1837 — 491,308		1851 — 523,846	
1838 — 501,552		1852 — 524,935	
1841 — 502,277		1857 — 531,502	

It must be emphasized that all the foregoing figures are only estimates, but they are provided by men who had access to the best information available.

APPENDIX B

Towns and Villages

Azompa
Cuilapan
Huayapan
Ixcotel
Jalatlaco
Oaxaca City
San Agustín de las Juntas
San Agustín Yatareni
San Andrés Ixtlahuaca
San Antonio de la Cal
San Bartolomé Coyotepec
San Felipe del Agua
San Francisco Tutla
San Jacinto Amilpas
San Juan Chapultepec

San Martín Mexicapan
San Pablo la Raya
San Pedro Ixtlahuaca
San Sebastián Tutla
Santa Catalina de Sena
Santa Cruz Amilpas
Santa Lucía del Camino
Santa María Coyotepec
Santa María del Tule
Santa María Oaxaca
   (Marquesado)
Tlalixtac
Tomaltepec
Xochimilco
Xoxocotlán

Haciendas

Aguilera
Aranjuez
Arrazola
El Carmen
La Compañía
Crespo

Nazareno
Panzacola
Quintas
El Rosario
San José
San Luis

Dolores	San Miguel
Montoya	Zorita
Murguía	Montaño

Ranchos

Aguayo	Jardín
Blanco	Manzano
Los Caciques	Pombo
El Carrizal	San Antonio
La Concepción	San Jacinto
La Cruz Blanca	La Soledad
Guadalupe	Tiracoces

Miscellaneous Designations

Barrio de Animas de Coyotepec
Labor de Cinco Señores
Labor de la Noria
Labor de la Sangre de Cristo
Molinos de Mantecón (Hermosa)
Molinos de Santo Domingo
Molinos de Tepetetutla
Trapiche de Candiani
Trapiche de San Javier
Trinidad de las Huertas

APPENDIX C

Collaboration and Historiography

The widespread collaboration in Oaxaca of Liberals with the Interventionist government raises important historiographical problems. Possible reasons for this cooperation with the imperialists have already been offered, but the fact that such support was readily forthcoming from an area that could be characterized, as of 1864, as "the last stronghold of the armed Republic" leads one to wonder if the other regions incorporated into the Empire did not also produce the same type of collaboration, perhaps to an even greater extent than in Oaxaca.

Although some historians contemporary with the Reform and later during the nineteenth century dealt with the problem of collaboration, they quickly and deprecatingly dismissed those who cooperated as traitors, egoists who put self above nation, or indifferent men who would serve anyone as long as they had the comforts of life. Such were the labels attached to Mexicans who accepted the Intervention by the stalwart republican historian and publicist, José María Iglesias, writing from Chihuahua in early 1865.[1] Later, Justo Sierra acknowledged the support given to Maximilian by many Liberals, somewhat less harshly attributing it to the great interest in and admiration for all things French on the part of the educated men of Mexico. Indeed, if they had not actually been educated in France, they had at least read French literature and used French textbooks. They were attracted to the authoritarianism of Napoleon III and fell victim to the personal magnetism and charm of Maximilian. And they were convinced that Juárez's dead or dying Republic could only be revived by intervention by the United States, a nation they had learned to distrust through hard and bitter experience.[2]

204

As decades passed and the triumph of the Republic became enshrouded in heroic, mythic glory, the Mexican historians of the predominant Liberal school forgot or consciously ignored how common was the cooperation with the Interventionist regime, primarily because recognition, mention, or emphasis of the phenomenon would not fit into their theses explaining the fact or significance of the Mexican victory, the triumph of democracy over monarchy, Liberalism over Conservatism, state over church, progress over the status quo, America over Europe, Mexican over foreigner. These twentieth-century historians of the Liberal school couch their discussions in lofty, philosophic, ethical terms, which cannot be squared with the facts.

For example, Ernesto de la Torre Villar sees the struggle between the Interventionists and republicans as one of illegitimacy and government outside the Mexican tradition opposed to the deeply held desire for absolute independence, free self-determination, and sovereign dignity. It was right that republicanism should win. He seems to think that any other outcome would be an admission that evil can triumph. Furthermore, the outstanding republican leaders of extraordinary qualities drew their strength from and had the support of the Mexican people, who were, indeed, the principal actors, shedding their blood for the Republic. Since the republican cause was so sacred and elicited such popular support, it could not be otherwise that victory was theirs.[3] Emilio Rabasa also pointed to patriotism and aroused nationalism to explain the Mexican victory. The proof of the patriotism could be seen in the way Mexicans everywhere supported the republican military commanders who in turn fought against the greatest of odds for a government that was virtually disarmed. In disaster and crisis, this physically weak goverment had at its disposal only its moral authority to summon the support of the people, but that was sufficient. "The war forged [a] nationality."[4] José C. Valadés likewise emphasized the moral strength and appeal of a constitution, a government that was not simply "a caprice of Juárez," institutions that had the loyalty of the people, and realistic republican leaders who guided Mexico to its rightful destiny of victory as the reasons for the triumph over the Intervention. The Mexican nation was "constituted by the will of its people."[5] More recently, Martín Quirarte summarizes the victory concisely: "If you want to explain [it] in a simple formula . . . you would have to affirm that it was the far-sightedness of the leaders [*clase directora*] that facilitated the victory." The secret of the success of the leaders lay in their "having known how to create a conscience of nationality" in a people who lacked such a sentiment when the struggle began.[6]

Such views are representative of the mainstream of Mexican historiographical writing on the topic of the Intervention. It is not to be denied that there is great attraction in the theory that the "right will prevail" in explaining historical processes, nor that a surge of nationalism, a high sense of moral right, realism on the part of leaders, and determination and sacrifice on the part of the people contributed to the victory of the Liberal republicans. But in light of the large-scale collaboration that went on, such lofty, abstract reasons cannot be accepted as the sole factors. They are not in accord with the evidence, which shows instead that leaders such as Porfirio Díaz earned the hatred of many Oaxacan Liberals; that state leaders by the dozens went over to the French and openly, sometimes enthusiastically worked to help the imperial administration function smoothly; and that patriotism or nationalism found little soil from which to draw nourishment in many areas. To a large extent, many Mexican historians have ignored facts and helped perpetuate myths.

APPENDIX D

Given the extent of Maximilian's Mexican Empire, severe lines of administrative centralization proved unworkable. To remedy this, there evolved over a period of months the system of control vested in imperial deputies and imperial visitors. These officers of the government were to be reputable Mexicans well known to the emperor. Each military district—of these there were eight, later nine—also formed the boundaries of the areas under the supervision of the deputies, who were to be Maximilian's personal, civilian representatives in those divisions. Placed there to insure that government machinery worked smoothly, that justice and equality prevailed, and that abuses and malfeasance were eliminated, the deputies were given a wide range of powers, from questioning prisoners to ordering the inventories of records to suspending and fining subordinate officials.

The visitors had similar powers but their appointments were of a more temporary, limited nature. Assigned when specific problems arose or when specific matters in the civil departments or military divisions needed special attention, the visitors were granted those powers Maximilian deemed necessary for the fulfillment of their missions. In short, the deputy was a kind of viceroy on a small scale, whereas the visitor resembled more that investigative officer in the Spanish colonial empire brought in to conduct *visitas* and *residencias*. The normal chain of command was from the emperor through his ministers to the deputies and visitors, but in cases of emergency or of paramount importance the last could go directly to the emperor and circumvent his cabinet.[1]

207

Within the Department of Oaxaca, the districts as defined in the law of March 1858, passed by the state legislature, still prevailed under the Empire. Instead of being administered by *jefes políticos,* however, they were now headed by subprefects who were to take orders directly from the departmental superior prefect, who in turn received his instructions from Juan Pablo Franco, the imperial visitor.[2]

APPENDIX E

A Note on the Value of the Disentailed and
Nationalized Properties in Oaxaca

When I began this study, I hoped to be able to arrive at some figure
that would express accurately the value of the disentailed and
nationalized property in the State of Oaxaca and to be able to compare it with the total value of property in that area. I was prompted to
attempt this by the controversy that has grown around the real or
imagined economic power of the church in Mexico in the nineteenth
century.

The more data I collected, however, the more confused the issue
became. And when all the data were coded for computer analysis, a
formula was worked out, and a program was arranged to produce
such comparative figures, the more firmly I was convinced that such
statistics were impossible to obtain.

The reasons for this are many. For example, the notaries were
not systematic in recording the information necessary to determine
the value of property. There were many figures used. Frequently the
value at the time of disentailment is given in the records of auctions
and sales, but just as frequently only the selling price is given. When
records of first sales were not available but records of subsequent sales
were, the properties could have been reappraised in the interim and
the relation of the selling price to the original valuation was not necessarily clear. Thus the data were not consistent. I obtained original
valuations on some properties, reappraised valuations on others, sale
prices on others, but seldom did I obtain all such information on any
given piece of property. For many properties, the only information
available was that it had been put up for sale and had previously been
owned by either a civil or ecclesiastical corporation. If a sale was

209

concluded and the price was stated, that price was frequently described as "two thirds of the official valuation plus a few pesos."

A few government reports of the era listed total values, but these are highly untrustworthy. How could officials claim validity for such statistics when at the same time they were complaining of the difficulties of record keeping and sending memoranda to each other begging for information in an attempt to bring their files up to date? Ramón Cajiga, borlado governor of the state in the early 1860s, included a summary of values in his report to the state legislature in 1861, but noted that the records for Oaxaca City were incomplete because the registry had been destroyed.[1]

The government reports, if issued at the national level, subtotaled the disentailed or nationalized properties according to states, thereby making it impossible to extract data pertinent to smaller geographical or political divisions, and frequently making it impossible to distinguish between civil and ecclesiastical real estate. A typical government report is that issued by Miguel Lerdo de Tejada in early 1857, which is full of inaccuracies and errors but which has nevertheless—and unfortunately—been accepted with great validity by historians.[2]

Even if such values could be established, there would arise the problem of the accuracy of the statistics. Did the church purposely undervalue its real estate in order to avoid paying heavy taxes or contributing money to the government based on property values? One can summon data, argue, debate ad infinitum, and yet all efforts would still result in unsure answers to such questions.

Futhermore, were it possible to arrive at an accurate figure for the value of disentailed property, such a figure, taken alone, has no intrinsic meaning; its meaning only becomes apparent when it can be compared with the total value of property, and this latter statistic is impossible to determine.

Lamentably, I must therefore conclude with the sentiments expressed by Andrés Portillo of Oaxaca in 1909: "It is today, as it was previously, a difficult or impossible task to establish the amount of rural and urban property administered by the civil and religious corporations of Oaxaca in the era in which the Laws of the Reform began to have their desired effects."[3]

LIST OF ABBREVIATIONS

AEO	Archivo del Estado de Oaxaca, Oaxaca City
AGN	Archivo General de la Nación, Mexico City
AMO	Archivo Municipal de Oaxaca, Oaxaca City
AN	Archivo de Notarías, Oaxaca City
APD	Díaz, Porfirio. *Archivo del General Porfirio Díaz: memorias y documentos.* Alberto María Carreño, ed. 29 vols. Mexico City, 1947–60.
BA	Bazaine Archives, 1862–67. 26 folders. The Nettie Lee Benson Latin American Collection, The University of Texas at Austin.
BLIM	Segura, José Sebastián. *Boletín de las Leyes del Imperio Mexicano o sea Código de la Restauración.* 4 vols. Mexico City, 1863–65.
BUBJO	Biblioteca de la Universidad "Benito Juárez" de Oaxaca, Oaxaca City
CCG	Private collection of Luis Castañeda Guzmán, Oaxaca City
CLD	*Colección de leyes y decretos del estado libre de Oaxaca.* 26 vols. in 22. Oaxaca City, 1851–1909.
CLDRI	*Colección de leyes, decretos y reglamentos que interinamente forman el sistema político, adminstrativo y judicial del imperio.* 8 vols. Mexico City, 1865–66.
Con.	*El Constituyente. Periódico Oficial del Gobierno de Oaxaca.* 1858.
Dem.	*La Democracia. Periódico del Gobierno de Oaxaca.* 1856–59.
DI	*El Diario del Imperio.* Mexico City, 1865–67.
Esp.-BJ	Oaxaca. Governor (Benito Juárez). *Esposición que*

211

	el gobernador del estado have . . . el día 2 de Julio de 1852. Oaxaca City, 1852.
HAHR	*The Hispanic American Historical Review*
HM	*Historia Mexicana*
Inf.—FM	Mexico. Secretaría de Hacienda y Crédito Público. *Informe presentado . . . el 16 de Setiembre de 1874 . . . por el C. Francisco Mejía.* 2 vols. Mexico City, 1874.
JLAS	*Journal of Latin American Studies*
LM	Dublán, Manuel and Lozano, José María. *Legislación mexicana, o colección completa de las disposiciones legislativas expedida desde la independencia de la república . . . .* 34 vols. Mexico City, 1876–1904.
*Mem.-*FD	Oaxaca. Governor (Félix Díaz). *Memoria que presenta el ejecutivo del Estado al H. Congreso . . . de 17 de Setiembre de 1869 a 16 de Setiembre del presente año* [1870]. Oaxaca City, 1871.
*Mem.-*JE	Oaxaca. Governor (José Esperón). *Memoria que el ejecutivo del estado presenta al congreso . . . hoy 17 de setiembre de 1875.* Oaxaca City, 1875.
*Mem.-*JMDO	Oaxaca. Governor (José María Díaz Ordaz). *Memoria que el governador del estado presenta al congreso . . . 1858.* Oaxaca City, 1858.
*Mem.-*LdeT	*Memoria presentada al exmo. sr. presidente . . . por el c. Miguel Lerdo de Tejada . . . .* Mexico City, 1857.
*Mem.-*MBC	Oaxaca. Governor (Miguel Bolaños Cacho). *Memoria administrativa presentada por el C. Lic. Miguel Bolaños Cacho . . . el 17 de Septiembre de 1902.* Oaxaca City, 1902.
*Mem.-*MC	Oaxaca. Governor (Miguel Castro). *Memoria que el ejecutivo del estado presenta al congreso . . . de 8 de Enero de 1872 a 16 de Setiembre del mismo año.* Oaxaca City, 1873.
*Mem.-*MG (1898)	Oaxaca. Governor (Martín González). *Memoria administrativa presentada por el c. General Martín González . . . el 17 de Septiembre de 1898.* Oaxaca City, 1899.
*Mem.-*MG (1899)	*Memoria administrativa presentada por el c. General*

	Martín González . . . el 17 de Septiembre de 1899. Oaxaca City, 1899.
Mem.-RC	Oaxaca. Governor (Ramón Cajiga). *Memoria que el c. Ramón Cajiga . . . presenta al segundo congreso . . . el 16 de Septiembre de 1861.* Oaxaca City, 1861.
MG-HO	Martínez Gracida, Manuel. Historia de Oaxaca, Años de 1852 a 1860. 6 vols. mss. (BUBJO).
Vic.	*La Victoria. Periódico del Gobierno de Oaxaca.* 1860–64.

NOTES

PREFACE

1. Thomas F. McGann, "Research Opportunities: Southern South America," *The Americas* 18 (April 1962): 375–79.

2. *Investigaciones contemporáneas sobre historia de México*, pp. 245–89; and Luis González y González, *Pueblo en vilo: microhistoria de San José de Gracia* (1968), translated by John Upton as *San José de Gracia: Mexican Village in Transition* (1974); and González's article, "Microhistoria para multiméxico," *HM* 21 (Octubre-Diciembre 1971): 225–41.

3. Quoted by Claude Morin, "Los libros parroquiales como fuente para la historia demográfica y social novohispana," *HM* 21 (Enero-Marzo 1972): 418.

CHAPTER 1

1. Jorge Fernando Iturribarría, "Alonso García Bravo, trazador y alarife de la villa de Antequera," *HM* 7 (Julio-Septiembre 1957): 84–86, for laying out the townsite; John K. Chance, *Race and Class in Colonial Oaxaca*, p. 34, for the colonial appearance; and Jorge Fernando Iturribarría, *Monografía histórica del Palacio de los Poderes del Estado de Oaxaca*, pp. 27, 35.

2. Andrés Portillo, *Oaxaca en el centenario de la independencia nacional*, p. 130. (Each 4th page of this book is numbered; hence the pages cited here and subsequently refer either to the numbered page on which the information appears or to the last previously numbered page before the one containing the information cited.)

3. G. F. von Tempsky, *Mitla*, p. 248.

4. Manuel Martínez Gracida, *Colección de los "cuadros sinópticos" de los pueblos, haciendas y ranchos del estado libre y soberano de Oaxaca*, p. 4.

5. Jorge Fernando Iturribarría, *El agua en la ciudad de Oaxaca desde los tiempos más remotos hasta el primer tercio del siglo XX*, pp. 11–13; *Dem.*, 4:7:4, Feb. 17, 1859, for one such notice of impending repairs (all newspaper citations give volume:issue:page, and date), and Juan Bautista Carriedo, *Ensayo histórico-estadístico del departamento de Oaxaca*, pp. 12–13, for a description of the trenches.

6. Carriedo, *Ensayo*, pp. 12–13, for the streets; *CLD*, 2:88–91 (decree of Oct. 4, 1852) and 2:120–25 (decree of Nov. 23, 1852), for subdivisions.

7. Désiré Charnay, *Le Mexique,* pp. 122–23. Charnay was in Oaxaca in late 1858 or early 1859. Tempsky, *Mitla,* p. 248, wrote of the solidity of construction of the homes of the wealthier residents.

8. The above follows closely the account given in the anonymous "Apuntes históricos de la vida en Oaxaca en el siglo XIX," pp. 6–9, in CCG. This ms. was found among the papers of Francisco Vasconcelos, uncle of José Vasconcelos of later fame, and Lic. Luis Castañeda Guzmán made a typescript copy for his collection, which copy the present writer used. The ms. probably dates from about 1910, and Vasconcelos, who left other signed mss., is probably the author; he will be so listed in subsequent citations. The work is full of valuable information of a social nature, although it is not clear just which social group is being described. It is in the form of a dialogue between Doña Bibiana, whose age is given as 90 and whose birth is set in 1820, and Antonia, a young laundress, who inquires of the old woman about life in Oaxaca in bygone days. These conversations took place at the end of the workday, and are divided into chapters called *veladas* ("evening gatherings"). Some pages in the typescript are numbered and some are not; in subsequent references to this work, when page numbers are not available the velada will be given.

9. Ibid., Velada sexta.

10. Ibid., Velada segunda. MG-HO, 1851, "Mal estado de la policía." In the municipal police ordinance of Jan. 21, 1851, found in the latter work, there is an article providing for the levying of fines on persons who met or congregated more than three in number on the streets after 10:30 P.M.

11. Manuel Martínez Gracida, *Efemérides oaxaqueñas, 1853–1892,* 1:passim. Although William B. Taylor's emphasis is on the villages of central Mexico and the Mixteca Alta in the eighteenth century, he provides some evidence of lawlessness and violence in regions near the state capital in the early nineteenth century. See his *Drinking, Homicide and Rebellion in Colonial Mexican Villages,* passim.

12. Twenty thousand deaths from cholera in the entire state were reported for the epidemic of August-December, 1853, and an equal number in the epidemic of two decades earlier. Jorge Fernando Iturribarría, *Historia de Oaxaca,* 1: *1821 a 1854,* 198–200, 422; MG-HO, 1852, "Beneficencia Pública."

13. *Mem.*-JMDO, pp. 14–16; Pedro Camacho, *Ensayo de monografía sobre los hospitales del estado,* pp. 1–10.

14. Portillo, *Oaxaca en el centenario,* p. 152.

15. *CLD,* 1:298; AEO, Ramo de Asuntos Varios, Carpeta negra, 1856, registro 304 (expediente 24) is a request by the village of San Miguel Tlalixtac to be allowed to hold a bullfight to celebrate the feast day of St. Michael. See Comte Mathieu de Fossey, *Le Mexique,* p. 356, for comments on dances.

16. Fossey, *Le Mexique,* pp. 356–57, and especially Vasconcelos, "Apuntes históricos," Velada cuarta, provide descriptions of these various festivals and processions.

17. Francisco Vasconcelos, "Reminiscencias de lo que fué en Oaxaca," pp. 3–4, in CCG. Arnold J. Bauer, "Rural Workers in Spanish America," *HAHR* 59 (February 1979): 55–56, notes that throughout Latin America charitable works of the church were declining both in quantity and quality in the late colonial period and onward. But in Oaxaca evidence suggests that the

church continued to play this significant social role, despite declining resources, at least until the mid-nineteenth century. The state had no commensurate funds to substitute for the welfare provided by the various ecclesiastical agencies and groups.

18. Brian Hamnett, "Dye Production, Food Supply and the Laboring Population of Oaxaca, 1750–1800," *HAHR* 51 (February 1971): 54, 64–67, 73, 76; and the same author's "The Appropriation of Mexican Church Wealth by the Spanish Bourbon Government," *JLAS* 1 (November 1969): passim.

19. For the details of this decline of personnel and erosion of economic strength, see Charles R. Berry, "La ciudad de Oaxaca en vísperas de la Reforma," *HM* 19 (Julio-Septiembre 1969): 36–43. Two articles by Asunción Lavrin, "Problems and Policies in the Administration of Nunneries in Mexico, 1800–1835," *The Americas* 28 (July 1971): 57–77, and "Mexican Nunneries from 1835 to 1860," *The Americas* 28 (January 1972): 288–310, suggest the growing impoverishment of most nunneries throughout the nineteenth century, although in many cases nunneries were able to hold their own against all odds.

20. José Bravo Ugarte, "Datos sobre la fundación de los seminarios diocesanos de México y sus confiscaciones," *Memorias de la Academia Mexicana de la Historia* 11 (Abril-Junio 1952): 144, for date of founding of seminary; Carriedo, *Ensayo*, pp. 37–38, for curriculum reform and reason for increase of students; Juan Bautista Carriedo, *Estudios históricos del estado libre de Oaxaca,* 1:111, for the number of students in 1831; and *Memoria del Ministerio de Justicia y Negocios Eclesiásticos, presentada a las augustas cámaras del Congreso General de los Estados-Unidos Mexicanos por el secretario del ramo, en el mes de Enero de 1851,* document 16, for the number of students in 1850 and other information on curriculum. Manuel Martínez Gracida et al., "Biografías de oaxaqueños distinguidos," in BUBJO, passim.

21. [Jose Mariano Galíndez], "De Nuestra Señora de la Soledad de Oaxaca. Sobre el Patronato de María Santísima" (preached Dec. 18, 1841), in *Sermones panegíricos y morales predicados en las grandes solemnidades de esta capital, por un seminarista oaxaqueño,* 1:193–196.

22. Carriedo, *Ensayo,* p. 15 fn.; Benito Juárez, "Apuntes para mis hijos," in Jorge L. Tamayo, ed., *Benito Juárez,* 1:95. The Institute evolved into the present state Universidad "Benito Juárez" de Oaxaca, but its contemporary status and influence are not nearly so great as a century ago.

23. Carriedo, *Ensayo,* pp. 36–37; Pedro Camacho, *Ligeros apuntes históricos del Instituto de Ciencias y Artes del Edo. de Oaxaca,* pp. 8–9; and the report by Manuel Dublán giving a history of the Institute in *DI,* 4:557:381–82, Nov. 6, 1866, all touch upon the curriculum changes, each varying slightly in the details given. Antonio Ramos-Oliveira, *La formación de Juárez,* p. 213, comments on the importance of the curriculum in the context of the mid-nineteenth century.

24. Ramón Pardo, *Berve estudio sobre la evolución del Instituto de Ciencias y Artes de Oaxaca,* pp. 3–7. This brief account seems to me the most reasoned statement concerning the Institute. Educational institutes of a similar nature were established in other states, such as Zacatecas, Guanajuato, and Jalisco, all of them fostering liberalism, but by far the most important and influential in

the long term was that of Oaxaca. See François Chevalier, "Conservateurs et liberaux au Mexique," in Arturo Arnáiz y Freg and Claude Bataillon, eds., *La Intervención francesa y el imperio de Maximiliano cien años después, 1862–1962,* p. 21. Also see Fidel López Carrasco, *Historia de la educación en el estado de Oaxaca,* pp. 26–34, for an estimate of Juárez's role.

25. Report of Juan Nepomuceno Bolaños, director of the Institute, to the Minister of Justice and Public Instruction, dated Oaxaca, Feb. 13, 1855, in MG-HO, 1855, "Santa Anna convierte el Instituto del Estado en Colegio de Estudios preparatorios." Carriedo, *Ensayo,* p. 37, describes the museum and library.

26. *Mem.*-JMDO, pp. 30–31. In 1827, when the Institute opened, its library contained 610 titles in 2,035 volumes; in 1857, there were 3,902 volumes. Portillo, *Oaxaca en el centenario,* p. 146.

27. The variations in courses, the texts used, and the professors teaching in the Institute in the years 1856–63 may be compared by consulting the following: *Con.,* pp. 3–4, May 15, 1856; *Dem.,* 1:7:3, Oct. 23, 1856; *Mem.*-JMDO, document 20; *Mem.*-RC, document 22; and *Vic.,* 3:50:1, Jan. 8, 1863.

28. Camacho, *Ligeros apuntes,* p. 9. A century later, in our contemporary period, the part-time academic who focuses his chief attention on the practice of his profession is the bane of academe, in Latin America and elsewhere. But in the era before the professionalized professoriate, surely there was worthwhile practical experience to be derived from contact with the men who both taught and followed their professions.

29. Portillo, *Oaxaca en el centenario,* p. 139; López Carrasco, *Historia de la educación,* pp. 15, 27–29; and Policarpo T. Sánchez, *Memoria de la Escuela Normal de Oaxaca en su inauguración 29 de Octubre de 1946,* pp. 12, 14. *Catecismo político dedicado a la instrucción primaria de la juventud oaxaqueña,* pp. 39 ff., delineates the curriculum.

30. To my knowledge, no accurate map of the Central District exists. The most satisfactory of the area is that by Cecil Welte, *Mapa de las localidades del Valle de Oaxaca,* but it does not contain the district boundary lines. Mr. Welte kindly sketched in the boundaries of the Central District on his map for me, and the map appearing in the text is based on his cartography.

31. Decree of Mar. 23, 1858, *CLD,* 2:389–441. When the Central District is mentioned here, it is understood to mean the district as detailed in the 1858 law, not the Central Department of earlier periods.

32. Benjamin H. Luebke, "Delineation of Rural Communities in the State of Oaxaca, Mexico" (Ph.D. diss., University of Florida, 1959), p. 55, comments that in the catholic villages of Oaxaca "church and local government are closely associated"—even today. Philip A. Dennis, *Conflictos por tierras en el Valle de Oaxaca,* concerns the longstanding disputes between San Andrés Amilpas and Santo Tomás Soyaltepec, 24 kms. from Oaxaca City. Hamnett, "Dye Production," pp. 51, 53, 59, also comments on the frequency of disputes between neighboring villages over lands and boundaries. Taylor, *Drinking, Homicide and Rebellion,* p. 136, notes that "boundary questions were a chronic occasion for violence in both [central Mexico and Oaxaca], but it is noteworthy that the Oaxaca examples (both from the Mixteca Alta and the

Valley of Oaxaca) of boundary wars and attacks on public officials in *vistas de ojos* were especially prolonged and acrimonious."

33. In 1861, Governor Ramón Cajiga expressed much dissatisfaction with the internal organization of the state. He noted that some regroupings of villages had been necessary so that they would come under the jurisdiction of the district to which they were tied economically and topographically. More such modifications needed to be made. The municipio should be the bulwark of the government, he pointed out, but the isolated locations of some pueblos and the ignorance of the people in many villages made the municipalities unreliable agencies of the Liberal regime. Nor could the political chiefs fulfill completely their role as overseers and intermediaries because of the isolation of so many pueblos. The governor thought that more and smaller districts might prove to be the solution, but this entailed more funds to pay the salaries of the additional political chiefs needed, and the funds did not exist. *Mem.*-RC, pp. 19–20. Of course, the Central District was an exception; because it was small and because roads were maintained comparatively well, no villages were completely isolated.

34. *Mem.*-MC, document 6. The presence of the Mixtecs, can be traced back to the preconquest era and to the early colonial period, when some resettlement of Indians was common for military defense or for the encomiendas. Chance, *Race and Class,* pp. 16–18; William B. Taylor, *Landlord and Peasant in Colonial Oaxaca,* p. 22; and Joseph Whitecotton, *The Zapotecs,* p. 183, comment on the presence of the Mixtecs in Zapotec areas.

35. For lack of figures prior to the Reform, the information on agriculture pertains to 1872 and is taken from *Mem.*-MC, document 6, on the assumption, which the author acknowledges may be misleading, that what obtained in 1872 probably could be applied to 1855 or thereabouts.

36. Enrique de Nassos [?] de Lafond, "1857. Estadística del Estado de Oaxaca" (legajo 760, expediente 2, Antigua Colección, Archivo Histórico, Biblioteca del Museo de Antropoligía e Historia, Mexico City), pp. 15, 24–26. These figures are surprisingly low, but Taylor, *Landlord and Peasant,* pp. 128–31, in discussing animals kept on Spanish estates in the colonial period, provides evidence of a marked decline of *ganado menor* ("sheep, goats, swine") on some Valley haciendas in the late eighteenth and early nineteenth centuries, while on the same estates *ganado mayor* ("cattle and horses") was maintained at a comparatively stable, but low, level. Taylor (p. 81) also includes figures from a census of *ganado mayor* in the Valley towns (not just the Central District) taken in 1826, which shows that approximately 50 per cent were oxen. If the ratio was also applicable to the Central District and held good three decades later, there would have been about 3,000 horses and beef cattle in the district at the time of Lafond's count.

37. *Mem.*-JMDO, pp. 18–19.

38. José María García, "Apéndice" to José María Murguía y Galardi, "Estadística antigua y moderna de la provincia, hoy estado libre, soberano e independiente do Guajaca," *Boletín de la Sociedad Mexicana de Geografía y Estadística* 7 (1859): 268–73.

39. Taylor, *Drinking, Homicide and Rebellion,* passim.

40. For information on the district's schools on the eve of the Reform, see MG-HO, 1852, "Instrucción primaria"; *Dem.*, 2:31:4, Oct. 15, 1857; Lafond, "1857. Estadística," p. 14; and Manuel Dublán, *Memoria que sobre instrucción pública presenta el director del Instituto al gobierno del estado* (dated Aug. 27, 1863), pp. 5–14.

41. E.g., *Mem.*-JMDO, pp. 20–21.

42. Whitecotton, *The Zapotecs*, p. 815; Chance, *Race and Class*, pp. 28–29; Hamnett, "Dye Production," pp. 51–53, 59, 69, 75; and Taylor, *Landlord and Peasant*, passim, all refer to the resistance by the Indians to losing their lands and working on creole-owned farms and haciendas.

43. *Inf.*-FM, 2:256. Four of the Dominican monasteries were empty and the other seven had a total of only seventeen monks. As to property held by the orders, evidence is contradictory. Hamnett, "Dye Production," pp. 54, 64–67, states that in the late eighteenth century revenue from rural estates owned by the Dominicans had declined considerably, and some estates were without equipment or cattle. On the other hand, Taylor, *Landlord and Peasant*, p. 194, concludes that although there were difficulties in the management of rural holdings by the various ecclesiastical entities—underused land, neglect and deterioration of some estates, tenure of lands that was of a "rather fluid and unsettled character"—"nineteenth-century documentation does suggest . . . that much Church property remained intact in the 50 years after independence." Chance, in his Ph.D. dissertation, "Race and Class in a Colonial Mexican City" (University of Illinois at Urbana–Champaign, 1974), p. 248 fn. 6, states that "by the end of the colonial period, combined church holdings amounted to as much as one-fourth of the Valley's productive rural property." He seems not to have transferred this information into his book, *Race and Class*. I have found that by the time the Reform began, the church and its agencies owned few rural estates but remained heavily invested in urban properties (see chap. 6). What is needed, of course, is a careful study of the church's real estate in the period from 1810 to 1856. Even then, the myth of rural property held widely throughout the Republic on a large scale by the church will be difficult to dispel.

44. *Mem.*-JMDO, p. 32.

45. José María Murguía y Galardi, "Extracto general que abraza la estadística toda en su 1a. y 2a. parte del estado de Guaxaca," 1:20–22, states that there were 129 members of the secular clergy residing in Oaxaca City in 1827.

46. Taylor, *Drinking, Homicide and Rebellion*, pp. 23, 142–43.

47. *Mem.*-RC, p. 38, reports that in 1861 there were 437 schools, attended by 17,696 students in a total population of 533,733. His figures include the Central District and Oaxaca City. Admittedly, these figures are rather meaningless; what would provide meaning is a comparison of in-school population with school-age population, but such statistics do not exist, nor can they be calculated from available documentation.

48. García, "Apéndice," p. 274, and *Mem.*-JMDO, p. 20 and document 13, for decline of production and revenues. (The calculations are erroneous in the Díaz *Memoria*. The income for 1774 is given as 3,408,398 pesos, and for 1851 as 527,962 pesos. I have corrected the sums as they appear in the text.) See also the decree of President Comonfort, dated Mar. 23, 1857,

which defines the measures to be taken to finance the registry office in years when production was too low to yield enough money to support the registry, in *Dem.*, 1:62:1, May 3, 1857.

49. *Mem.*-MC, document 15; *APD*, 2:155–56. John Tutino, "Indian Rebellion at the Isthmus of Tehuantepec," *Actes du XLIIe Congrès International des Americanistes* (1976), 3:205, on the Maqueo family. For a discussion of cochineal production in the late colonial period, see two studies by Hamnett, "Dye Production," passim, and *Politics and Trade in Southern Mexico, 1750–1821*, passim.

50. *Mem.*-RC, pp. 60–63.

51. Ibid., document 24. Textile manufacturing was carried on in the early years of the nineteenth century, when 500 looms produced cheap cloth for the lower classes, but competition presented by even cheaper imported English cloth caused them to shut down. Carlos María Bustamante, *Memoria estadística de Oaxaca y descripción del valle del mismo nombre, estractada de la que en grande trabajó el señor don José Murguía y Galardi*, p. 18. Also see Enrique Florescano and Isabel Gil, comps., *Descripciones económicas generales de Nueva España, 1784–1817*, pp. 50–57, for information on textile production and grain and sugar mills.

52. *Balanza mercantil del departamento de Oaxaca, correspondiente al año de 1843*, passim. In 1858, the value of goods imported was estimated at 2,500,000 pesos. From other areas of Mexico came cacao, sugar, flour, and salt. From foreign countries the Oaxacans imported fabrics such as chintz, muslin, linen, and lace, and also cinnamon, white wax, brandy, and, until the late 1850s, iron. By 1858, enough iron was being mined within the state not to have to import it, thanks to the efforts of one Agustín López, who had opened an iron mine in 1842. *Mem.*-RC, pp. 60–63.

53. The information on roads and communications is taken from diverse sources. See *Dem.*, 2:4:4, Aug. 13, 1857, for slowness of mails; ibid., 1:45:4, Mar. 5, 1857, for schedules of stage travel; *Mem.*-JMDO, pp. 18–19, and *Vic.*, 2:18:4, Oct. 3, 1861, for efforts to improve the highway to Tehuacán.

CHAPTER 2

1. Rafael de Zayas Enríquez, *Benito Juárez*, pp. 95–96, analyzes the situation in Oaxaca State when Comonfort sent Juárez to assume the governorship. The isthmus had seceded in November 1855, the federal garrison had pronounced against the Juárez Law in December, the National Guard had opposed the federal garrison, and when Juárez arrived in the state capital, not only did he find all the work of his previous administration undone but there was an attempt to keep him from becoming governor.

2. The various ceremonies and festivities honoring Juárez upon his return are enumerated and described in MG-HO, 1856.

3. For decree on elections, see *CLD*, 2:182; for reopening of the Institute, ibid., pp. 182–83; for matters regarding the public health program, see decree dated July 16, 1856, in ibid., pp. 231–32, and 292–96, and the communication from Luis María Carbó, governor of the Central Department, to

Pedro Ramírez, president of the medical committee of Oaxaca City, May 26, 1856, in *Con., Suplemento de Actas,* June 1, 1856, p. 8. For the public works projects, see *Con., Suplemento de Actas,* May 15, 1856, p. 4.

4. The liberal creed is thoroughly analyzed in such works as Jesús Reyes Heroles, *El liberalismo mexicano,* 3 vols. (1957–61); Charles Hale, *Mexican Liberalism in the Age of Mora, 1821–1853* (1968); and Francisco López Cámara, *La génesis de la conciencia liberal en México* (1954). It is also expounded in the writings of such nineteenth-century Mexican Liberals as Lorenzo de Zavala, José María Luis Omra, Mariano Otero, and Melchor Ocampo. The political aspects of the Liberal program are discussed in Walter Scholes, *Mexican Politics during the Juárez Regime, 1855–1872* (1957). Conservatism is less well served. Modern scholarship tends to ignore the Conservatives, and this needs to be rectified. Hale pays some attention to that ideology by contrast with liberalism in his book on Mora, and some procatholic writers have offered interpretations of Mexican history from a Conservative orientation. See, for example, Mariano Cuevas, *Historia de la nación mexicana,* 2d ed., 3 vols. (1952–53); José Bravo Ugarte, *Historia de México,* 3 vols. (1944); and Paul V. Murray, *The Catholic Church in Mexico,* vol. 1: *1519–1910* (1965). The principal spokesman of nineteenth-century conservatism was Lucas Alamán, whose published works fill 12 volumes *(Disertaciones sobre la historia de la república megicana; Documentos diversos;* and *Historia de Méjico).* Alamán has received some attention by historians: see Moisés González Navarro, *El pensamiento político de Lucas Alamán* (1952); and José C. Valadés, *Alamán, estadista e historiador* (1938). On perfectability, see Edmundo O'Gorman, "Epílogo: El triunfo de la República en el horizonte de su historia," pp. 333–431, in *A cien años del triunfo de la República.*

5. In his autobiographical sketch, Juárez described his law of Nov. 23, 1855, as "the spark that ignited the blaze of the Reform that later consumed the worm-eaten edifice of abuses and conventions; it was, in fact, a challenge to a duel, flung at the privileged classes. . . ." Benito Juárez, "Apuntes para mis hijos," in Jorge L. Tamayo, ed., *Benito Juárez,* 1:225.

6. *CLD,* 2:182–84; *Esp.*-BJ, pp. 7–8; Jorge Fernanado Iturribarría, "Los abogados generales del Instituto de Ciencias y Artes" (unpublished essay in the possession of Iturribarría).

7. *Alcance al Número 32 de El Constituyente,* Aug. 15, 1856, is devoted to reprinting the *reglamento.*

8. *Dem.,* 1:2:2, Oct. 5, 1856.

9. Circular of Lafragua to state governors, dated Aug. 19, 1856, in *LM,* 8:246–47. For action to be taken against the priests, see José María Lafragua to Juárez, dated Mexico City, Sept. 6, 1856, in Tamayo, ed., *Benito Juárez,* 2:209–10.

10. *Dem.,* 1:2:3–4, Oct. 5, 1856.

11. Antonia Martínez Báez, ed., *Representaciones sobre la tolerancia religiosa,* pp. 40–41, reprints the letter. In the summer of 1856, Domínguez was in his sixtieth year and approaching the third anniversary of his installation as diocesan bishop. Born on the Hacienda of Prío in the parish of Zaachila, not far from Oaxaca City, Domínguez had spent his entire life in his native state and since his youth had served the church. Educated in the seminary in

Oaxaca City, he became a professor in that institution and later vice-rector; then he served as a parish priest in nearby Tlacolula, a Zapotec Indian town, and at Nochixtlán in the Mixteca Alta. He received appointment as a canon of the cathedral and gradually moved upward to become dean of the chapter. When his predecessor, Bishop Mantecón, died, the cathedral canons elected him vicar capitular, then nominated him as bishop, in which post he was confirmed by Rome in April 1854. His portrait in the chapter room of the cathedral shows him tall and thin with a long, solemn face and hard eyes that stare back at the intruder. Eutimio Pérez, *Recuerdos históricos del episcopado oaxaqueño*, pp. 113–20; Emetrio Valverde Téllez, *Bio-bibliografía eclesiástica mexicana (1821–1943)*, 1:283–85; Eulogio G. Gillow, *Apuntes históricos*, pp. 117–18. Jorge Fernando Iturribarría, *Porfirio Díaz ante la historia*, p. 1, makes Domínguez the uncle of Porfirio Díaz. They were, in fact, distant cousins.

12. On Mar. 22, 1857, the national charter was proclaimed in Oaxaca City and the oath to uphold it, required by the government of all public officials, was taken the following day. The oath-taking ceremony was held in the Marquesado on Mar. 27, and in the surrounding towns and the rest of the state on the 30th. Decree of Juárez, dated Mar. 21, 1857, setting forth the plans for the celebration and the schedule of events of the ceremonies, in *Dem.*, 1:50:3, Mar. 22, 1857; and Félix Romero's description of the events in ibid., 52:3–4, Mar. 29, 1857.

13. For the resignations, removals, and replacements of officials, see *Dem.*, 1:50:3–4, Mar. 22, 1857; 1:53, Apr. 2, 1857; and 1:55:1, Apr. 2, 1857. Brokers were involved in many types of business transactions, such as banking, dealings in stocks and bonds, and buying and selling foodstuffs and real estate. Their profession was so highly regulated by legal statutes that they might be considered quasi–public officials. See Jan Bazant, *Alienation of Church Wealth in Mexico*, pp. 87–88.

14. See the article entitled "¡¡¡Mentis!!!" in *Dem.*, 1:65, May 14, 1857, which refutes an article written by a "cura oaxaqueño" in the *Diario de Avisos*, num. 155, and contains copies of the letters that passed between Juárez and Domínguez. This Te Deum controversy is reported in detail, for it has been misstated by many historians who point to the fact that the ceremony was held as an indication of the enthusiastic reception of the Constitution of 1857 in Oaxaca by the local clergy and hierarchy. See, for example, John Lloyd Mecham, *Church and State in Latin America*, p. 365; Alfonso Toro, *La iglesia y el estado en México*, p. 260; Helen Phipps, *Some Aspects of the Agrarian Question in Mexico*, p. 83 fn. 28; and Robert Knowlton, "The Disamortization and Nationalization of Ecclesiastical Property in Mexico, 1856–1910" (Ph.D. diss., State University of Iowa, 1963), p. 87. Knowlton later corrected this in his "La iglesia mexicana y la Reforma," *HM* 18 (Abril-Junio 1969):522–25. Charles Allen Smart, *Viva Juarez!*, p. 146, gives an interesting but inaccurate twist by stating that the cathedral chapter, which opposed the bishop and the constitution, was absent at the time of the promulgation of the constitution and therefore Domínguez, whom he characterizes as "conciliatory," allowed the Te Deum to be sung.

15. *Libro de Cordilleras* (typescript selections made by Lic. Luis Castañeda Guzmán in 1959 and located in CCG). The *Libro de Cordilleras* was kept in each

parish church; in it were recorded all circulars sent out by the bishop before being passed on to the next church for recording. Thus each parish would have a complete file of such communications and would be fully informed, though sometimes very late, of all dispositions emanating from the chancery office. A copy of this same circular is also in MG-HO, 1857. Knowlton, "La iglesia mexicana y la Reforma." pp. 521–22, reports on the other dioceses.

16. Ignacio de la Llave to state governors, Apr. 1, 1857, in Tamayo, ed., *Benito Juárez*, 2:242–43.

17. MG-HO, 1857, for Prieto; *Dem.*, 1:55:8, Apr. 9, 1857, for Anaya.

18. AEO, Ramo de Asuntos Varios, Carpeta negra, 1857, registro 3823: "Averiguación de las palabras subversivas dichas en el 'Encuentro' de Xochimilco por un fraile franciscano." The words attributed to Ruiz are contained in the investigation report. Also see registro 3819: "Parra, Francisco.—Expediente instruido contra las palabras subversivas que profinó dicho S. Cura en el sermón que predicó en el atrio de la Trinidad."

19. *LM*, 8:431–32.

20. Circular of Apr. 24, 1857, *Libro de Cordilleras*.

21. Carriedo was a prominent Conservative, although he held many interests in common with the Liberals, such as reform, statistics, progress, which led him to write the informative *Estudios históricos y estadísticos del estado libre de Oaxaca* and the *Ensayo histórico-estadístico del departamento de Oaxaca . . . Año de 1843*. For the dispute over his newspaper, see *Dem.*, 1:75:2–3, June 7, 1857; and 93:3–4, July 19, 1857.

22. It was Miguel Castro to whom Juárez entrusted his illegitimate daughter, Susana, to raise when the governor left Oaxaca to enter Comonfort's cabinet late in 1857. Marcos Pérez was the mentor of the young Porfirio Díaz and had been responsible for bringing him into the ranks of the Liberal party.

23. Biographical material on these men is widely dispersed, and, as in the case of biographies of most Mexicans, it is a matter of picking up a piece of information here and there. To cite all the sources from which such bits were gathered to make the above comments would require too much space. The reader is referred particularly to Andrés Portillo, *Oaxaca en el centenario de la independencia nacional*, passim; *Diccionario Porrúa de historia, biografía y geografía de México;* Manuel Martínez Gracida et al., "Biografías de oaxaqueños distinguidos y de escritores y personajes relacionados con la cultura e historia de Oaxaca," passim; and Jorge Fernando Iturribarría, *La generación oaxaqueña del 57*, passim.

24. *Dem.*, 1:88:1–2, 3, 4, July 7, 1857; 93:2, July 19, 1857.

25. Ibid., *Alcance al núm. 85*, June 30, 1857; and 87:4, July 5, 1857.

26. Juárez received over 98,000 votes, while a host of other candidates received 12,000-odd votes combined. Statewide, Cenobio Márquez was Juárez's closest opponent; at that, the Conservative drew only 2,968 votes. The reports of the balloting in the Central Department are in *Dem.*, 1:89:1, July 9, 1857; the statewide totals are in ibid., 91:1-2, July 14, 1857; and for a report on the voting in general, see ibid., 70:1, May 26, 1857.

27. Angel Taracena, ed., "Don Benito Juárez y los Tedeums oficiales, 1857," *Boletin del Archivo General de la Nación* 9 (Octubre-Diciembre

1938):782–86, reprints copies of the correspondence that passed between the governor and the bishop.

28. Juárez, "Apuntes," in Tamayo, ed., *Benito Juárez*, 1:259–69.

29. A handful of priests in Oaxaca renounced their vows in mid-1857: Cortés was the first, followed by Carvajal in July, who was in turn followed by the presbyters Francisco Gracida and Manuel Eligio Vigil and the deacon Manuel Mendoza. The most important was Carvajal, a friend of Juárez, whom the governor appointed to the second position in his secretariat. Ordained in 1840, he had a reputation for being a brilliant orator. He was also known for his Liberal sentiments. Because of these he had been exiled by Santa Anna and had never been popular with his superiors in the Oaxaca hierarchy, who had assigned him to a parish in the isolated coastal region of the diocese. He held a captain's commission in the National Guard and had served one term in the national congress and two terms in the state legislature. Martínez Gracida et al., "Biografías de oaxaqueños distinguidos," 1:136–50; *Dem.*, 1:95:4, July 23, 1857, announces Carvajal's appointment by Juárez; MG-HO, 1857.

30. These political chiefs were required to reside in their districts, to make a complete tour of their areas at least once a year, and to remain at their posts unless the governor gave them permission to leave. They were appointed for two years and could be reappointed at the governor's discretion. Neither the legislative nor the judicial branch had any effective check on them, and it is readily seen that they could easily become henchmen for a dishonest governor, to whom they owed allegiance and their jobs. The state constitution is found in *CLD*, 2:307–29.

31. Ibid.

32. There is disagreement about certain points. Jorge Fernando Iturribarría, *José María Díaz Ordaz*, p. 14, maintains he was born in 1814 or 1815 and that his family owned Rosario Hacienda. Circumstantial evidence suggests a later birthdate and there is mention of his purchase of the hacienda in the disentailment records of 1856.

33. *Dem.*, 2:52:2–3, Dec. 3, 1857, reports the incident.

34. *CLD*, 2:387–88, for the decree; *Boletín Oficial*, Núm. 2, Dec. 15, 1857, for the bishop's message. This newspaper replaced the official gazette, *La Democracia*, in the period from Dec. 12, 1857 to Feb. 26, 1858, during and immediately following the Cobos siege.

35. Gustavo Pérez Jiménez, *Las constituciones del estado de Oaxaca*, p. 139–40.

36. *Boletín Oficial*, Núm. 1, Dec. 12, 1857.

37. *APD*, 1:123.

38. Ms. memoirs of Ignacio Mejía, as quoted in Jorge Fernando Iturribarría, *Oaxaca en la historia*, p. 193. Among those fleeing with the generals was a young lieutenant-colonel, Manuel González, who later changed sides to support the Liberals. He would become president of Mexico in 1880. The above account of the siege and the repulse on Jan. 16, 1858, follows closely that of MG-HO, 1857 and 1858. Martínez had access to the ms. diaries of Ignacio Mejía and Tiburcio Montiel, both of whom were participants and who recorded their eyewitness accounts. These mss. are either in private hands or

lost. Colonel Manuel Balbontín, *Memorias,* pp. 249–50, gives a slightly different account, emphasizing the poor state of Cobos's forces, ill-equipped and without enough ammunition. Balbontín participated in a later siege of Oaxaca City, that of Feb.-May 1860, and talked with many men who fought in the battle of Jan. 16, 1858. Francisco Salazar, "Compendio de la historia de Oaxaca. Cuarta parte: Vida independiente de Oaxaca" (typescript copy in CCG), holds that several officers, including Captain Porfirio Díaz, opposed the retreat in the council of war and names Ignacio Mejía as the leader of this group.

CHAPTER 3

1. MG-HO, 1859, "19. Prisioneros políticos," and "31. Brigada de Oaxaca al servicio del Sr. Juárez"; also "Apéndice letra (e): Diario llevado por un prisionero en su prisión en esta capital, con continuación de lo sufrido por otro en las galeras de Veracruz," in *La democracia en Oaxaca.* This last is a pamphlet written by an anonymous Conservative who interprets the course of affairs in Oaxaca from a viewpoint different from that generally available to the historian.

2. For the effects of the first siege on Oaxaca City and the surrounding area, see *Boletín Oficial,* Núms. 8, 14, and 18, Jan. 22 and Feb. 7 and 18, 1858; *Dem.,* 2:55:3–4, Feb. 28, 1858; and MG-HO, 1858, "11. Hechos de la Reacción."

3. The Central District was the smallest in area but had the largest population. "Decreto. División permanente política y judicial del territorio del Estado de Oaxaca," dated Mar. 23, 1858, in *CLD,* 2:399–441.

4. MG-HO, 1858, "31. Brigada de Oaxaca al servicio del Sr. Juárez."

5. On the tax structure of Oaxaca in this period, see *Catecismo político dedicado a la instrucción primaria de la juventud oaxaqueña,* pp. 35–36; *Mem.-JMDO,* p. 35 and document no. 28. For the *tres al millar* legislation, see decrees of Oct. 3 and 7, 1850, *CLD,* 1:701–7.

6. Decrees of Apr. 21 and May 11, 1858, *CLD,* 2:443–48 and 499 respectively.

7. AMO, Libro de Tesorería Municipal, 1854 a 1859, Tomo 7, unnumbered *hojas.*

8. *Dem.,* 3:32:4, Aug. 26, 1858.

9. The decree calling for the gubernatorial election is dated Apr. 1, 1858, *CLD,* 2:442. MG-HO, 1858, "38. Convocatoria para elección de Gobernador," gives the votes.

10. MG-HO, 1858, "39. Convocatoria para elecciones de Diputados al Congreso del Estado." The seven borlados elected were Joaquín Septién, Esteban Maqueo, Cristóbal Salinas, José I. Carrasquedo, Agustín Castañeda, Juan de Mata Vázquez, and Antonio Mimiaga. The two *puros* were Ignacio Mejía and Luis Maria Carbó. The five uncommitted Liberals were Miguel Castro, who represented the Central District, Manuel Canseco, Nicolás Rojas, José Irribarren, and José Antonio Gamboa. The last two probably sympathized more with the rojos than with the borlados.

11. Jorge Fernando Iturribarría, "El Partido 'Borlado,' " *HM* 3(Abril-

Junio 1954):473. Jesús Reyes Heroles, *El liberalismo mexicano*, 2:419–54, compares the moderate and radical Liberals. Rafael de Zayas Enríquez, *Benito Juárez*, pp. 60–61, 156, speaks harshly of the moderates, characterizing them as irresolute and cowardly; not to be trusted because one never knew what they were thinking; the bats of politics, living in church ruins to make the Conservatives think they were fellow rats, flying out at sunset to make the Liberals think they were swallows; taking advantage of victories to which they did not contribute and making themselves the masters of the situation.

12. Various lists of the adherents to the two factions exist, some more extensive than others, with some contradictions, which might indicate a frequent crossing of party lines depending on the issues of the moment. See Iturribarría, "El Partido 'Borlado,' " passim; MG-HO, 1860, "División del partido liberal oaxaqueño;" Manuel Martínez Gracida, *Efemérides oaxaqueñas, 1853–1892*, 1:87–88; Manuel Martínez Gracida et al., "Biografías de oaxaqueños distinguidos y de escritores y personajes relacionados con la cultura e historia de Oaxaca," 2:504 (reverse)–5; and Francisco Vasconcelos, "Memorias," pp. 22–27.

13. This interpretation is in accord with Andrés Molina Enríquez, *Juárez y la Reforma*, p. 101, which characterizes the moderate faction as the party of businessmen and proprietors, interested in security.

14. *Mem.*-JMDO, passim, elaborates Governor Díaz Ordaz's principles and his program. A similar but fuller statement of Liberal principles is contained in the manifesto "El gobierno constitucional a la Nación," issued at Veracruz on July 7, 1859, and signed by Juárez, Melchor Ocampo, Manuel Ruiz, and Miguel Lerdo de Tejada, the last of whom may have been its author. Melchor Ocampo, *Obras completas*, 2:113–42.

15. MG-HO, 1858, "54. Sale a la campaña el Gobernador Díaz Ordaz"; and 1859, "Depone el Gobierno del mando de la Brigada al Sr. Díaz Ordaz." An account of these developments may be found in Jorge Fernando Iturribarría, *Historia de Oaxaca*, 2:175–78.

16. *LM*, 8:680–83.

17. Ibid., 683–88.

18. Eulogio Gillow, *Apuntes históricos*, "Apéndice," p. 118. So inflamed were the times that all kinds of rumors concerning Domínguez's death circulated and gained credence. Alexis de Gabriac, the French chargé in Mexico City, in late August wrote a dispatch to his foreign minister in which he reported that the bishop, "dignified, old, forced to flee, died on the road." Lilia Díaz López, ed., *Versión francesa de México*, 2:105.

19. An anonymous Conservative claimed that the bishop abandoned the clergy through his timidity and left them divided and without guidance, ill-prepared and leaderless for battle. "Few were the ones who out of persuasion and zeal fulfilled the duties of their holy ministry in those critical circumstances; many, more careful of their own interests rather than their obligations, declared themselves peaceful spectators of the events." *La Democracia en Oaxaca*, pp. 19–20. For the bishop's attempt to reform the clergy, see José Agustín Domínguez, *Edicto pastoral que el Escmo. e Illmo. Sr. Dr. D. José Agustín Domínguez, dignísimo obispo de Oaxaca, dirige a todo el clero de la diócesis a 11 de Diciembre de 1854*, passim.

20. *Dem.*, 4:75:4, July 26, 1859.

21. Márquez to Dean and chapter of cathedral, Aug. 4, 1859, and circular of Aug. 2, 1859, *Libro de Cordilleras*. The date of this circular in the *Cordilleras* book is given as Aug. 2; it is probably an error made by the priest copying it before sending it on to the next church. The same circular is given in MG-HO, 1859, "Destierros de encumbrados sacerdotes," ·with the date of Aug. 5, and is also referred to in Martínez Gracida et al., "Biografías de oaxaqueños distinguidos," 1:224–30, as bearing the date of Aug. 5.

22. Vicente Fermín Márquez Goyeneche y Carrizosa (1811-1887) would become Bishop of Oaxaca in 1868 and serve there until his death. He attended the Vatican Council in 1870. Emetrio Valverde Téllez, *Bio-bibliografía eclesiástica mexicana (1821–1943),* 2:68–71, and V[icente] de P[aula] A[ndrade], *Apéndices a la obra Noticias de México de D. Francisco Sedano,* pp. 295–98.

23. Alvarez y Castillejos (1818–59), prothonotary apostolic by grace of Pope Gregory XVI and domestic prelate by appointment of Pius IX, held a doctorate in theology and had taught for many years both in the Oaxaca seminary and in the Institute of Sciences and Arts. Antonio Gay, *Necrolojía del Ilustrísimo Señor . . . Vicario Capitular del Obispado de Oaxaca Doctor D. José María Alvarez y Castillejos,* passim; Martínez Gracida et al., "Biografías de oaxaqueños distinguidos," 1:9–13; Andrade, *Apéndices,* 263–65. For early education, see "Libro en que constan los sugetos qe. visten beca desde 18 de octubre de 1803 en el Rl. y Pontifico Seminario de Oaxaca . . ." (typescript copy in CCG).

24. MG-HO, 1859, "Leyes del Registro Civil." There seems to be some disagreement as to the date of the suppression, which may have taken place sometime immediately prior to Aug. 10. See the circular of Alvarez y Castillejos in the *Libro de Cordilleras,* dated Aug. 10, 1859. Governor Díaz Ordaz, in his annual message to the state legislature in September 1858, reported that there were only twenty-three regular clergy in the entire state. *Mem.*-JMDO, pp. 32–33. Also see Andrés Portillo, *Oaxaca en el centenario de la independencia nacional,* p. 106. Maldonado first asked for his money in late July 1859, immediately after the promulgation of the Law of July 12. In November 1860, he was still trying to collect, an indication of the poor state of records and the bankruptcy of the government treasury. AEO, Ramo de Asuntos Varios, Carpeta negra, 1860, registro 3889: "Maldonado, Margarito.—Presbítero, solicita se le den $500.00 por haber acatado a tiempo la ley del 12 de Julio de 1859 sobre exclaustración." Juan Riveras, guardian of the monastery of San Francisco, to General José María Cobos, Tehuacán, Aug. 1, 1859, in MG-HO, 1859, "Leyes de Reforma," reports on the reaction of the people and the one Franciscan who remained in the monastery.

25. Martínez Gracida et al., "Biografías de oaxaqueños distinguidos," 2:487 ff.

26. Circular of Aug. 10, 1859, issued by Vicar Alvarez y Castillejos, *Libro de Cordilleras.*

27. See, for example, AEO, Ramo de Asuntos Varios, Carpeta negra, 1860, registro 3893: "Varela, José A.—Juicio promovido por dicho presbítero contra D. Jacinto Castro sobre goce de un beneficio eclesiástico." This relates how Varela, a Dominican, was assigned upon the suppression of the

monasteries as the curate of Ocotlán with the enjoyment of all the corresponding emoluments. He remained there for three months and then returned to the reopened monastery, which had been returned to the order by Cobos in his second occupation of Oaxaca (see below). When Cobos was driven out in August 1860, the monasteries were once again closed and Varela returned to Ocotlán. Another secular priest, Padre Castellanos, had appeared with a letter from the parish priest, Padre Castro, who was away for reasons of health and in whose absence Varela was serving; the letter charged Castellanos with appointment as parish priest during the remainder of Castro's absence, and Varela was thus left out in the cold.

28. Circular of Ocampo to governor of Oaxaca, Aug. 22, 1859, *LM*, 8:712. On the valuations, see, for example, the ms. "Valuo del Monasterio de Santa Catalina" (dated May 25, 1859, the valuation made by J. M. Escandón), in La Iglesia en México. Conventos, hospitales, iglesias, etc., 1580–1869, The Nettie Lee Benson Latin American Collection, The University of Texas at Austin.

29. *Dem.* 4:79:1, Aug. 4, 1859, for editorial comment; *LM*, 8:691–95, for the text of the law.

30. *LM*, 8:696–702. Carlos Pereyra, *Historia del pueblo mejicano*, 2:137, comments on this law.

31. *LM*, 8:702–5.

32. Ibid., 710, 716–17.

33. *CLD*, 2:572–75. This tax was decreed on July 18. Five days earlier, a forced loan of 100,000 pesos, levied statewide, was decreed (ibid., 578–80), but probably with word reaching the state of the impending passage of the Law of Nationalization of Church Property and in consideration of the money that would accrue to the state as a result of the property sales, the governor decided to annul the large loan and replace it by the contribution in the form of a property tax. Many complaints were received from residents in Oaxaca City. The Spanish vice-consul in the state capital, Agustín Aguirre, appealed to the governor on July 24 in behalf of the Spaniards residing there but to no avail. See the reply, Ramón Cajiga to Aguirre, ibid., 562–65, dated July 25, 1859.

34. MG-HO, 1859, "La Brigada de Oaxaca en campaña," and "Causas que motivaron la Derrota de la Brigada de Oaxaca."

35. For Castro's actions, see proclamation and decree both dated Nov. 2, 1859, in *CLD*, 2:575–77. On November 4, Josefa Bustamante, who rented the market from the ayuntamiento and in turn sublet stalls to the vendors and merchants, wrote the city council that with the announcement of the state of siege, the rent from the market had diminished daily and would continue to decline as long as the disturbances continued. AMO, Libro de Tesorería Municipal, 1854 a 1859, Tomo 7, unnumbered *hoja*. See Vasconcelos, "Memorias," p. 6, for details of the evacuation.

36. The three commissioners were Juan Pablo Franco, who would play a prominent role later; Esteban Esperón, brother of the borlado leader José; and Antonio Díaz. See MG-HO, 1859, "Ocupación de Oaxaca por el Gral. Cobos."

37. See Martínez Gracida, *Efemérides oaxaqueñas*, 1:98–99, for José María

Cobos's entry; and Portillo, *Oaxaca en el centenario,* p. 168, for his residence.

38. Information on Cobos's reception by the churchmen and his relations with them may be found in various communications and circulars from Nicolás Vasconcelos to his priests in the *Libro de Cordilleras* under dates of Nov. 10, 22, 25, and 30, 1859. Marcelino Ruiz Cobos's decree of Nov. 9, 1859, declaring the right of the church to receive back all alienated property is in BUBJO. The Zuloaga laws of Jan. 28, 1858, annulling the Lerdo Law and the law regulating fees charged by priests and the regulatory statute of the former are in Basilio José Arrillaga, *Recopilación de leyes, decretos, bandos, reglamentos, circulares y providencias de los supremos poderes y otras autoridades de la República Mexicana,* 1:25–26, 46–53. Additional information on the matter may be found in MG-HO, 1859, "El Gobierno de Cobos y el Gobierno Eclesiástico."

39. MG-HO, 1859, "Caridad cristiana," and "Préstamo al clero." The terms of this loan are contained in the contract made between Father Manuel Río y Hermosa, acting for the diocese, and F. Robleda, tax collector of the Department of Oaxaca, dated Jan. 9, 1860, in *Vic.,* 1:31:3–4, Dec. 2, 1860. Of the 100,000 pesos the clergy only paid 62,338 pesos, which were never returned. *Vic.,* 1:33:2–3, Dec. 9, 1860.

40. MG-HO, 1859, "Contribución reaccionaria." For forced loans, see ibid., 1860, "Préstamos forzosos." One such loan was for 43,000 pesos, which 56 designated citizens were to pay. See ibid., 1859, "Fusilamientos, prisiones de damas, consignaciones, etc.," for arrests.

41. Francisco Salazar, "Compendio de la historia de Oaxaca. Cuarta parte: Vida independiente de Oaxaca," chap. xl, para. 659.

42. Juárez was in close contact with his countrymen in Ixtlán. The communications link between the Sierra of Oaxaca and Veracruz via Tuxtepec was open despite the Conservatives' siege of the port city. MG-HO, 1859, "Tanteo de los liberales."

43. *Mem.*-RC, document 1, gives the strength of Díaz Ordaz's column. *APD,* 1:98–100, details the difficulties of Díaz and his battle against Ruiz. In his memoirs, Díaz noted, "This was the first defeat that I suffered in my military career, which, of course, mortified me very much" (quote from p. 100). Díaz erroneously gives the date of the battle as Jan. 21—it took place on Jan. 23.

44. For imprisonments and ransom demands, see Martínez Gracida, *Efemérides oaxaqueñas,* 1:111, 118, 147; Salazar, "Compendio. Cuarta parte," chap. xl, para. 659; MG-HO, 1860, "Persecuciones de liberales;" and AN, *Libro de Protocolo* de Ambrosio Ocampo, Tomo 10, 1858–59–60–61. Año de 1860, 13 *vuelta*–15 *vuelta,* which contains eleven "fianzas de cárcel," all dated in the spring of 1860. At least two had to pay bail of 1,000 pesos. For impressments into the army and work gangs and other demands on villagers, see *Vic.,* 1:15:1, Oct. 7, 1860; MG-HO, 1860, "Leva para fortificaciones," "Reemplazos," "Impuesto de fusiles para extraer dinero," and "Saqueos a los propietarios." For the deteriorating relations with the priests, see Martínez Gracida, *Efemérides oaxaqueñas,* 1:113, and MG-HO, 1860, "Nuevo préstamo a propietarios, comerciantes y curas." In February 1860, the priests were forced to pay 21,000 pesos, proportioned among individual clergymen. *Vic.,* 1:4:1,

Aug. 30, 1860, contains a list of priests and the amount each was to pay.

45. Manuel Balbontín, *Memorias,* p. 255. Balbontín was a lieutenant-colonel on Rosas Landa's staff.

46. Ibid., pp. 255 and 259; Salazar, "Compendio. Cuarta parte," chap. x1, para. 663. The number of troops, as of Feb. 7, 1860, was given as 1,406 with 72 horses. *Mem.*-RC, document no. 3. From his arrival in mid-February and into April, Rosas Landa sent Juárez several letters, all carping and complaining. These are reprinted in Jorge L. Tamayo, ed., *Benito Juárez,* 2:610–11 (letter of Feb. 14, 1860); 615–16 (Feb. 21, 1860); 617 (Feb. 25, 1860); 676 (Mar. 29, 1860); 677–78 (Apr. 2, 1860); and 680–81 (Apr. 7, 1860).

47. AEO, Ramo de Asuntos Varios, Carpeta negra, 1860, registro 3880: "El Marquesado.—El Ayuntamiento pide que se separen del Batallón 'Bravos,' los vecinos de aquella Villa." This long and eloquent letter, dated Apr. 10, 1860, and signed by six councilmen of the suburb and addressed to Rosas Landa, gives an excellent description of the plight of the valley towns caught up in the war.

48. For the decision to withdraw, see Rosas Landa to Minister of War, May 12, 1860, *APD,* 1:251. On the assassination attempt, see ibid., 111 and 255. And on Rosas Landa's departure, see his letter to Juárez in Tamayo, ed., *Benito Juárez,* 2:706–7.

49. *APD,* 1:113–18; MG-HO, 1860, "5 de Agosto de 1860." The cousins Cobos were soon afterwards killed. Marcelino was shot by a firing squad at Capulalpan in the autumn of 1861; and José María was executed two years later in Matamoros. Marcelino's head was cut off, taken to Mexico City, and displayed in a basket in the national congress. Agustín Rivera y Sanromán, *Anales mexicanas,* pp. 87, 1159; and José María Vigil, *La Reforma,* p. 484.

50. For the decree of Nov. 8, 1860, separating Pérez from the governorship, see *CLD,* 3:24. For Cajiga's comments on this turn of events, see *Mem.*-RC, p. 12.

51. Decree of Feb. 14, 1861, *CLD,* 3:146–47.

52. Hernández to governor of state [Marcos Pérez], Oct. 25, 1860, in MG-HO, 1860, "El Cabildo Eclesiástico nombra Vicario Capitular al cura D. Rafael Hernández;" and circular of Oct. 26, 1860, *Libro de Cordilleras.* Hernández was made a subdeacon in 1838 at age 21, and a year and a half later was ordained a priest. He taught philosphy in the seminary for many years. See the "Libro en que constan los sugetos qe. visten beca." *Vic.,* 1:21:1, Oct. 28, 1860, comments on the prospects of church-state relations.

53. Circulars of Dec. 5, Nov. 6, 1860; June 7, Sept. 10 and 14, 1861, *Libro de Cordilleras.*

54. The law of religious toleration was promulgated in Oaxaca on Jan. 4, 1861. *Vic.,* 1:42:1, Jan. 10, 1861. Order of Jan. 17, 1861, exiling the bishops, signed by José de Emparán, minister of gobernación, *LM,* 9:12. *LM,* 9:32, ordering the reduction of the nunneries.

55. Circular of Nov. 21, 1861, *Libro de Cordilleras.*

56. Salinas showed little inclination for politics. Although elected a delegate to the national congress in 1847, he renounced the honor and refused to attend. When Bishop Mantecón of Oaxaca died in 1852, the new bishop, Domínguez, made Salinas vicar general until he could take charge of the

diocese. Salinas would in time become bishop of Durango, where he was destined to serve for a quarter of a century until his death in 1894. Valverde Téllez, *Bio-bibliografía eclesiástica,* 2:291–95. Vicente de Paula Andrade, *Noticias biográficas sobre los ilustrísimos prelados de Sonora, de Sinaloa y de Durango,* pp. 300–301.

57. Circular of July 3, 1861, *Libro de Cordilleras,* announces the arrival of the holy oils. Ibid., circular of Dec. 5, 1860, concerns the seminary. Ibid., circular of Jan. 5, 1862, concerns the conciliar pensions. *Vic.,* 3:75:4, Apr. 5, 1863, reports on Easter week. Throughout the republic, churches took on a desolate and abandoned appearance in this period. One contemporary author wrote of the darkness of the edifices, the sighing of the wind through the empty interiors, and the broken windows. Manuel Ramírez Aparicio, *Los conventos suprimidos en México* (published in 1862), quoted in Francisco Santiago Cruz, *La piqueta de la Reforma,* p. 19.

58. Salazar, "Compendio. Cuarta parte," chap. xl, para. 670, and *Vic.,* 2:62, Mar. 7, 1862, concerning the transfer of the sisters. *Vic.,* 2:65:4, Mar. 16, 1862, on the discovery of the guns.

59. *Vic.,* 2:62:4, Mar. 7, 1862. See the annexes 1–7 of the letter from Juan María Maldonado to Félix Díaz, ibid., 6:33, Apr. 24, 1867 and Apr. 25, 1867; and Fuente to Cajiga, Nov. 22, 1862, in *LM,* 9:553. Also see discussion of how this matter was covered up by the borlados in chap. 5 below.

60. Martínez Gracida, *Efemérides oaxaqueñas,* 1:252; *Mem.-RC,* pp. 69–70; and *Vic.,* 2:58:2, Feb. 20, 1862, give information on these properties. For the methods by which the conventual establishments were disposed of in central Mexico, see Jan Bazant, *Alienation of Church Wealth in Mexico,* passim.

61. For proclamation, see *CLD,* 3:282–86; for measures taken by Cajiga, see his decree of Dec. 18, 1861, ibid., 286–88.

62. Manuel Santibáñez, *Reseña histórica del cuerpo de ejército de Oriente,* 1:46–52.

63. *Vic., Alcance al núm. 63,* Mar. 9, 1863, for the special edition; and ibid., 2:68:2, Mar. 27, 1862, on the committee of charity.

64. Ibid., 3:43:4, Dec. 14, 1862; and 44:2, Dec. 18, 1862.

65. Ibid., 48:4, Jan. 1, 1863; 50:1, Jan. 8, 1863; 52:4, Jan. 15, 1863. This spurt of cultural activity in Oaxaca City continued intermittently throughout the remainder of the period of the Reform until 1868, with the appearance of magicians, at least two traveling companies of actors, and concerts.

66. *APD,* 2:41–45. The Army of the East consisted of men from San Luis Potosí, Sinaloa, and central Mexico as well as from Oaxaca.

67. Adrián Valadés, "La marcha de Díaz hacia Oaxaca durante la Intervención," *HM* 7(Julio-Septiembre 1957): 97–102. Valadés participated in this march.

68. *APD,* 2:46, 243–44, concerning Cajiga's lukewarm support of the war effort. Lázaro Pavía, *Apuntes biográficos de los miembros más distinguidos del poder judicial de la República Mexicana,* 1:23–25, on Romero's mission. Santibáñez, *Reseña histórica,* 2:139, comments on the need to force aid from Cajiga.

69. Martínez Gracida, *Efemérides oaxaqueñas,* 1:241–42, mentions the Cajiga-Esperón meeting. For the exchange of notes and the resignations, see *APD,* 2:44–45, and Salazar, "Compendio. Cuarta parte," chap. xl, para. 672.

CLD, 4:3, 57–58, concerns Díaz's administrative and military responsibilites and the appointment of General Ballesteros.

70. For the numerous measures taken by Díaz, see the various decrees and orders issued by him and Ballesteros in *CLD,* 4:3–158; for the exiling of citizens, one of whom was Manuel Dublán, see *APD,* 2:57; and AN, *Libro de Protocolo* de Felipe Sandoval, 1864, Tomo 11, *hoja* 264, for the exile of the priest Ortigosa; for recruiting see *APD,* 2:46.

CHAPTER 4

1. Justo Sierra, *Political Evolution of the Mexican People,* pp. 325, 327.

2. *APD,* 2:46, Minute de Dépêche, Bazaine to Ministre de la guerre, Huajuapan, Jan. 9, 1865, in BA, 11, fol. 2102. Support for the Empire in the Mixteca Alta can be accounted for not only by the Indians' hatred of Díaz and his highhanded treatment but also by their traditional orientation toward conservative Puebla, which made liberalism unpopular and weak in the area. Sherburne F. Cook and Woodrow Borah, *The Population of the Mixteca Alta, 1520–1960,* p. 49, and William Taylor, "Town and Country in the Valley of Oaxaca, 1750–1812," p. 74, in Ida Altman and James Lockhart, eds., *Provinces of Early Mexico.* Jean Meyer, *Problemas campesinos y revueltas agrarias, 1821–1910,* pp. 8, 17–18, and T. G. Powell, *El liberalismo y el campesinado en el centro de México (1850 a 1876),* pp. 101 ff., show that there was widespread support for Maximilian among the Indians throughout Mexico, partly because of the alienation of Indian lands sponsored by the Liberals. Carleton Beals, *Porfirio Díaz,* p. 124, concocts a picture of Mixtec support for the Liberals and harassment of the advancing French. "A French soldier dared not stick his nose out alone. Villages refusing to recognize the benign Emperor were razed to the ground; with each razing, a hundred men sprang to arms." This is a figment of Beal's imagination!

3. Gustave Niox, *Expédition du Mexique, 1861–1867,* pp. 439–50.

4. Genaro García, ed., *Documentos inéditos o muy raros para la historia de México,* 24: *La intervención francesa en México según el archivo del Mariscal Bazaine, 7a parte,* document no. xxv, 115.

5. "Proyecto sumario de ataque a la ciudad de Oaxaca," dated Jan. 11, 1865, made by Lieutenant-colonel Brissonet, in BA, 11, foll. 2104-2109.

6. "Rapport," dated San Felipe del Agua, Jan. 22, 1865, by Colonna D'Ornano, commander of the 2nd African Battalion, in Intervención francesa: Documentos misceláneos, 1862–1867, The Nettie Lee Benson Latin American Collection, The University of Texas at Austin.

7. Adrián Valadés, "La marcha de Díaz hacia Oaxaca durante la Intervención," *HM* 7(Julio-Septiembre 1957):112, comments on the desertions. *APD,* 2:65–69; and Beals, *Porfirio Díaz,* p. 125, discuss the Treviño desertion.

8. Ramón Fernández del Campo, "Sitio de Oaxaca por el ejército francés (1865–1865)," ms. diary in BUBJO; José María Vigil, *La Reforma,* p. 697; Beals, *Porfirio Díaz,* p. 125; Manuel Gamboa, in a long report from Oaxaca to Emperor Maximilian, undated but probably written soon after the surrender of Oaxaca to the French, contained in Jorge L. Tamayo, ed., *Benito Juárez,* 9:694–702; and Brissonet in his reconnaissance report of Jan. 11, 1865

(see fn. 5 above), all comment on the anger of the Oaxacans towards General Díaz or the destruction of property outside the quadrilateral. In addition, Gamboa comments several times on the insignificant number of Conservatives in Oaxaca City (pp. 695, 699, 701).

9. Fernández del Campo, "Sitio de Oaxaca," pp. 21–24; *APD*, 2:73.

10. *APD*, 2:76–78, contains a detailed account of the night's activities and the negotiations with Bazaine.

11. Manuel Santibáñez, *Reseña histórica del cuerpo de ejército de Oriente*, 2:243–44 (quote from p. 243); and *APD*, 2:79–80.

12. "Minuta de comunicación, Núm. 2," Maximilian to Bazaine, Chapultepec, Feb. 14, 1865, BA, 11, fol. 2175.

13. Maximilian to Napoleon III, May 26, 1865, as quoted in Egon C. Corti, *Maximilian and Charlotte of Mexico*, 2:503.

14. Ibid., 488.

15. Franco played an important role during the Intervention and deserves more attention than he has received. Information on him is very scattered and the above material upon his career before 1864 has been drawn from various sources. Manuel Martínez Gracida et al., "Biografías de oaxaqueños distinguidos y de escritores y personajes relacionados con la cultura e historia de Oaxaca," 1:245–47, gives the fullest sketch, but has inaccuracies. There is a long letter from Franco to the ayuntamiento of Oaxaca City, dated Aug. 4, 1858, protesting the amount of taxes levied against him, which gives much biographical information, in AMO, Tesorería Municipal, 1854 a 1859, Tomo 7, unnumbered *hoja*. Also see José Sebastián Segura, ed., *BLIM*, 2: "Apéndice," 329–30, for the greeting to Maximilian by the Oaxacans dated June 16, 1864; and *Vic.*, 1:50:1, Feb. 7, 1861, and 5:43:1–2, Sept. 20, 1864.

16. AMO, Borrador de Actas del año de 1865, session of Feb. 21, 1865.

17. *DI*, 1:56:226, Mar. 9, 1865, and a printed announcement, dated Mar. 28, 1865, Oaxaca, issued by Noriega, Secretario General del Despacho, in BUBJO, contain information on the sums allotted. Letter from Noriega to Fagoaga, Mar. 31, 1865, in AMO, Libro de Tesorería Municipal, 1859 a 1867, Tomo 8, unnumbered *hoja;* and records of ayuntamiento sessions of Apr. 3 and 25, 1865, in AMO, Borrador de Actas, 1865, contain information on reconstruction. Fagoaga to Ayuntamiento, Mar. 24, 1865, in AMO, Tesorería municipal, 1859 a 1867, Tomo 8, unnumbered *hoja;* Franco to Ministro de Guerra, Mar. 25, 1865, in *DI*, 1:76:303, Apr. 1, 1865, provide information on the distribution of food. D'Ornano, "Rapport" of Jan. 22, 1865, in Intervención francesa: Documentos misceláneos, 1862–1867; Bazaine to General Comandante de la Artillería del Ejército, Oaxaca, Feb. 11, 1865, BA, 11, fol. 2169; General Mangin to Bazaine, Oaxaca, Mar. 2, 1865, BA, 11, foll. 2197–98, concern, among other things, the return of the bells.

18. Marshal Bazaine's secretary to Colonel Flon, Montoya, Feb. 3, 1865, BA, 11, fol. 2144, concerns the fines against the villages. Order, "Excepción del derecho de capitación," dated Hacienda Blanca, Jan. 23, 1865, BA, 11, fol. 2133; and Bazaine to Franco, Hacienda Blanca, Jan. 23, 1865, BA, 11, fol. 2137. Bazaine to Cacho, Oaxaca, Feb. 14, 1865, BA, 11, fol. 2173.

19. Alfred Hannah and Kathryn Hannah, *Napoleon III and Mexico*, pp.

134–35, point out that in the national imperial administration Maximilian had little success in attracting Liberals to hold positions in his government, but that in the provincial administrations "hundreds of men, presumably Juaristas at heart, manned the lesser jobs of the imperial government because a job was a job." Carlos Pereyra, *Historia del pueblo mejicano*, 2:185, points out that "those Liberals without faith" who accepted the Empire "consoled themselves thinking that the death of the Republic did not imply the destruction *of the liberal reformist work of the Republic*" (italics his).

20. Mangin to Bazaine, Oaxaca, Mar. 2, 1865, BA, 11, foll. 2197–98. Signers with their official positions are given in the printed letter from leading citizens of Oaxaca to Maximilian, dated Apr. 18, 1865, thanking the emperor for his generosity, which serves as an index of the degree to which the state leaders were supporting the Empire. A copy is in BUBJO.

21. D'Ornano to Mangin, Mar. 4, 1865, BA, 12, fol. 2214.

22. Printed decree of Lieutenant-colonel Carteret, Commandante Superior de la Subdivisión de Oaxaca, Oaxaca, Mar. 25, 1865, concerning civilian-military relations, firearms, sale of liquor, etc., in BUBJO; printed decree of Manuel María de Fagoaga, Alcalde Municipal, Oaxaca, May 26, 1865, concerning merchandizing regulations, in BUBJO; Sublieutenant Blanck (?) to Franco, Oaxaca, Mar. 15, 1865, in García, *Documentos inéditos*, 27: *La intervención francesa . . . 8a parte*, document no. xiv, 47–50, concerning spies and vigilance of police; printed *bando* of Fagoaga, Oaxaca, June 9, 1865, concerning the Austro-Mexican police force, in BUBJO.

23. Maximilian's Oct. 3, 1865, court-martial decree was printed and promulgated in Oaxaca on Oct. 12, over the signature of Fagoaga. Copy of the printed decree is in BUBJO. Circular from Secretary of Justice, dated Sept. 9, 1864, in *Leyes, decretos, circulares y providencias de la intervención, el supremo poder ejecutivo provisional, la regencia y el imperio*, 3:112, contains the earlier court-martial measure. "Minute d'ordre, No. 1," Oaxaca, Mar. 1, 1865, BA, 11, fol. 2188, orders the court-martial procedures implemented. Captain Vosseur to Mangin, Oaxaca, Mar. 10, 1865, in García, *Documentos inéditos*, 27: *la intervención francesa . . . 8a parte*, document no. v, 26–30, discusses Castro's execution; and Mangin to Bazaine, Oaxaca, Mar. 24, 1865, BA, 12, fol. 2232, discusses the deserter's sentence. I found mention of only one case in which patriots, the Heras brothers from Cuicatlán, were executed after condemnation by a court-martial, and that took place on Dec. 10, 1865. Manuel Martínez Gracida, *Efemérides oaxaqueñas 1853–1892*, 1:286, 2:60.

24. Luis B. Santaella, *Discurso pronunciado en la noche del día 15 de Setiembre de 1865 en el portal del Palacio de la prefectura Superior del Departamento*, pp. 16–17.

25. AMO, Libro de Tesorería Municipal, 1859 a 1867, Tomo 8, expediente: "Curiosas noticias del año de 1865," gives a list of members of the ayuntamiento for that year and also the committee assignments.

26. Vicente de Paula Andrade, *Datos biográficos de los señores capitulares de la Santa Iglesia Catedral de México*, pp. 59–63.

27. "51. Oajaca le 10 fevrier," and "52. Oajaca 10 fevrier," Tomo 2, Ordres de la Subdivision de Oajaca, 7a, Archivo histórico del Mariscal Bazaine, AGN; and Andrés Portillo, *Oaxaca en el centenario de la independencia*

nacional, p. 168, mention the return of the real estate. See the *Edictos pastorales que los illmos. sres. obispos de Oaxaca, Dr. D. José Agustín Domínguez y Dr. D. José María Covarrubias y Mejía, dirigieron a todo el clero de la diócesis.* Circular of July 3, 1865, *Libro de Cordilleras,* orders the prayers. Circular of Dec. 14, 1865, *Libro de Cordilleras,* concerns support for the seminary.

28. Letter from Covarrubias to the dean and chapter of the Oaxaca cathedral, Apr. 4, 1865. Ms. in BUBJO.

29. Maximilian's decree regarding ecclesiastical property was promulgated on Feb. 26, 1865. For a fuller discussion of this in relation to Oaxaca, see chap. 6 below. Robert Knowlton, *Church Property and the Mexican Reform, 1856–1910,* pp. 149–67, discusses the revision in a national setting. The civil registry law was promulgated on Nov. 1, 1865, and is in *CLDRI,* 6:189–98. The civil registry law decreed that the municipal alcaldes would keep the books and serve as registrars. In Oaxaca, this task fell to Manuel María de Fagoaga. The books of reigstry that he certified and kept during the occupation, oddly enough, do not cite the imperial law but rather state that the books are certified in accordance with the registry law promulgated by the Juárez administration in 1859. That this republican statute was referred to as supreme law of the land by a Mexican official of the Empire suggests how closely the two governments lay in principle. AEO, Ramo de Registro Civil, *Libros de testimonios de las actas de fallecimientos,* 1865, 1866; *Libros de testimonios de las actas de casamientos,* 1865; *Libros de testimonios de las actas de nacimientos,* 1865, 1866. Fagoaga continued certifying the registry books through Jan. 1, 1867, two months after the Intervention ended in Oaxaca. The decree on religious toleration also came on Feb. 26, 1865, the same date as the property decree, and is in *DI,* 1:48:193, Feb. 27, 1865.

30. José María Covarrubias, *Esposición que el illmo. sr. obispo de la diócesis de Oaxaca . . . elevó a S. M. el Emperador de México,* passim. There were several points to which Covarrubias objected. For one, the civil law set the ages of eighteen for boys and fifteen for girls as the earliest years in which marriage could be contracted; canon law allowed boys as young as fourteen and girls of twelve to marry. Second, the civil law did not recognize close degrees of consanguinity as impediments to marriage as did canon law.

31. José María Covarrubias, *Tercera carta pastoral,* passim. On Protestantism in Mexico in this period, see James Helms, "Origins and Growth of Protestantism in Mexico to 1929" (Ph.D. diss., The University of Texas at Austin, 1955), passim; for Protestantism in Oaxaca, see Portillo, *Oaxaca en el centenario,* p. 137; for the cooperative efforts of the Mexican prelates in opposing Maximilian's decree of religious toleration, see Jesús García Gutiérrez, *La iglesia mejicana en el segundo imperio,* pp. 75–82.

32. Decree of Maximilian dated Mar. 3, 1865, in Segura, ed., *BLIM,* 4, núm. 111, 234–53. Ejutla and Teposcolula were separate departments only briefly and were soon reincorporated into the Department of Oaxaca. Edmundo O'Gorman, *Historia de las divisiones territoriales de México,* p. 165 fn. 7, states the reintegration took place in August, 1865, but later cites a law of Sept. 27, 1865, as the basis for the modification (p. 306). There is some indication this change took place even earlier, by June 1865. See, for example, the communication from Siliceo, Minister of Public Instruction, to Franco,

June 12, 1865, in *DI,* 2:152:11, July 4, 1865. In Maximilian's decree setting forth departmental budgets for May-December, 1866, in *DI,* 3:422:516–23, May 28, 1866, Ejutla and Teposcolula are listed as subprefectures of the Department of Oaxaca.

33. See Martínez Gracida et al., "Biografías de oaxaqueños distinguidos," 1:245–47, for the appointment as Imperial Visitor; and Gustavo Pérez Jiménez, *Las constituciones del estado de Oaxaca,* p. 255, for the superior prefects.

34. See *CLDRI,* 4:41–43, for the second military district. Thun was the commander of the 6,000-man Austrian contingent sent to Mexico to support Maximilian. His brother, Count Guido Thun-Hohenstein, was the Austrian ambassador to the Mexican court. Arnold Blumberg, *The Diplomacy of the Mexican Empire, 1863–1867,* pp. 31, 64–65. The suggestion regarding a ninth military district was made probably sometime in May 1866, when Franco dined with Maximilian at Chapultepec Palace. Reasons given for the new division were the overextension of the Puebla District and the elimination of difficulties with the Austrians. At the same interview, Franco expressed his disgust with the situation in Oaxaca and mention was made of his being given the Ministry of Gobernación, an indication of the high regard Maximilian had for him and his importance in the imperial government. The meeting and the conversation are summarized in an unsigned, undated note in BA, 21, fol. 4056.

35. But one French commander in Oaxaca, soon after the fall of the city, reported to Bazaine: "The political Prefect, with whom I have always had excellent relations, is losing a little of that spirit of independence which he manifested at the beginning; he seems to understand that there is a necessity to rely upon us . . . ." "Rapport politique No. 110," Carteret to Marechal Commandant en chef, 1 au 15 Mars 1865, BA, 12, foll. [2222]–23.

36. Aceval to Franco, Yanhuitlán, Aug. 20, 1865, in García, *Documentos inéditos,* 30: *La intervención francesa . . . 9a parte,* document no. lxv, 194–96.

37. Franco to Bazaine, Nacaltepec, Sept. 11, 1865, BA, 14, fol. 2644.

38. José María L. Carrasco to Sr. Secretario General Provincial del Departamento de Oaxaca [Noriega], Sept. 19, 1865, BA, 14, fol. 2682.

39. General Thun to Franco, Puebla, Sept. 17, 1865, in García, *Documentos inéditos,* 33: *La intervención francesa . . . 10a parte,* document no. x, 40–41; Franco to Thun, Oaxaca, Sept. 26 [*sic* for 28], 1865, in ibid., document no. xxiv, 87–95.

40. Franco to Bazaine, Oaxaca, Sept. 28, 1865, BA, 14, fol. 2706.

41. Federico Larrainzar to his uncle Ramón, Oaxaca, Sept. 29, 1865, in García, *Documentos inéditos,* 33: *La intervención francesa . . . 10a parte,* document no. xxxiv, 115–21.

42. Larrainzar to his uncle Ramón, Oaxaca, Sept. 30, 1865, in ibid., document no. xxxvi, 124–26.

43. Franco to Bazaine, Oaxaca, Feb. 17, 1866, enclosing copies of correspondence from Thun to Franco, Zacapoaxtla, Feb. 5, 1866 (Annex N), and Franco to Thun, Oaxaca, Feb. 17, 1862 (Annex Ñ), BA, 18, foll. 3485–89.

44. "Nota 152," signed by Loysel, Feb. 25, 1866, BA, 18, fol. 3541.

45. Franco to Bazaine, Oaxaca, Mar. 26, 1866, BA, 19, foll. 3710–11.

46. Confidential letter, Larrainzar to Bazaine, Mexico City, Apr. 17, 1866, BA, 19, foll. 3797–3800.

47. Secret letter, Larrainzar to Bazaine, Mexico City, Apr. 20, 1866, BA, 20, foll. 3853–54.

48. This note in Bazaine's handwriting appears at the bottom of a communication from Maximilian to Bazaine, Mexico City, June 18, 1866, in which the emperor asks the marshal his opinion on Thun's proposals regarding combating Díaz in Oaxaca. BA, 21, fol. 4185.

49. Franco to Bazaine, Oaxaca, Sept. 27, 1865, AGN, Archivo histórico del Mariscal Bazaine, 3, *hoja* 483. Rafael de Zayas Enríquez, *Benito Juárez,* p. 270, contains details of Díaz's guerrilla activities after his escape.

50. See David L. Miller, "Porfirio Díaz and the Army of the East" (Ph.D. diss., University of Michigan, 1960), p. 130, for the size of Díaz's guerrilla army. Díaz to Romero, Atoyaquillo, Oaxaca, Feb. 2, 1866, and Díaz to Juárez, Atoyaquillo, Feb. 2, 1866, in U.S. Congress, House, *Message of the President of the United States, of March 20, 1866,* Part 1, pp. 462–63. There were many difficulties in communicating with the national government from Díaz's isolated positions. The quickest way to get in touch with Juárez in Paso del Norte was through Romero in Washington, and this took months. On October 13, 1865, for example, Romero wrote to Juárez that Díaz had made his escape. Juárez received his note on December 30. But the president had already heard from a man in Puebla in contact with the imprisoned Díaz that his general was intending to escape. On the assumption that Díaz was successful, Juárez had reinstated him as chief of the Line of the East—this on November 12. The general, however, did not receive word of his new assignment until February 2, 1866. *APD,* 2:107–10.

51. *APD,* 2:81 ff.

52. Ibid., 144–45.

53. See Franco to Bazaine, Tehuantepec, Sept. 8, 1866, BA, 23, foll. 4530–31, acknowledging that he was returning to Oaxaca. The summary of the strength of the 9th Military Division, given by Alejo Barreiro, Gefe de la Dirección, to the Ministro de Guerra, dated Mexico City, October 13, 1866, is in AGN, Archivo histórico del Mariscal Bazaine, 4, *hoja* 924.

54. *APD,* 2:155.

55. Ibid., 139–50 and 153–54.

56. Ibid., 191, details Covarrubias's overtures and Díaz's reply. Circular of Nov. 8, 1866, *Libro de Cordilleras,* for appointment of Márquez.

57. The above account of the developments from the battle of Miahuatlán to the surrender of Oaxaca City follows *APD,* 2:149–70. The terms of surrender are given in ibid., 3:199–200. Santibáñez, *Reseña histórica,* 2:481, 493, 503–8, supplies details concerning the location of the negotiations, the number of military prisoners, and the names of civilian prisoners.

CHAPTER 5

1. Daniel Cosío Villegas, *La república restaurada. La vida política,* vol. 1 of his *Historia moderna de México,* 67–70; Hubert H. Bancroft, *History of Mexico,* 6:350–51.

2. Gabriel Esperón to Matías Romero, Oaxaca, Jan. 27, 1867, in Archivo Histórico de Matías Romero, document 1507. This long letter summarizes the capture of Franco. An account may also be found in *APD*, 2:191–92 and 341–52.

3. Porfirio Díaz to Lieutenant-colonel Guillermo Carbó, Acatlán, Feb. 6, 1867, *APD*, 4:75. *DI*, 2:192:177, Aug. 21, 1865, contains Carbó's appointment as agent in the Oaxaca office of nationalized property. Francisco Vasconcelos, "Memorias," p. 12, mentions Carbó's editorship of the newspaper. *Vic.*, 6:29:3, Apr. 11, 1867, contains a notice of Carbó's capture in Puebla.

4. The 1863 decree is in *LM*, 9:652–54; the 1867 modification is in 10:42–43. The list of the 249 traitors is in *Vic.*, 6:84:2–3, Dec. 6, 1867. There are 250 names, but one man is listed twice. The notice concerning the removal of the punishments for all but two of the men is in *Vic.*, 6:84:3, Dec. 6, 1867.

5. The reason for Cházari's fine is unknown to this writer. He was a member of the town council, but if he held higher positions under the tutelage of the French or in any other way compromised himself, the evidence could not be found. The heavy fine against Sandoval probably was the result of his complicity in the campaign undertaken in September 1865, by Franco to destroy the four villages that had given aid to the Liberals. Sandoval had been sent by the imperial visitor to seek permission from Maximilian to mount the military expedition against the villages. Jorge Fernando Iturribarría, *Historia de Oaxaca*, 3:172.

6. *Vic.*, 6:31:3, Apr. 18, 1867. Names appearing in the newspapers and documents of the following decade would suggest that a sizeable number of former Austrian and French soldiers took up permanent residence in Oaxaca State and became active in business, mining, and agriculture.

7. *CLD*, 4:184.

8. Félix Díaz to Maldonado, Apr. 18, 1867, in *Vic.*, 6:32:2, Apr. 21, 1867.

9. Maldonado to Félix Díaz, Apr. 24, 1867, in ibid., 33:1–2, Apr. 25, 1867.

10. Félix Díaz to José Esperón and Esperón to Díaz, both letters dated May 4, 1867, in ibid., 36:2, May 5, 1867.

11. The two letters, Porfirio Díaz to Maldonado and Maldonado to Díaz, dated Apr. 23 and May 8 respectively, are in ibid., 37:1–2, May 9, 1867. Félix Díaz's official statement is on p. 4. The Apr. 23 letter reveals that Porfirio Díaz had called the closure law to Maldonado's attention about Apr. 8.

12. These laws are also in *LM*, 9:594–95, 598–601.

13. The freedom spoken of in the law rings false, since so many restrictions were placed on the nuns.

14. Decree of Governor Maldonado, dated May 10, 1867, in *Vic.*, 6:38:1, May 12, 1867.

15. *CLD*, 4:202.

16. Throughout Mexico the question of closing the convents was an emotional issue whenever implementation of the 1863 law was undertaken. Mexican males normally were chivalrous towards women of gentility, as the nuns were by their profession of vows. Thus it was natural for male government officials to delay the closings whenever possible. Also it was common for

the removal of the nuns to be carried out after dark, as happened in Mexico City on the night of Feb. 13, 1861. Robert Knowlton, *Church Property and the Mexican Reform,* p. 114. *Vic.,* 6:39:4, May 16, 1867, describes the removal and transfer. As to the number of nuns involved, the sources disagree. Andrés Portillo, *Oaxaca en el centenario de la independencia nacional,* pp. 106–7, gives the number as seventy-six. Francisco Salazar, "Compendio de la historia de Oaxaca. Cuarta parte: Vida independiente de Oaxaca," chap. xlii, para. 695, states, ". . . about one hundred nuns were removed from the convents and divided among various private houses in the city." Manuel Martínez Gracida, "El estado de Oaxaca y su estadística del culto católico," *Boletín de la Sociedad de Geografía y Estadística de la República Mexicana,* 3a. época, 6(1882): 56–66, states that up to 1870, eighty-one nuns had registered in the books of Civil Registry but the numbers he gives for each convent total only seventy-eight, probably the most accurate figure. Of these seventy-eight, there were twelve Augustinian Recollets, five Dominican Sisters, fourteen Conceptionists, seventeen Indian and thirty Spanish Capuchinesses.

17. An example of how closely guarded was their self-imposed isolation is the letter from Sor Ana María de Nuestra Señora Santa Mónica, prioress of Soledad convent, to Bishop Domínguez, undated but from Domínguez's reply probably mid-1857, in which the prioress asks the renewal of the licenses of chaplains and confessors to enter the convent to administer the sacraments, and for permission for the nuns to allow entry to doctors and surgeons for matters the nuns themselves could not handle and for burial of the dead; to the administrator in matters pertaining to the business affairs of the convent; to masons and bricklayers; to charcoal burners and woodsellers; to the boys who cared for the refectory gardens and took out the garbage; to the man who worked in the orchard three days each week; and to the clock repairman whenever he offered to do work. Typescript extract from the Archivo del Santuario de la Soledad in CCG.

18. Eulogio Guillow [*sic*], "Apuntes históricos sobre el Obispado de Antequera y Arzobispado de Oaxaca," pp. 86–87 (typescript copy of extracts from Gillow's unpublished writings made by Luis Castañeda Guzmán, in CCG).

19. For the statement of election, see "Libro, en que se Asientan, Las Elecciones y Releciones, de las Rdas. Mmes. Augnas. Recoletas, del Comvto. de Nrã. Me. y Sra. de la Soledad. de Oaxca. Año de Mill Seiscientos y Nobenta y Siete" (Typescript copy in CCG; the elections are recorded from 1697–1889). Biographic material on Sister María Encarnación is taken from the "Libro de Entradas" and the "Libro de professiones de el Combento de Religosas Augustinas Recoletas de Nuestra Madre, y Señora de la Soledad de esta Ciudad de Oaxaca, desde su fundación" (typescript copies in CCG). Agustin Echeverría, *Memorias religiosas y ejemplares noticias de la fundación del Monasterio de Nuestra Señora de la Soledad,* p. iii, mentions that Sister María Encarnación was the lone survivor of the community. Guillow [*sic*], "Apuntes históricos," pp. 86–87, states that only four were alive in 1908.

20. Frank S. Falcone, "Federal-State Relations during Mexico's Restored Republic: Oaxaca, A Case Study, 1867-1872" (Ph.D. diss., University of Massachusetts, 1974), pp. 131–40, gives a narrative and analysis of the political

developments that are different in some details and interpretations from Jorge Fernando Iturribarría, "El Partido 'Borlado,' " *HM* 3(Abril-Junio 1954):480–81.

21. Jorge Fernando Iturribarría, *Porfirio Díaz ante la historia*, p. 10; *Diccionario Porrúa de historia, biografía y geografía de México*, 1:641.

22. Falcone, "Federal-State Relations," pp. 143–50, discusses the appointments and indicates that of the twenty-one *jefes políticos* named by Félix Díaz, six were Porfiristas, six were Juaristas-borlados, and nine were Felicistas (p. 149).

23. Ibid., passim, but especially chap. 5.

24. Lawrence to Fish, Feb. 3, 1872, U.S. Department of State, Despatches from U.S. Consuls in Oaxaca, Sept. 15, 1869–Mar. 31, 1878, Microcopy no. M-328, roll 1 (U.S. National Archives, Record Group 59: General Records of the Department of State).

25. There is no clear explanation of the grievances of the isthmians, but a considerable amount of literature touches casually on the situation at the eastern end of the state and reveals that there were longstanding complaints and tensions of diverse origin. Jean Meyer, *Problemas campesinos y revueltas agrarias, 1821–1910*, pp. 11–20, hints at a long history of disturbances in the region and lists six rebellions centered in the Isthmus between 1845 and 1870. John Tutino, "Indian Rebellion at the Isthmus of Tehuantepec: A Socio-Historical Perspective," *Actes du XLIIe Congrès International des Americanistes* (1976), 3:197–214, surveys Indian disturbances and focuses attention on disputes in the 1840s and 1850s, in which Juchitán was heavily involved. Miguel Covarrubias, *Mexico South*, pp. 159–60, 225–30, sheds some light on the rivalry between the towns of Juchitán and Tehuantepec and gives some information on the former's opposition to Félix Díaz. Charles Ètienne Brasseur de Bourbourg, *Voyage sur l'isthme de Tehuantepec*, p. 115, comments on the disorders in the Isthmus—political factionalism, armed bands of robbers, the pillaging of villages—and implies that such troubles were of ancient origin. Arcadio Molina, *Historia de Tehuantepec, San Blas, Shihui y Juchitán, en la intervención francesa en 1864*, passim, although poorly organized and largely narrative, gives some details on rivalries that developed between towns and individuals in the early 1860s. Falcone, "Federal-State Relations," pp. 154–55, analyzes the role of Félix Díaz in the intervention into isthmian affairs. José de Garay, *Survey of the Isthmus of Tehuantepec in the Years 1842 and 1843*, pp. 107, 109, 112, 151–52, provides some statistical information on the industry, agriculture, and population of the area, as does J. J. Williams, *The Isthmus of Tehuantepec*, pp. 250–51. The latter estimates the population of the town of Juchitán at 6,000, of the town of Tehuantepec at 13,000, and the total population of the Isthmus at 61,393, in the period under discussion.

26. Rosendo Pérez García, *La Sierra Juárez*, 2 vols., provides the most complete information on the economy, politics, and society of the sierra. See especially 1:227–41, 260–67, 275, 327–28, 371–78, and 2:15–28, 61–64. Joseph Whitecotton, *The Zapotecs*, p. 319 fn. 5, provocatively analyzes the commitment of the serranos to Liberalism. Lucio Mendieta y Núñez, ed., *Los Zapotecos*, p. xlv, briefly analyzes the contemporary conditions of the sierra, which indicate little improvement in the intervening century. Pérez García,

1:371, 374, 378, gives figures placing the total population of the Sierra de Ixtlán in the period under discussion at between roughly 15,000 (1857) and 23,500 (1876). Ixtepeji, the largest town, had a population of 2,441 in 1878, and Ixtlán de Juárez a population of 959 for the same year. Cosío Villegas, *La república restaurada. La vida política,* pp. 645–49, devotes full attention to the defeat of the serranos by the Díaz forces in the summer of 1871 because it was a prelude to the Noria Rebellion.

27. For example, in late December 1871, Félix Díaz declared an extraordinary levy of 12,000 pesos on the merchants and property owners of Oaxaca City in order to finance the defense of the capital against an invading army, which aimed at putting down the military movement to place Porfirio Díaz in the presidency. *CLD,* 5:457–58. Also see Frank Knapp, *The Life of Sebastián Lerdo de Tejada, 1823–1889,* p. 152, and Laurens B. Perry, *Juárez and Díaz,* p. 170.

28. Decree no. 27, *CLD,* 5:437–39.

29. Ibid., 6:6–7.

30. The most thorough treatment of La Noria revolt is contained in Cosío Villegas, *La república restaurada. La vida política,* pp. 575–766. The lengthy section of his general survey was extracted and published separately as *Porfirio Díaz en la Revuelta de la Noria.* For additional details, see Bancroft, *History of Mexico,* 6:379–84; Pérez García, *La Sierra Juárez,* 2:62–64; and Perry, *Juárez and Díaz,* pp. 153–76.

31. *CLD,* 6:14, 16.

32. Cosío Villegas, *La república restaurada. La vida política,* pp. 662–66; Jorge Fernando Iturribarría, *Oaxaca en la historia,* p. 225. Perry, *Juárez and Díaz,* p. 172, incorrectly places the assassination in Juchitán.

33. John W. Foster, *Las memorias diplomáticas de Mr. Foster sobre México,* p. 55.

34. This information was gleaned from several sources. See especially Francisco Calderón, *La república restaurada. La vida económica,* vol. 2 of Daniel Cosío Villegas, ed., *Historia moderna de México,* passim, but particularly pp. 47, 91, 125, 306, 353–55, 559, 575, 709. Also, Falcone, "Federal-State Relations," passim, but especially chap. 5; *Mem.-FD, Mem.-MC,* and *Mem.-JE,* passim, all provide much information on the economy of the state in the early 1870s.

35. Calderón, *La república restaurada. La vida económica,* pp. 76, 101–2, 408–13.

36. Foster, *Las memorias diplomáticas,* pp. 55–58; Bancroft, *History of Mexico,* 6:367.

37. *Mem.-JE,* p. 5. The tone of Félix Díaz's report to the state legislature in 1870 is that everything was functioning smoothly and progress was being made in a variety of endeavors, including the economy and education. *Mem.-FD,* passim.

38. The Castro report to the state legislature in 1873 summarizes the political conditions in Oaxaca in the wake of La Noria. *Mem.-MC,* passim, but especially pp. 4–12. See also Falcone, "Federal-State Relations," p. 49.

39. Vicente Riva Palacio, *Historia de la administración de D. Sebastián Lerdo de Tejada,* pp. 420–22, accurately narrates the tangled dispute between Castro and the legislature. Also see Iturribarría, "El partido 'Borlado,' " pp. 485–96,

and *Oaxaca en la historia,* pp. 226–28; Manuel Payno, *Compendio de la historia de México para el uso de los establecimientos de instrucción pública de la República Mexicana,* p. 286; and Perry, *Juárez and Díaz,* pp. 191–92.

40. Knapp, *The Life of Sebastián Lerdo de Tejada,* p. 120. On Lerdo's alliance with the moderates, his use of state governors, and his centralism, see pp. 119–20, 170, 178–82; Bancroft, *History of Mexico,* 6:366 fn. 7, and 377; and Perry, *Juárez and Díaz,* pp. 177–200.

41. These and other grievances are summarized in the preamble to the Plan de Tuxtepec. Pérez García, *La Sierra Juárez,* 2:65–67.

42. Circular no. 17, Secretaría del Gobierno del Estado de Oaxaca to the district political chiefs, Apr. 12, 1875, *CLD,* 7:227–28.

43. Pérez García, *La Sierra Juárez,* 2:89, 131–33.

44. There is much confusion surrounding the Plan de Tuxtepec. Iturribarría, "El partido 'Borlado,' " p. 488, and the same author's *Oaxaca en la historia,* pp. 229–30, give Jan. 5, 1876, as the date of proclamation. Cosío Villegas, *La república restaurada. La vida política,* p. 798, gives Jan. 10. And Pérez García, *La Sierra Juárez,* 2:65–67, gives the date of Jan. 15. The best of modern scholarship and the most reliable analysis are offered by Cosío.

45. Pérez García, *La Sierra Juárez,* 2:68.

46. Ibid., 68–71, contains a letter from Hernández to Díaz narrating the events of the week of Jan. 21–28, and following pages recount the movements and military engagements of Hernández's army.

47. Cosío Villegas, *La república restaurada. La vida política,* pp. 767–925, and Perry, *Juárez and Díaz,* passim, treat the national aspects of the Tuxtepec Revolution. See also Bancroft, *History of Mexico,* 6:419–29; Wigberto Jiménez Moreno, José Miranda, and María Teresa Fernández, *Historia de México,* pp. 533–34; and Knapp, *The Life of Sebastián Lerdo de Tejada,* pp. 251–52, for comments on the battle of Tecoac. Laurens B. Perry, "The Dynamics of the Insurrection of Tuxtepec" (Ph.D. diss., University of Michigan, 1971), is a thorough treatment of the rebellion.

CHAPTER 6

1. Letter from Juan María Maldonado, political chief of the Central District, to president of ayuntamiento of Oaxaca City, Nov. 9, 1858, asking for a list of properties disentailed, complaining tht his registry book of property transactions had been carried off by the Cobos army, and also implying that the *tres al millar* tax rolls had been destroyed. AMO, Libro de Tesorería Municipal, 1854 a 1859, unnumbered sheet. Michael Costeloe, *Church Wealth in Mexico,* pp. 110–11, 120–21, also notes the disorder in notarial records and states the confusion was a major obstacle to postindependence governments in their efforts to obtain precise information on ecclesiastical wealth. The official gazettes constitute the other major primary source available to the researcher for material pertaining to the properties that were disentailed. Containing a wealth of information, these newspapers were published almost continuously throughout the Reform decade in the Central District. There are only two gaps: the nine months in 1859–60 when the Cobos army oc-

cupied Oaxaca City and its environs, and the eighteen months in 1865–66 when the Interventionist army was in control of the district.

2. See, for example, the statement by Manuel Ruiz, refuting the authorship of Miguel Lerdo de Tejada of some of the Reform statutes, in Jorge Fernando Iturribarría, *La generación oaxaqueña del 57*, pp. 172–79. Melchor Ocampo makes these comments in a letter to Juárez written on Feb. 28, 1861, which is contained in Ocampo's *Obras completas*, 2:151–204. Francisco Bulnes, positivist critic of the Reform, characterizes the laws as "without philosophic criteria, without clarity, without practicality, without logic, without study, without awareness of possible consequences." See his *Juárez y las revoluciones de Ayutla y de la Reforma*, pp. 276–77.

3. A few months after the promulgation of the Law of Disentailment, Miguel Lerdo de Tejada, its author, took notice of the mass of government statements necessary to implementation of the decree, but blamed the amount of paper work on the opposition of the Conservatives and the fears and doubts they aroused. In Lerdo's report, there are 148 documents—letters, circulars, supplementary decrees, and so forth—clarifying and explaining the law, all issued within six months following its promulgation. *Mem.*-LdeT, p. 9 and appendices of attached documents.

4. For the establishment of the Office for the Liquidation of Ecclesiastical Properties, see *Dem.*, 4:76:4, July 28, 1859; for Carvajal's office, see ibid., 5:1:4, Sept. 25, 1859; and for the office designated to collect rents, see ibid., 5:9:4, Oct. 13, 1859. For information regarding the two state funds designated to receive endowments in the form of unsold disentailed properties, see fn. 31 below.

5. The revenue office was called the Tesorería y Dirección General de Rentas del Estado de Oaxaca. See the announcement in *Vic.*, 5:7:4, June 17, 1864. The first major action of the army in Oaxaca regarding property is embodied in the decree issued in the name of Porfirio Díaz by his secretary, José María Ballesteros, on Jan. 10, 1864, in *CLD*, 4:43–45. Several subsequent decrees relating to the property questions, too numerous to cite here, were issued by Díaz throughout 1864, and may be found in the same compilation of laws.

6. Andrés Portillo, *Oaxaca en el centenario de la independencia nacional*, passim.

7. William Taylor, *Landlord and Peasant in Colonial Oaxaca*, p. 173, accounts for a total of 870 houses in Oaxaca City in 1792 owned by monasteries and convents. Fausto Mejía, comp., "Bienes desamortizados" (typescript in CCG), accounts for 742 houses owned by all ecclesiastical agencies of the Oaxaca diocese and alienated during the Reform. Mejía did not use notary books and relied solely on notices of sale in the newspapers. Even more helpful than the number of houses would be a comparison of the monetary values of disentailed properties and the total value of all property held in the district. This is impossible to determine. For a discussion of this problem, see Appendix E.

8. Helen Phipps, *Some Aspects of the Agrarian Question in Mexico*, p. 79, surmises that "the usual price for improved agricultural land was about 2 pesos per acre." This is out of all proportion to the price in Oaxaca. The price

per acre for Carmen Hacienda was about 50 pesos.

9. A *capellanía,* or "chaplaincy," was an endowment in the form of cash, real estate, or mortgages for the support of a priest, who, in return for the income, was required to celebrate a stipulated number of masses for the soul of the donor. The property tied up in the different types of chaplaincies was required to be disentailed by the Reform laws. For a good, brief discussion, see Robert Knowlton, "Chaplaincies and the Mexican Reform," *HAHR* 48 (August 1968):421–37. For a detailed study of the chaplaincy in the era before the Reform, see Costeloe, *Church Wealth,* passim.

10. AN, Protocolo de Juan Rey, 1856, Tomo 5, *hojas* 698–718, 719. The same Vasconcelos who administered the Hacienda of San Antonio for the Dominican Sisters of Santa Catarina convent, was also accused of stripping that estate of implements and cattle when it was sold in auction in late July 1856. San Antonio was located in the neighboring District of Tlacolula. *El Constituyente, Suplemento de Actas y Decretos Oficiales,* Aug. 3, 1856, 3d page; and Aug. 21, 1856, 2d page. AEO, Ramo de Asuntos Varios, Carpeta negra 1863, registro 759: "Esperón Gabriel.—Pide se le levante el embargo de su Hacienda de Montoya," gives information on the plea for tax relief.

11. *Vic.,* 1:55:1, Feb. 24, 1861.

12. AN, Protocolo de Felipe Sandoval, 1861, Tomo 8, *hojas* 112–12 *vuelta,* 114–16, 118–21.

13. See, for example, Phipps, *Some Aspects of the Agrarian Question,* pp. 80, 92; and Robert Knowlton, *Church Property and the Mexican Reform, 1856–1910,* pp. 123–24.

14. All three of these items are listed in *Mem.-LdeT,* pp. 426–41, and Aguirre's purchase is also recorded in AN, Protocolo de Juan Rey, 1857, Tomo 6, *hojas* 1–26 *vuelta.*

15. This contrasts with what Bazant found to have happened in Central Mexico, where, he states, "most tenants chose to claim their properties." Jan Bazant, *Alienation of Church Wealth in Mexico,* p. 54.

16. Agustín Cue Cánovas, *La reforma liberal en México,* pp. 66–69, characterizes the denouncers as generally an immoral and greedy lot who were permitted by the Lerdo Law to accumulate great wealth. Lucio Mendieta y Núñez, *El problema agrario de México,* p. 112, describes them as *gente acomodada,* of few scruples and of great economic capacity. He sees them as having a distinct advantage over those who did not denounce properties as far as purchasing in auctions was concerned because of the substantial discount the denouncers earned. He also blames them for contributing to latifundism because they bought large estates intact and thereby hindered any movement toward dividing up the estates into smaller parcels. Manuel Aguilera Gómez, *La reforma agraria en el desarrollo económico de México,* pp. 53–54, reasons that one cause of the Reformers' failure to distribute land as they planned to do was because denunciations were made only by the great landlords. Thus in the eyes of some Mexican analysts, the denouncers were major obstacles in the fulfillment of the Reform laws, were responsible for subverting the laws, and were enormously greedy in their acquisitions. As in other instances, the Oaxaca disentailment does not support these generalizations.

17. Knowlton, *Church Property,* pp. 99–100, notes that depreciated values

continued to characterize the real estate market on into the early 1860s and beyond.

18. AN, Protocolo de Felipe Sandoval, 1857, Tomo 5, *hojas* 719–32, concerns the two clergymen who were fined. Costeloe, *Church Wealth,* pp. 131–32, notes that the Lerdo Law was not universally condemned by churchmen, but even among those priests who supported it there was refusal to cooperate with the authorities. See AN, Protocolo de Felipe Sandoval, 1857, Tomo 4, *hojas* 289–99 *vuelta,* for Esperón's refusal to cooperate.

19. William Taylor, "Town and Country in the Valley of Oaxaca, 1750–1812," in Ida Altman and James Lockhart, eds., *Provinces of Early Mexico,* pp. 83–84, shows that rural properties in the Valley were heavily mortgaged to the church in the late eighteenth century.

20. Decree of Feb. 5, 1861, in *LM,* 9:54–62. *Vic.,* 3:12:4, Aug. 28, 1862; 3:27:4, Sept. 19, 1862; 3:61:4, Feb. 15, 1863; 3:70:4, Mar. 19, 1863; 3:73:4, Mar. 29, 1863; and 3:74:4, Apr. 2, 1863, list the devolutions required by the 1861 decree. Of the 176 properties returned, 140 were put up for resale before the end of 1867 and 118 were sold.

21. Anselmo de la Portilla's charge that speculators reaped immense profits, which he made in 1858 in his book *Méjico en 1856 y 1857* (pp. 69–70), has stuck in the minds of many who have written generally or specifically about the Reform; for example, Manuel Cambre, *La guerra de tres años,* p. 286, but most especially does the charge appear in the writings of conservative Mexican churchmen. See, for example, Regis Planchet, *La cuestión religiosa en México,* pp. 228–34; Mariano Cuevas, *Historia de la nación mexicana,* 3:50; and José Bravo Ugarte, *Historia de México,* 3:231–32. The charge has also crept into works on Mexico in English: Eyler Simpson, *The Ejido,* p. 25; Lesley Simpson, *Many Mexicos,* p. 243; Walter Scholes, *Mexican Politics during the Juárez Regime, 1855–1872,* p. 16; Knowlton, *Church Property,* pp. 85–86; and Nicholas Cheetham, *A History of México,* (London; R. Hart-Davis, 1970), p. 163, are but a few examples. But Phipps, *Some Aspects of the Agrarian Question,* p. 86, surmises, and I think correctly, that speculators were not generally active throughout Mexico. Certainly the example of Oaxaca does not support the generalization that speculation was a prominent feature of disentailment.

22. Robert P. Swierenga, *Pioneers and Profits: Land Speculation on the Iowa Frontier,* pp. 4–6.

23. This man of wealth is Joaquín Rómulo Vasconcelos. The transactions are found in several notarial books, too numerous to cite here.

24. Knowlton, *Church Property,* pp. 85–86, 99–100. Bazant, *Alienation of Church Wealth,* pp. 90–91, fully discusses these bonds and how they were used. Although he seems to believe that speculation took place in the area he studied, he also concludes that a decade after the Reform laws, "the value of clerical property was still lower than that of comparable real estate" (p. 282).

25. For the donation to Saavedra, see AMO, Libro de Tesorería Municipal, 1854 a 1859, "Año de 1856 Noviembre," unnumbered page. A week earlier, the council gave another lot worth 80 pesos to Miguel Canseco as partial compensation for the 114.25 pesos owed to him in back pay as assistant to the warden of the jail. AN, Protocolo de Juan Rey, 1856, Tomo 5, *hojas* 664 *vuelta*–70. On Aug. 18, 1857, Antonio Ramos bought seven lots belonging to

the town council in the Trinidad de las Huertas section on the southern edge of the city, paying various prices. Ramos was not able to retain all these lots, although the reason for his inability is not specified. Three were returned to the agencies in charge of nationalized properties at an unspecified date. In March 1862, two of the lots were auctioned, but there were no purchasers. Finally the lots were ceded to three city employees in June and July 1863, in partial payment for unpaid salaries. AN, Protocolo de Ambrosio Ocampo, 1862–1864, Tomo 11, *hojas* 136 *vuelta*–37 and 159 *vuelta*–60, and Protocolo de Juan Rey, 1863–1864, Tomo 8, *hojas* 44–46 *vuelta*. One of the thirteen properties given in lieu of salaries involved the National Guard. A house that had previously belonged to the convent of La Concepción, valued at 1,123.25 pesos, was ceded to Battalion Commander Vicente Lozano sometime in 1864. Lozano was due 1,013 in back pay, and the transfer of title was ordered by the state government and the general headquarters of the Guard. Since the officer received property worth more than the salary owed him, he was required to pay back the difference of 110.25 pesos. AN, Protocolo de Juan Rey, 1863–1864, Tomo 8, *hojas* 119 *vuelta*–21.

26. AN, Protocolo de Juan Rey, 1857, Tomo 6, *hojas* 466 *vuelta*–74 *vuelta*.

27. Protocolo de Felipe Sandoval, 1862, Tomo 9, *hojas* 302 *vuelta*–36 *vuelta*, 308–15.

28. Decree of Feb. 11, 1860, in *LM*, 8:738–39, and decree of Mar. 25, 1860, ibid., 740–41. AN, Protocolo de Juan Ocampo formado por J. M. Ruiz, 1867, *hojas* 208–10, gives the details of the donation.

29. AN, Protocolo de Felipe Sandoval, 1864, Tomo 11, *hojas* 563 *vuelta*–67.

30. AN, Protocolo de Gregorio Fernández Varela, 1864–1867, Tomo 3, *hojas* 42–46. After the promulgation of the Law of Nationalization in 1859, mortgages held by ecclesiastical institutions on disentailed property were also confiscated and were then sold just as was the confiscated corporate real estate. Presumably the traffic in mortgages was heavy, but as previously stated, it has been impossible to compile systematic data on them because the notarial documents are far from complete.

31. The Law of Nationalization of 1859 provided that states would receive one-fifth of the value of the confiscated property and mortgages to be used for public improvement. In December 1860, the Oaxaca legislature set aside the state's share as endowments for education and such charitable work as hospitals, orphanages, and asylums. In addition to this endowment, the state agency for education (Fund for Public Instruction) received substantial amounts of other properties from the national government. Most of the properties were in such a ruinous state of repair, however, that insufficient revenue was realized from them. Because of this, the Fund was given permission to sell many of its properties and mortgages at greatly reduced rates. With the intensification of the war effort in 1863–64, General Porfirio Díaz decreed that the endowments be cancelled and all properties and mortgages accrue to the Army of the East, which would use the income to help finance the war effort. Upon the cessation of hostilities in 1867, the endowments were returned to education and welfare, except those properties valued at less than 1,000 pesos, which were to be given to widows and orphan children of soldiers

killed while fighting during the Reform and Intervention. *CLD,* 3:70; 4:47–49, 60–64, 184–86; and Manuel Dublán, *Memoria que sobre instrucción pública presenta el director del Instituto al govierno del estado,* passim.

32. *Mem.*-FD, document 49; *Mem.*-MC, p. 36 and document 49; *Inf.*-FM, 2:255 fn. 99 *Mem.*-JE, document 23. *Mem.*-MG (1898), document 3; and *Mem.*-MBC, document 45, list a number of rural properties that had been disentailed. But in late 1898-early 1899, at least 36 municipal lots in Oaxaca City were adjudicated to their tenants. See *Mem.*-MG (1899), document 4.

33. Scholes, *Mexican Politics during the Juárez Regime,* p. 16 fn. 32.

34. In addition to Bazant, many other commentators hold that foreigners benefited most from disentailment, or at least were extremely active in purchasing the alienated properties, because they had money available to invest whereas Mexicans were short of capital. See, for example, Martín Quirarte, *Visión panorámica de la historia de México,* p. 111; Justo Sierra, *The Political Evolution of the Mexican People,* p. 273; Cue Cánovas, *La reforma liberal en México,* pp. 20, 38; Cambre, *La guerra de tres años,* p. 286; Moisés González Navarro, "Tenencia de la tierra y población agrícola (1877–1960)", *HM* 19 (Julio-Septiembre 1960):62–86; and Rafael Ramos Pedrueza, who gives a Marxist view in his *La lucha de clases a través de la historia de México,* 1:201–2. It is not surprising that such a generalization has penetrated popularized accounts in English, such as Henry Parkes, *A History of Mexico* (Boston: Houghton Mifflin Co., 1969), p. 235, and J. Patrick McHenry, *A Short History of Mexico* (Garden City, N.Y.: Doubleday 9 Co., 1962), p. 122. It is probably correct to say that *in some areas* foreigners invested heavily in disentailed real estate and benefited greatly, but, as the case of Oaxaca shows, the generalization cannot be applied universally to Mexico.

35. Of necessity, the foregoing breakdowns according to sex, nationality, and profession or occupation do not reflect accurately the total number of persons involved. This is true in those cases where one person served in several capacities or held various positions. As an example, a lawyer who taught at the Institute may have held appointment as a judge, served as regidor and sindic in the ayuntamiento, acted as *jefe político* of one of the state's districts, served in the state legislature and later in the national congress, in which case he would have been counted several times.

36. Some historians who have written of the Reform suggest that there were few small transactions. See, for example, Manuel López Gallo, *Economía y política en la historia de México,* p. 141, and Aguilera Gómez, *La reforma agraria en el desarrollo económica de México,* p. 53–54. Bazant, *Alienation of Church Wealth,* passim, primarily as a result of his methodology, which led him to concentrate on the larger investments and buyers, also leaves this impression. A specific example of Bazant's "elitism" may be found on pp. 200–201, in which he analyzes the buyers listed in the 1862 Disentailment Report. About 1,000 persons are listed who redeemed values and mortgages or disentailed chaplaincies, and the total value of sales exceeded 16,000,000 pesos. In order to get an identifiable group from these thousand buyers, he took those whose investments amounted to 40,000 pesos or more. Seventy-eight persons fell into this category, and of those seventy-eight, sixty-seven were identifiable. Throughout his otherwise excellent study, Bazant ignores small purchasers of

properties like rooms, portals, and small pieces of land such as garden plots, which the church owned prior to disentailment and which were acquired by private citizens of the poorer classes as a result of the Lerdo Law.

37. For the "rich-getting-richer" thesis, see Portilla, *Méjico en 1856 y 1857*, pp. 69–70; Planchet, *La cuestión religiosa en México*, pp. 228–34; Bravo Ugarte, *Historia de México*, 3:231–32; López Gallo, *Economía y política en la historia de México*, p. 141; Simpson, *The Ejido*, p. 23; Phipps, *Some Aspects of the Agrarian Question*, p. 80; and the popular textbook, Hubert Herring, *A History of Latin America* 3d ed. (New York: Alfred A. Knopf, 1968), p. 315. Luis Gonzalez y González, "El agrarismo liberal," *HM* 7 (Abril-Junio 1957): 487, summarizes this idea by writing that "no poor person remedied his poverty with the Lerdo Law; but many wealthy landowners and merchants augmented their fortunes. . . ."

38. Napoleon III to Forey, July 13, 1862, quoted in Jack A. Dabbs, *The French Army in Mexico, 1861–1867*, p. 32; Napoleon III to Bazaine, July 30, 1863, quoted in ibid., p. 61.

39. Budin to Forey, May 22, 1863, in José Sebastián Segura, *BLIM*, 1: núm. 5, 19–20.

40. Decree of May 22, 1863, ibid., 20–21, establishes the review board in Puebla; decree of July 1, 1863, ibid., núm. 42, 95–96, decree of July 6, 1863, ibid., núm. 48, 113, apply the Puebla formula to other areas.

41. Decree of Feb. 26, 1865, ibid., 4: núm. 94, 194–98.

42. Taylor, *Landlord and Peasant*, pp. 171–74, asserts that in the colonial era the church in Oaxaca did not concentrate on obtaining agricutural lands but placed emphasis on accumulating urban properties. This tendency changed in the late eighteenth century to the extent that some agencies acquired more land than they could use and were forced to let some estates fall into decay and remain vacant. He also notes that some estates acquired by the monasteries and convents were sold with considerable frequency.

43. See the list given in *Inf.*-FM, *Documentos anexos*, p. 256.

44. Bazant, *Alienation of Church Wealth*, pp. 108–10.

45. Donald Fraser, "La política de desamortización en las comunidades indígenas, 1856–1872," *HM* 21 (Abril-Junio 1972):615–52, has demonstrated that the despoliation of Indian lands was not some evil manifestation of Porfirian greed or disregard for Indians but instead had a strong base in Liberal thought prior to the issuance of the Lerdo Law in 1856. In this respect, as in others, Díaz did not pervert Liberal principles but merely carried them to their logical conclusion.

46. Mendieta y Núñez, El *problema agrario de México*, pp. 53–65. This study is probably the definitive work on Indian lands in Mexico, having now gone into its ninth edition. But other scholars have categorized and analyzed the types of Indian lands in other ways. See, for example, Phipps, *Some Aspects of the Agrarian Question*, p. 21; Luis G. Labastida, *Colección de leyes, decretos, reglamentos, circulares, órdenes y acuerdos relativos a la desamortización de los bienes de corporaciones civiles y religiosas y a la nacionalización de los que administraron las últimas*, pp. 19–23; and George McBride, *The Land Systems of Mexico*, p. 124. Taylor, *Landlord and Peasant*, p. 68, details six types of Indian holdings in Oaxaca in the colonial era: the *fundo legal;* communal lands worked collec-

tively to support festivals and meet other community expenses; communal woodlands and pastures; communal barrio lands, which were frequently divided and worked separately by individuals and families of the community's barrios, or sections; communal tracts allotted to landless townsmen; and privately owned tracts. For a discussion of the canonical confraternities (as distinct from Indian confraternities), see Héctor Martínez Domínguez, "Las cofradías en la Nueva España, 1700–1859," *Primer Anuario*, pp. 45–71.

47. Taylor, *Landlord and Peasant*, p. 73. Also see his "Cacicazgos coloniales en el Valle de Oaxaca," *HM* 20(Julio-Septiembre 1970):1–41. Brian Hamnett, "Dye Production, Food Supply and the Laboring Population of Oaxaca, 1750–1800," *HAHR* 51 (February 1971):51–78; and the same author's *Politics and Trade in Southern Mexico*, passim.

48. AN, Protocolo de Felipe Sandoval, 1856, Tomo 3, *hojas* 158–70.

49. AN, Protocolo de Ambrosio Ocampo, 1855–1857, Tomo 9, *hojas* 292–95. San Bartolomé's residents were not the only ones who bought or sold the communal lands. Forty-two citizens of the village of Cuilapan denounced the land set aside to endow the parish, the products of which "since time immemorial have been used for the benefit of the priest of the parish." The priest refused to have anything to do with the process of alienation because his bishop would not allow it. He would neither appoint an appraiser nor sign any papers. But the law provided for such a contingency and the subprefect of the district acted in behalf of the priest. The appraisal was made on October 18 and fixed at 340 pesos, and the registration of the sale took place on November 3. AN, Protocolo de Felipe Sandoval, 1856, Tomo 3, *hojas* 361–77. Cuilapan also had confraternity lands lying some distance from the village. One hundred ninety-two citizens of the village of Jalpan, near which the land was located, asked to buy Cuilapan's tracts and were allowed to do so. The Jalpan citizens rented the lands from Cuilapan and their purchase was therefore in the form of adjudication prescribed by the Lerdo Law by which tenants could acquire the land rented during the 3-month period. The 192 citizens paid 1,666.33 pesos and the registration of sale was made on Sept. 20, 1856. *El Constituyente, Suplemento de Actas y Decretos Oficiales*, Sept. 28, 1856, 1st page. Cuilapan also had a rancho as part of the municipal lands that it lost in November 1856. The farm was rented to Doña Guadalupe Gamboa de Mejía, the wife of a prominent Oaxacan lawyer. The lease had been made in 1847 for 9 years, and the señora paid the municipality an annual rent of 36 pesos. On Oct. 4, 1856, the husband, Manuel María Mejía, asked that the lands be sold to his wife in accordance with the law. The case became rather complicated because the Mejías had sublet the rancho and the subtenant also claimed the right to adjudicate the land. Finally all difficulties were settled, the Mejías bought the land for 594 pesos, and the village was to hold the mortgage, which carried 6 per cent interest. AN, Protocolo de Ambrosio Ocampo, 1855–1857, Tomo 9, *hojas* 346–72.

50. Asunción Lavrin, "The Execution of the Law of *Consolidación* in New Spain," *HAHR* 53 (February 1973):42, 47, found that Indians willingly cooperated in the Consolidación procedures of the early nineteenth century by relinquishing two-thirds of their communal funds as required by the law.

51. AEO, Ramo de Asuntos Varios, Carpeta negra 1863, registro 725:

"Xoxocotlán.—Adjudicación de terrenos.—1863."

52. See reports in *Dem.*, 1:6:3, Oct. 19, 1856; 1:7:2–3, Oct. 23, 1856; 1:8:3, Oct. 26, 1856: 1:12:3, Nov. 9, 1856. These reports come from Zimatlán, Etla, Yautepec, and other districts.

53. *Mem.*-LdeT, pp. 28–29, for the response to the Juárez inquiry. *LM*, 8:324, for the letter to Fomento.

54. *LM*, 8:712–13.

55. Ibid.

56. *CLD*, 2:570–71.

57. Ibid., 3:146.

58. Ibid., 184–87.

59. Ibid., 324.

60. *Vic.*, 1:63:3, Mar. 24, 1861 (Teposcolula); 1:62:3, Mar. 21, 1861 (Tehuantepec); 1:65:2, Mar. 31, 1861 (Yanhuitlán); 1:76:1, May 5, 1861 (Villa Alta); 3:11:2, Aug. 24, 1862 (Juquila—1 adjudication); 1:92:2, July 5, 1861, and 2:15:2, Sept. 29, 1861 (Jamiltepec—some activity reported); 1:67:3, Apr. 7, 1861 (Choapan—no properties to be disentailed, a statement repeated in 1:83:3, June 2, 1861).

61. *CLD*, 4:52–54.

62. *Mem.*-MBC, document 45.

63. The late José Miranda, in his article "La propiedad comunal de la tierra," *Cuadernos Americanos* 25 (Noviembre-Diciembre 1966):168–81, pointed out that disentailment of communal lands was never totally accomplished, due in large part to Indian resistance, and that by 1910, 41 per cent of the Indian communities in Mexico still retained their ancient lands.

64. The number of persons involved in five transactions was large but could not be determined precisely.

65. William Taylor, "The Valley of Oaxaca: A Study of Colonial Land Distribution" (Ph.D. diss., University of Michigan, 1969), p. 292; Jan Bazant, "La desamortización de los bienes corporativos de 1856," *HM* 16(Octubre-Diciembre 1966):193–212.

66. *Esp.*-BJ, document 5; *Mem.*-RC, document 18. The political chief of Etla district reported in 1861 that many pueblos attempted to keep from revealing the exact amount of their municipal revenues so that they could continue spending their funds on masses, church functions, banquets, and other festivities, as they had traditionally spent their revenues in the past. *Vic.*, 1:96:1–2, July 18, 1861.

67. Report of district chief in *Vic.*, 1:66:2, Apr. 4, 1861.

Appendix C

1. José María Iglesias, *Revistas históricas sobre la intervención francesa*, p. 529. (This is a collection of Iglesias's journalistic articles written to support the republican effort. Not strictly history, there is a strong historical sense throughout the articles.)

2. Justo Sierra, *The Political Evolution of the Mexican People*, p. 326.

3. Ernesto de la Torre Villar, ed., *La intervención francesa y el triunfo de la república*, pp. 55–57.

4. Emilio Rabasa, *La evolución histórica de México,* pp. 48–49.

5. José C. Valadés, *Historia del pueblo de México,* 3:99, 106.

6. Martin Quirarte, *Historiografía sobre el imperio de Maximiliano,* pp. 45–56.

Appendix D

1. Four imperial decrees concern the offices of imperial deputy and imperial visitor. In chronological order they are: decree of Nov. 9, 1864, in *CLDRI,* 2: núm. 13 (pages unnumbered); the "Estatuto Provisional del Imperio Mexicano," decreed on Apr. 10, 1865, in *DI,* 1:83:333–36, Apr. 10, 1865; and the decrees of Oct. 11, 1865, and July 1, 1866, both in Segura, *BLIM,* 2, pt. 1, Boletín núm. 7, núm. 109, 241–46, and Boletín núm. 14, núm. 252, 148–67, respectively.

2. Decree of Franco, Apr. 10, 1865, *DI,* 2:201:214, Aug. 31, 1865.

Appendix E

1. *Mem.*-RC, document 33.

2. *Mem.*-LdeT, passim.

3. Andrés Portillo, *Oaxaca en el centenario de la independencia nacional,* p. 106.

BIBLIOGRAPHY

Archival and Manuscript Sources

Austin. The Nettie Lee Benson Latin American Collection. The University of
    Texas at Austin.
    Bazaine Archives, 1862–1867. Genaro García Collection.
    Documentos relativos a la Reforma y a la Intervención francesa, 1850–
    1867. Genaro García Collection.
    La Iglesia en México. Conventos, hospitales, iglesias, etc. 1580–1869.
    Genaro García Collection.
    Intervención francesa. Documentos misceláneos, 1862–1867. Genaro
    García Collection.
    Murguía y Galardi, José María. "Extracto general que abraza la estadís-
    tica toda en su la y 2a parte del estado de Guaxaca, y ha reunido de
    orden del supremo gobierno el intendente de provincia en clase de los
    cesantes José Ma. Murguía y Galardi." 2 vols. 1827. (Ms.).
Mexico City. Biblioteca del Museo de Antropología e Historia. Archivo His-
    tórico, Antigua Colección.
    "1857. Estadística del Estado de Oaxaca formada por el Sor Dn Enrique
    de Nassos [?] de Lafond Comisionado al efecto por el Supror gobo de la
    Nación." (ms., legajo 760, exp. 2).
————. Archivo General de la Nación.
    Archivo histórico del Mariscal Bazaine.
————. Archivo Histórico de Matías Romero.
Oaxaca. Archivo del Estado.
    Ramo de Asuntos Varios, 1855–1867.
    Ramo de Registro Civil.
————. Archivo de Notarías.
    Libros de Protocolos del Notario Gregorio Fernández Varela (1860–67);
    Manuel María Martínez (1867–69); Ambrosio Ocampo (1855–67);
    Juan Ocampo (1865–67); Juan Rey (1856–60, 1863–67); José María
    Ruiz (1856–64, 1867); and Felipe Sandoval (1856–64, 1866–67).
————. Archivo Municipal.
    Borrador de Actas del año de 1865 [includes 1866 and 1867].
    Inventorio general de los libros y demás documentos que forman el
    archivo de la Secretaría del Exmo. Ayuntamiento de la capital, revisado
    y arreglado en Junio de 1865, por el Secretario que suscribe. Tomo 1.
    Libros de Tesorería Municipal de 1848 a 1868. Tomos 6–11.

———. Biblioteca de la Universidad "Benito Juárez" de Oaxaca.

Fernández del Campo, Ramón. "Sitio de Oaxaca por el ejército francés (1864–1865)." (Ms. dated Oaxaca, 1890).

Martínez Gracida, Manuel. "Historia de Oaxaca. Años de 1856 a 1860." (Ms. in bound vols. dated Oaxaca, 1891–93).

Martínez Gracida, Manuel; Brioso y Candiani, Miguel; Esteva, Cayentano; and Salazar, Francisco. "Biografías de oaxaqueños distinguidos y de escritores y personajes relacionados con la cultura e historia de Oaxaca." (Typescript in 2 bound vols.).

Miscellaneous ms. letters of Bishop José María Covarrubias, Vicente Márquez, and Juan Pablo Franco.

Miscellaneous printed decrees and *bandos* of Manuel María de Fagoaga, Juan Pablo Franco, Noriega, Juan María Santaella, and Generals Carteret, José María Cobos, and Marcelino Ruiz Cobos.

———. Colección de Lic. Luis Castañeda Guzmán

"Año de 1830. Quaderno que manifiesta las Casas pertenecientes a los Conventos de Capuchinas de esta Cuidad que como su Admor. son à mi cargo pa. su cobro de alquileres desde lo. de Enero de 1830. Quado. 2o." (Ms.).

"Archivo del Santuario de la Soledad." (Typescript extracts).

Castañeda Guzmán, Luis. "Templo de los Siete Príncipes y Monasterio de Nuestra Señora de los Angeles." (Unpublished typescript).

Guillow [*sic*], Monseñor Eulogio G. "Apuntes históricos sobre el Obispado de Antequera y Arzobispado de Oaxaca." (Typescript).

"Libro de Entradas, Y abitos, en este convento De augustis, Recoletas de nra. Señora de la Soledad, Desta siudad—De hoaxaca. Asentadose dia—mes. Y año." (Ms.).

"Libro de la fundación del Convento. Y monasterio: de monjas intitulado Sancta Catharina de Sena, de la orden de los Predicadores. Fundado en la Cuid. de Antequera De los Valles de Oaxaca. Bulas, Pontificias, Estatutos, Constituciones, Ordenaciones, y Partidas de las Religiosas profesas." (Typescript copy).

"Libro de las casas que tiene este convento de la Merced y se hizo el dia lo. de Enero de 1856, por orden del R. P. Comendador Fr. José Ignacio Ortiz." (Ms.).

"Libro de professiones de el Combento de Religosas Augustinas Recoletas de Nuestra Madre, y Señora de la Soledad de esta Cuidad de Oaxaca, desde su fundación." (Typescript copy).

"Libro en que constan las Boletas que mensualmente se remiten á las Reverendas Madres del Convento de N. S. de la Concepción Regina Coeli de esta Ciudad de Oajaca, pr. su Administrador Dn. Ignacio Morales, y principió en lo. de Enero de 1830." (Ms.).

"Libro en que constan los sugetos qe. visten beca desde 18 de octubre de 1803 en el Rl. y Pontificio Seminario de Oaxaca. Los que sirven las catedras [,] merito exercicios literarios y funciones públicas." (Typescript copy).

"Convento de la Soledad. Libro, en que se Asientan, Las Elecciones y Releciones, de las Rdas. Mmes. Augnas. Recoletas. del Comvto. de Nrã.

Me. y Sra. de la Soledad. de Oaxca. Año de Mill Seiscientos, y Nobenta y Siete." (Typescript copy).

"Libro 2o. de Cordilleras del Sagrario de Esta Santa Iglesia Catedral, comenzado en 30 de Septiembre de 1820 años." (Typescript copies of extracts).

Mejía Muñozcano, Fausto, comp. "Bienes desamortizados según la ley llamada 'Ley Juárez' [*sic*] de 25 de Junio del año de 1856. Lista de bienes desamortizados a instituciones religiosas en las calles de la Cuidad de Oaxaca. Nomenclatura de la Cuidad de Oaxaca antes del año de 1884 comparada con la actual." (Typescript dated Oaxaca, Aug., 1931).

Rosas Lavaria, Lucas Pedro de. "Apuntes de la fundación y fábrica de la Iglesia de San José y Convento." (Typescript).

Salazar, Francisco. "Compendio de la Historia Oaxaca. Primera parte: Epoca precortesiana. Segunda parte: Dominación española. Tercera parte: Guerra de independencia. Cuarta parte: Vida independiente de Oaxaca." (Typescript).

Vasconcelos, Francisco [?]. "Apuntes históricos de la vida en Oaxaca en el siglo XIX." (Typescript).

————. "Memorias." (Typescript).

————. "Reminiciencias de lo que fué en Oaxaca el culto externo órdenes religiosas y algunos actos que aunque quedan en parte fueron unidos en la época a que esta reseña se refiere y es antes de que estubieran en vigor las leyes de la Reforma." (Ms.).

Washington, D. C. United States National Archives.

Record Group 59: General Records of the Department of State. Despatches from U.S. Consuls in Oaxaca, Sept. 15, 1869–Mar. 31. 1878. Micro-copy no. M-328, roll 1.

Published Sources

A cien años del triunfo de la República. Mexico City: Secretaría de Hacienda y Crédito Públic, 1967.

Aguilera Gómez, Manuel. *La reforma agraria en el desarrollo económico de México.* Mexico City: Instituto Mexicano de Investigaciones Económicas, 1969.

Altman, Ida, and Lockhart, James, eds. *Provinces of Early Mexico: Variants of Spanish American Regional Evolution.* Los Angeles: UCLA Latin American Center Publications, 1976.

A[ndrade], V[icente] de P[aula]. *Apéndices a la obra Noticias de México de D. Francisco Sedano.* Mexico City: Imprenta de J. R. Barbedillo, 1880.

————. *Datos biográficos de los señores capitulares de la Santa Iglesia Catedral de México.* Mexico City: n. p., 1908.

————. *Noticias biográficas sobre los ilustrísimos prelados de Sonora, de Sinaloa y de Durango.* . . . 3d ed. Mexico City: Imprenta del Museo Nacional, 1899.

Arnaiz y Freg, Arturo, and Bataillon, Claude, eds. *La Intervención francesa y el imperio de Maximiliano cien años despuès, 1862–1962.* Mexico City: Asociación Mexicana de Historiadores, Instituto Francés de América Latina, 1965.

Arrillaga, Basilio José. *Recopilación de leyes, decretos, bandos, reglamentos, circu-*

lares y providencias de los supremos poderes y otras autoridades de la República Mexicana. 9 vols. Mexico City: Imprenta de A. Boix, à cargo de M. Zornoza, 1861–66.

Balanza mercantil del departamento de Oaxaca, correspondiente al año de 1843. Oaxaca: Impresa por I. Candiani, 1844.

Balbontín, Manuel. *Memorias del Coronel Manuel Balbontín.* Colección de obras históricas mexicanas, 4. 1896. Reprint. Mexico City: Editorial "Elede," 1958.

Bancroft, Hubert Howe. *The Works of Hubert Howe Bancroft.* Vol. 14: *History of México, 1861–1867.* San Francisco: The History Company Publishers, 1888.

Bauer, Arnold J. "Rural Workers in Spanish America: Problems of Peonage and Oppression," *The Hispanic American Historical Review* 59: 34–63.

Bazant, Jan. *Alienation of Church Wealth in Mexico: Social and Economic Aspects of the Liberal Revolution, 1856–1875.* Edited and translated by Michael P. Costeloe. Cambridge Latin American Studies, no. 11. Cambridge: Cambridge University Press, 1971.

———. "La desamortización de los bienes corporativos de 1856." *Historia Mexicana* 16:193–212.

Beals, Carleton. *Porfirio Díaz, Dictator of Mexico.* 1932. Reprint. Westport, Conn.: Greenwood Press, 1971.

Berry, Charles R. "La ciudad de Oaxaca en vísperas de la Reforma." *Historia Mexicana* 19:23–61.

"Bibliografía de Don Manuel Martínez Gracida." *Boletín de la Biblioteca Nacional,* Segunda época, 6:48–72.

Blumberg, Arnold. *The Diplomacy of the Mexican Empire, 1863–1867.* Transactions of the American Philosophical Society, New Series, vol. 61, part 8. Philadelphia: The Ameican Philosophical Society, 1971.

Borah, Woodrow. "The Cathedral Archive of Oaxaca." *The Hispanic American Historical Review* 28:640–45.

———. "Notes on Civil Archives in the City of Oaxaca." *The Hispanic American Historical Review* 31:723–49.

Brasseur de Bourbourg, Charles Ètienne. *Voyage sur l'isthme de Tehuantepec, dans l'état de Chiapas et la république de Guatémala, exécute dans les années 1859 et 1860.* Paris: A. Bertrand, 1861.

Bravo Ugarte, José. "Datos sobre la fundación de los seminarios diocesanos de México y sus confiscaciones." *Memorias de la Academia Mexicana de la Historia* 11:140–57.

———. *Historia de Mexico.* 3 vols. Mexico City: Jus, 1944.

Bulnes, Francisco. *Juárez y las revoluciones de Ayutla y de la Reforma.* Mexico City: n. p., 1905.

Bustamante, Carlos María de. *Memoria estadística de Oaxaca y descripción del valle del mismo nombre, estractada de la que en grande trabajó el señor Don José Murguía Galardi. . . .* Veracruz: Imprenta Constitucional, 1821.

Camacho, Pedro. *Ensayo de monografía sobre los hospitales del estado y particularmente sobre el Hospital General de esta ciudad.* Oaxaca: Talleres de Imprenta y Encuadernación del Gobierno del Estado, 1927.

———. *Ligeros apuntes históricos del Instituto de Ciencias y Artes del edo. de Oaxaca.* Mexico City: Talleres Gráficos "Excelsior," Cia. Editorial, 1927.

Cambre, Manuel. *La guerra de tres años: apuntes para la historia de la Reforma.* 1892. Reprint. Guadalajara (?): Biblioteca de Autores Jaliscienses, 1949.

Carriedo, Juan Bautista. *Ensayo histórico-estadístico del Departamento de Oaxaca . . . Año de 1843.* Oaxaca: Imprenta del Estado, 1889.

————. *Estudios históricos y estadísticos del estado libre de Oaxaca.* Biblioteca de autores y de asuntos oaxaqueños, 1. 2d ed. 2 vols. Mexico City: Talleres Gráficos de A. Morales S., 1949.

Castañeda, Carlos E., and Dabbs, Jack A. *Guide to the Latin American Manuscripts in the University of Texas Library.* Committee on Latin American Studies, American Council of Learned Societies, Miscellaneous Publication, no. 1. Cambridge, Mass.: Harvard University Press, 1939.

Catecismo político dedicado a la instrucción primaria de la juventud oaxaqueña . Oaxaca: Imprenta de I. Rincón, 1857.

Chance, John K. *Race and Class in Colonial Oaxaca.* Stanford: Stanford University Press, 1978.

Charnay, Desiré. *Le Mexique: souvenirs et impressions de voyage.* Paris: E. Dentu, 1863.

Cobos, José María. *Manifiesto del General José María Cobos a la República Mejicana.* New York: n. p., 1862.

Colección de las leyes, decretos, circulares y providencias relativas a la desamortización eclesiástica, á la nacionalización de los bienes de corporaciones, y á la reforma de la legislación civil que tenía relación con el culto y con la iglesia. 2 vols. Mexico City: Imp. de J. Abadiano, 1861.

Colección de leyes, decretos y reglamentos que interinamente forman el sistema político, administrativo y judicial del imperio. 8 vols. Mexico City: Imprenta de Andrade y Escalante, 1865–66.

Colección de leyes y decretos del estado libre de Oaxaca. 26 vols. in 22. Oaxaca: Impreso por M. Rincón, 1851–1909.

Colección de los aranceles de obvenciones y derechos parroquiales que han estado vigentes en los obispados de la República Mexicana y que se citan en el supremo decreto de 11 de abril de 1857. Mexico City: Imprenta de I. Cumplido, 1857.

Cook, Sherburne F., and Borah, Woodrow. *The Population of the Mixteca Alta, 1520–1960.* Ibero-Americana, no. 50. Berkeley: University of California Press, 1968.

Corti, Count Egon Caesar. *Maximilian and Charlotte of Mexico.* Translated by Mrs. C. A. Phillips. 2 vols. New York: Alfred A. Knopf, 1928.

Cosío Villegas, Daniel, ed. *Historia moderna de Mexico.* 10 vols. Vol. 1: *La república restaurada: la vida política,* by Daniel Cosío Villegas. Vol. 2: *La república restaurada: la vida económica,* by Francisco Calderón. Mexico City: Editorial Hermes, 1955–72.

————. *Porfirio Díaz en la Revuelta de la Noria.* Mexico City: Editorial Hermes, 1953.

Costeloe, Michael P. *Church Wealth in Mexico: A Study of the "Juzgado de Capellanías" in the Archbishipric of Mexico, 1800–1856.* Cambridge Latin American Studies, no. 2. Cambridge: Cambridge University Press, 1967.

Covarrubias y Mejía, José María. *Carta pastoral . . . dirigida a todos sus diocesanos.* Oaxaca: Impreso por M. Rincón, 1865.

————. *Esposición que el illmo. sr. obispo de la Diócesis de Oaxaca . . . elevó a S. M. el*

Emperador de México, el día de Enero de 1866, sobre la ley de registro civil promulgada el 18 de Diciembre de 1865. Oaxaca: Impreso por M. Rincón, 1866.

————. *Tercera cara pastoral que el illmo. sr. obispo de Oaxaca, dirige a sus diocesanos.* Mexico City: Imprenta de J. M. Lara, 1866.

Covarrubias, Miguel. *Mexico South: The Isthmus of Tehuantepec.* 1946. Reprint. New York: Alfred A. Knopf, 1962.

Cruz, Francisco Santiago. *La piqueta de la Reforma.* Figuras y episodios de la historia de México, no. 55. Mexico City: Editorial Jus, 1958.

Cue Cánovas, Augustín. *La reforma liberal en México.* Mexico City; Ediciones Centenario, 1960.

Cuevas, Mariano. *Historia de la nación mexicana.* 2d ed. 3 vols. Mexico City: Buena Press, 1952–53.

Dabbs, Jack A. *The French Army in Mexico, 1861–1867: A Study in Military Government.* Studies in American History, no. 2. The Hague: Mouton & Co., 1963.

La democracia en Oaxaca. Apuntes históricos que contienen lo ocurrido en ella, desde el Plan de Ayutla hasta fines de Mayo de 1859. Primera Parte. Mexico City: n. p., 1859.

Dennis, Phillip A. *Conflictos por tierras en el Valle de Oaxaca.* Translated by Celia Paschero. Mexico City: Instituto Nacional Indigenista y Secretaría de Educación Pública, 1976.

Díaz, Porfirio. *Archivo del General Porfirio Díaz: memorias y documentos.* Edited by Alberto María Carreño. 29 vols. Mexico City: Editorial "Elede," 1947–60.

Díaz López, Lilia, ed. and trans. *Versión francesa de México. Informes diplomáticos.* 3 vols. Mexico City: El Colegio de México, 1963–65.

Diccionario Porrúa de historia, biografía y geografía de México. 3d ed. 2 vols. Mexico City: Editorial Porrúa, 1970.

[Domínguez, José Agustín]. *Edicto pastoral que el Escmo. e Illmo. Sr. Dr. D. José Agustín Domínguez, dignísimo obispo de Oaxaca, dirige a todo el clero de la diócesis, a 11 de Diciembre de 1854.* Oaxaca: Impreso por José Ignacio Candiani, 1854.

————. *Pastoral del Escmo. e Illmo. Sr. Obispo de Oaxaca Dr. D. José Agustím Domínguez, dirigida a sus diocesanos con motivo de la declaración dogmática del misterio de la Inmaculada Concepción de María Santísima Señora Nuestra.* Oaxaca: Impreso por Ignacio Rincón, 1855.

Dublán, Manuel. *Memoria que sobre instrucción pública presenta el director del Instituto al gobierno del estado.* Oaxaca: Tipografía del Instituto del Estado, 1863.

————, and Lozano, José María. *Legislación mexicana, o colección completa de las disposiciones legislativas expedidas desde la independencia de la república. . . .* 34 vols. Mexico City: Imprenta del Comercio, 1876–1904.

Echeverría, Agustín. *Memorias religiosas y ejemplares noticias de la fundación Monasterio de Nuestra Señora de la Soledad.* Oaxaca: Manuel M. Vázquez, Impresor, 1906.

Edictos Pastorales que los Illos. Sres. Obispos de Oaxaca, Dr. D. José Agustín Domínguez y Dr. D. José María Covarrubias y Mejía dirigieron a todo el clero de la Diócesis, el primero el 11 de Julio de 1854, y el segundo el 26 de Junio de 1865, y que el Illmo. Sr. Dr. D. Vicente Fermín Márquez y Carrizosa, como actual Obispo de la diócesis, manda reimprimir como vigente. Oaxaca: J. Mariscal en la Tipografía de L. San-Germán, 1879.

Florescano, Enrique, and Gil, Isabel, comps. *Descripciones económicas generales de Nueva España, 1784–1817.* Fuentes para la historia económica de México, no. 1. Mexico City: Instituto Nacional de Antropología e Historia, Seminario de Historia Económica, 1973.

Fossey, Comte Mathieu de. *Le mexique.* Paris: H. Plon, 1857.

Foster, John Watson, *Las memorias diplomáticas de Mr. Foster sobre México.* Edited by Genaro Estrada. Archivo histórico diplomático mexicano, no. 29. 1929. 2d ed. Mexico City: Editorial Porrúa, 1970.

Fraser, Donald. "La política de desamortización en las comunidades indígenas, 1856–1872." *Historia Mexicana* 21:615–52.

[Galíndez, José Mariano]. *Sermones panegíricos y morales predicados en las grandes solemnidades de esta capital, por un seminarista oaxaqueño.* 4 vols. in 2. Oaxaca: Impreso por Ignacio Candiani, 1844–45.

Garay, José de. *Survey of the Isthmus of Tehuantepec in the Years 1842 and 1843, with the Intent of Establishing a Communication between the Atlantic and Pacific Oceans.* London: Ackermann and Co., 1844.

García, Genaro, ed. *Documentos inéditos o muy raros para la historia de México.* 36 vols. Mexico City: Vda. de C. Bouret, 1905–11.

García, José María. "Apéndice." *Boletín de la Sociedad Mexicana de Geografía y Estadística* 7:264–75.

García Gutiérrez, Jesús. *La iglesia mejicana en el segundo imperio.* Figuras y episodios de la historia de México, no. 28. Mexico City: Editorial Campeador, 1955.

García Martínez, Bernardo. *El Marquesado del Valle: tres siglos de régimen señorial en Nueva España.* Centro de Estudios Históricos, Nueva Serie no. 5. Mexico City: El Colegio de México, 1969.

Gay, Antonio. *Necrolojía del Ilustrísimo Señor . . . Vicario capitular del Obispado de Oaxaca Doctor D. José María Alvarez y Castillejos.* Mexico City: Imprenta de Andrade y Escalante, 1864.

Gillow, Eulogio G. *Apuntes históricos.* Mexico City: Imprenta del Sagrado Corazón de Jesús, 1889.

González Navarro, Moisés. "Tenencia de la tierra y población agrícola (1877–1960)." *Historia Mexicana* 19:62–86.

González y González, Luis. "El agrarismo liberal." *Historia Mexicana* 7:469–96.

———. *Invitación a la microhistoria.* Mexico City: Secretaría de Educación Pública, 1973.

———. "Microhistoria para multimexico." *Historia Mexicana* 21:225–41.

———. *Pueblo en vilo: microhistoria de San José de Gracia.* Centro de Estudios Históricos, Nueva serie, 1. Mexico City: El Colegio de México, 1968.

———. *San José de Gracia: Mexican Village in Transition.* Translated by John Upton. The Texas Pan American Series. Austin: The University of Texas Press, 1974.

Hale, Charles A. *Mexican Liberalism in the Age of Mora, 1821–1853.* Caribbean Series, no. 11. New Haven: Yale University Press, 1968.

Hamnett, Brian. "The Appropriation of Mexican Church Wealth by the Spanish Bourbon Government: The 'Consolidación de Vales Reales,'

1805–1809." *Journal of Latin American Studies* 1:85–113.

———. "Dye Production. Food Supply and the Laboring Population of Oaxaca, 1750–1800." *The Hispanic American Historical Review* 51:51–78.

———. *Politics and Trade in Southern Mexico, 1750–1821.* Cambridge Latin American Studies, no. 12. Cambridge: Cambridge University Press, 1971.

Hannah, Alfred J., and Hannah, Kathryn Abbey. *Napoleon III and Mexico: American Triumph over Monarchy.* Chapel Hill: The University of North Carolina Press, 1971.

Iglesias, José María. *Revistas históricas sobre la intervención francesa en México.* 2d ed. Mexico City: Editorial Porrúa, 1966.

Iguiniz, Juan B. *Bibliografía biográfica mexicana.* Mexico City: Imprenta de la Secretaría de Relaciones Exteriores, 1930.

Investigaciones contemporáneos sobre historia de México: Memorias de la Tercera Reunión de historiadores Mexicanos y Norteamericanos, Oaxtepec, Morelos, 4–7 de noviembre de 1969. Mexico City: Universidad Nacional Autónoma de México and El Colegio de México, 1971.

Iturribarría, Jorge Fernando. *El agua en la ciudad de Oaxaca desde los tiempos más remotos hasta el primer tercio del siglo XX.* Oaxaca: Talleres Gráficos del Gobierno del Estado, 1943.

———. "Alonso García Bravo, trazador y alarife de la Villa de Antequera." *Historia Mexicana* 7:80–91.

———. *La generación oaxaqueña del 57. Síntesis biográfica.* Mexico City: Talleres de Impresión de Estampillas y Valores, 1956.

———. *Historia de Oaxaca, 1821–1877.* 4 vols. Oaxaca: various publishers, 1933–56.

———. *José María Díaz Ordaz: breves apuntes biográficos.* Cuadernos de lectura popular, serie La victoria de la República. Mexico City: Secretaría de Educación Pública, Subsecretaría de Asuntos Culturales, 1967.

———. *Monografía histórica del Palacio de los Poderes del Estado de Oaxaca: 1576–1940.* N.p., 1940.

———. *Oaxaca en la historia (de la época proecolombina a los tiempos actuales).* Mexico City: Editorial Stylo, 1955.

———. "El partido 'Borlado." *Historia Mexicana* 3:473–96.

———. *Porfirio Díaz ante la historia.* Mexico City: n. p., 1967.

Jiménez Moreno, Wigberto; Miranda, José; and Fernández, María Teresa. *Historia de México.* 1963. 6th ed. Mexico City: Editorial E.C.L.A.L.S.A., 1971.

Knapp, Frank A., Jr. *The Life of Sebastián Lerdo de Tejada, 1823–1889: A Study of Influence and Obscurity.* Latin American Studies, no. 12. Austin: The University of Texas Press, 1951.

Knowlton, Robert. "Chaplaincies and the Mexican Reform." *The Hispanic American Historical Review* 48:421–37.

———. *Church Property and the Mexican Reform, 1856–1910.* The Origins of Modern Mexico series. DeKalb: Northern Illinois University Press, 1976.

———. "La iglesia mexicana y la Reforma." *Historia Mexicana* 18:516–34.

Labastida, Luis G. *Colección de leyes, decretos, reglamentos, circulares, órdenes y acuerdos relativos a la desamortización de los bienes de corporaciones civiles y re-*

ligiosas y a la nacionalización de los que administraron las últimas. Mexico City: Tipografía de la Oficina Impresora de Estampillas, 1893.

Lavrin, Asunción. "The Execution of the Law of *Consolidación* in New Spain: Economic Aims and Results." *The Hispanic American Historical Review* 53:27–49.

———. "Mexican Nunneries from 1835 to 1860: Their Administrative Policies and Relations with the State." *The Americas* 28:288–310.

———. "Problems and Policies in the Administration of Nunneries in Mexico, 1800–1835." *The Americas* 28:57–77.

Lemoine V., Ernesto. "Ensayo de división municipal del estado de Oaxaca." *Yan* 3:69–74.

Leyes, decretos, circulares y providencias de la intervención, el supremo poder ejecutivo provisional, la regencia y el imperio. 3 vols. Oaxaca: Impreso por Manuel Rincón, 1865–66.

López Cámara, Francisco, *Los fundamentos de la economía mexicana en la época de la reforma y la intervención; la vida agrícola e industrial de México según fuentes y testigos europeos.* Congreso Nacional de Historia para el Estudio de la Guerra de Intervención, 7. Mexico City: n. p., 1962.

———. *La génesis de la conciencia liberal en México.* Mexico City: El Colegio de México, 1954.

López Carrasco, Fidel. *Historia de la educación en el estado de Oaxaca.* Mexico City: Publicaciones del Museo Pedagógico Nacional, 1950.

López Gallo, Manuel. *Economía y política en la historia de México.* 1965. 10th ed. Mexico City: Ediciones "El Caballito," 1975.

McBride, George M. *The Land Systems of Mexico.* Research Series, no. 12. New York: American Geographical Society of New York, 1923.

Maillefert, Eugenio, comp. *Directorio del comercio del Imperio Mexicano para el año de 1867.* Mexico City: E. Maillefert, 1867.

Martínez Báez, Antonio, ed. *Representaciones sobre la tolerancia religiosa.* Colección "El Siglo XIX." Oaxaca: Ediciones Técnicas Jurídicas del Gobierno del Estado de Oaxaca. 1959.

Martínez Domínguez, Héctor. "Las cofradías en la Nueva España, 1700–1859." *Primer Anuario* (Centro de Estudios Históricos, Facultad de Humanidades, Universidad Veracruzana) (n.d.):45–71.

Martínez Gracida, Manuel. *Colección de "cuadros sinópticos" de los pueblos, haciendas y ranchos del estado libre y soberano de Oaxaca. Anexo número 50 a la memoria adminisrativa presentada al H. congreso del mismo el 17 de Setiembre de 1883.* Oaxaca: Impr. del Estado, 1883.

———. *Efemérides oaxaqueñas, 1853–1892.* 2 vols. Mexico City: Tipografía de "El Siglo XIX," 1892.

———. "El estado de Oaxaca y su estadística del culto católico." *Boletín de la Sociedad de Geografía y Estadística de la República Mexicana,* 3a. epoca, 6:57–66.

Martínez Ríos, Jorge. *Bibliografía antropológica y sociológica del Estado de Oaxaca.* Mexico City: Instituto de Investigaciones Sociales de la Universidad Nacional, 1961.

Mecham, John Lloyd. *Church and State in Latin America: A History of Politico-*

Ecclesiastical Relations. Rev. ed. Chapel Hill: University of North Carolina Press, 1966.

Mendieta y Núñez, Lucio. _El problema agrario de México._ 9th ed. Mexico City: Editorial Porrúa, 1966.

————, ed. _Los Zapotecos: monografía histórica, etnográfica y económica._ Mexico City: Imprenta Universitaria, 1949.

Mexico. Ministerio de Justicia y Negocios Eclesiásticos. _Memoria del Ministerio de Justicia y Negocios Eclesiásticos presentada a las augustas cámaras del Congreso general de los Estados-Unidos Mexicanos por el secretario del ramo en el mes de Enero de 1851._ Mexico City: Imprenta de Cumplido, 1851.

Mexico. Secretaría de Hacienda y Crédito Público. _Informe presentado al congreso de la unión el 16 de Setiembre de 1874, en cumplimiento del precepto constitucional por el C. Francisco Mejía, Secretario de Estado y del Despacho de Hacienda y Crédito Público de los Estados Unidos Mexicanos._ 2 vols. Mexico City: Imprenta del Gobierno en Palacio, 1874.

————. _Memoria presentada al exmo. sr. presidente sustituto de la república por el C. Miguel Lerdo de Tejada dando cuenta de la marcha que han seguido los negocios de la hacienda pública en el tiempo que tuvo a su cargo la secretaría de este ramo._ Mexico City: Imprenta de Vicente García Torres, 1857.

Meyer, Jean A. _Problemas campesinos y revueltas agrarias, 1821–1910._ Sep-Setentas, no. 80. Mexico City: Secretaría de Educación Pública, 1973.

Miranda, José. "La propiedad comunal de la tierra y la cohesión social de los pueblos indígenas mexicanas." _Cuadernos Americanos_ 25:168–81.

Molina, Arcadio G. _Historia de Tehuantepec, San Blas, Shihui y Juchitán, en la intervención francesa en 1864._ Tehuantepec (?): Tip. de San-Germán hermanos, 1911.

Molina Enríquez, Andrés. _Juárez y la Reforma._ Mexico City: Editora Ibero-Mexicana, 1956; 1st published as _La Reforma y Juárez: estudio histórico-sociológico,_ 1906.

Monroy Huitrón, Guadalupe, ed. _Archivo histórico de Matías Romero. Catálogo descriptivo. Correspondencia recibida._ Vol. 1: _1837–1872._ Mexico City: Banco de México, 1965.

Murguía y Galardi, José María. "Estadística antigua y moderna de la provincia, hoy estado libre, soberano e independiente de Guajaca." _Boletín de la Sociedad Mexicana de Geografía y Estadídística_ 7:161–275.

Murray, Paul. _The Catholic Church in Mexico. Historical Essays for the General Reader._ Vol. 1: _(1519–1910)._ Mexico City: Editorial E. P. M., 1965.

Niox, Gustave Léon. _Expédition de Mexique, 1861–1867:récit politique & militaire._ Paris: J. Dumaine, 1874.

Oaxaca. Governor (Miguel Bolaños Cacho). _Memoria administrativa presentada por el C. Lic. Miguel Bolaños Cacho, gobernador interino constitucional del estado de Oaxaca, a la XXI legislature del mismo, en cumplimiento de lo prevenido en la fracción X del Artículo 61 de la constitución politica local el 17 de Septiembre de 1902._ Oaxaca: Imprenta del Comercio, 1902.

————. (Ramón Cajiga). _Memoria que el C. Ramón Cajiga, gobernador constitucional del estado, presenta al segundo congreso de Oaxaca en el primer período de sus sesiones ordinarias el 16 de Septiembre de 1861._ Oaxaca: Imprenta de Ignacio Rincón, 1861.

————. (Miguel Castro). *Memoria que el ejecutivo del estado presenta al congreso del mismo del período de la administración pública de 8 de Enero de 1872 a 16 de Setiembre del mismo año.* Oaxaca: Imprenta del Estado, 1873.

————. (Félix Díaz). *Memoria que presenta el ejecutivo del estado al H. congreso del mismo del período de la administración pública de 17 de Setiembre de 1869 a 16 de Setiembre del presente año* [1870]. Oaxaca: Tipografía del Estado, 1871.

————. (José María Díaz Ordaz). *Memoria que el gobierno del estado presenta al primer congreso constitucional de Oaxaca en sus sesiones ordinarias de 1858.* Oaxaca: Imprenta de Ignacio Rincón, 1858.

————. (José Esperón). *Memoria que el ejecutivo del estado presenta al congreso del mismo sobre los ramos de la administración pública, hoy 17 de Setiembre de 1875.* Oaxaca: Imprenta del Estado, 1875.

————. (Martín González). *Memoria administrativa presentada por el C. General Martín González, gobernador constitucional del estado de Oaxaca, a la XIX legislatura del mismo, en cumplimiento de lo prevenido en la fracción X del artículo 61 de la constitución política local, el 17 de Septiembre de 1898.* Oaxaca: Imprenta del Estado, 1899.

————. (Martín González). *Memoria administrativa presentada por el C. General Martín González, gobernador constitucional del estado de Oaxaca, a la XIX legislatura del mismo, en cumplimiento de lo prevenido en la fracción X del artículo 61 de la constitución política local, el 17 de Septiembre de 1898.* Oaxaca: Imprenta del Estado, 1899.

————. (Benito Juárez). *Esposición que el gobernador del estado hace en cumplimiento del artículo 83 de la constitución al soberano congreso al abrir sus primeras sesiones ordinarias el día 2 de Julio de 1852.* Oaxaca: Impreso por Ignacio Rincón, 1852.

Ocampo, Melchor. *Obras completas.* 3 vols. Mexico City: F. Vázquez, 1900–1901.

O'Gorman, Edmundo. *Historia de las divisiones territoriales de México.* Colección "Sepan cuantos," no 45. Mexico City: Editorial Porrúa, 1968.

Ordenanzas municipales de la capital del estado de Oaxaca. Oaxaca: Impreso por M. Rincón, 1868.

Pardo, Ramón. *Breve estudio sobre la evolución del Instituto de Ciencias y Artes de Oaxaca.* Oaxaca: Imprenta del Estado, 1926.

Parkes, Henry B. *A History of Mexico.* 1938. 3d ed. rev. Boston: Houghton Mifflin Co., 1969.

Pavía, Lázaro. *Apuntes biográficos de los miembros más distinguidos del poder judicial de la República Mexicana.* Mexico City: Tip. y lit. de F. Barroso hno. y co., 1893.

Payno y Flores, Manuel. *Compendio de la historia de México para el uso de los establecimientos de instrucción pública de la República Mexicana.* 6th ed. Mexico City: Imprenta de F. Díaz de León, 1880.

Pereyra, Carlos. *Historia del pueblo mejicano.* 2 vols. Mexico City: J. Ballescá y ca., n.d.

Pérez, Eutimio. *Recuerdos históricos del episcopado oaxaqueño.* Oaxaca: Imprenta de Lorenzo San-Germán, 1888.

Pérez García, Rosendo. *La Sierra Juárez.* 2 vols. Mexico City: Gráfica Cervantina, 1956.

Pérez Jiménez, Gustavo, *Las constituciones del estado de Oaxaca.* Oaxaca: Ediciones Técnicas Jurídicas del Gobierno del Estado de Oaxaca, 1959.

Perry, Laurens B. *Juárez and Díaz: Machine Politics in Mexico.* The Origins of Modern Mexico series. DeKalb: Northern Illinois University Press, 1978.

Phipps, Helen. *Some Aspects of the Agrarian Question in Mexico: A Historical Study.* University of Texas Bulletin no. 2515, Studies in History, no. 2. Austin: The University of Texas Press, 1925.

Planchet, Régis. *La cuestión religiosa en México.* 5th ed. Mexico City: n. p., 1956.

Portilla, Anselmo de la. *Méjico en 1856 y 1857: Gobierno del General Comonfort.* New York: Imprenta de S. Hallet, 1858.

Portillo, Andrés. *Oaxaca en el centenario de la independencia nacional. Noticias históricas y estadísticas de la ciudad de Oaxaca y algunas leyendas tradicionales.* Oaxaca: H. Santaella, 1910.

Powell, T. G. *El liberalismo y el campesinado en el centro de México (1850 a 1876).* Translated by Roberto Gómez Ciriza. SepSetentas, no. 122. Mexico City: Secretaría de Educación Pública, 1974.

Quirarte, Martín. *Historiografía sobre el imperio de Maximiliano.* Serie de historia moderna y contemporánea, no. 9. Mexico City: Universidad Nacional Autónoma de México, Instituto de Investigaciones Históricas, 1970.

———. *Visión panorámica de la historia de México.* 1965. 7th ed. Mexico City: Librería Porrúa Hnos. y Cia., 1976.

Rabasa, Emilio. *La evolución histórica de México.* 1920. 2d ed. Mexico City: Editorial Porrúa., 1956.

Ramos-Oliveria, Antonio. *La formación de Juárez: el paisaje y el hombre en Oaxaca.* Mexico City: Compañia General de Ediciones, 1972.

Ramos Pedrueza, Rafael. *La lucha de clases a través de la historia de México. Ensayo marxista.* 2d ed. Mexico City: Talleres Gráficos de la Nación, 1936.

Reyes Heroles, Jesús. *El liberalismo mexicano.* 3 vols. Mexico City: Editorial Cultura, 1957–61.

Rincón, Francisco. "Estadística. Noticia que manifiesta el censo del Estado de Oaxaca, con expresión del que a cada distrito pertenece, formada en virtud del decreto del congreso de la unión, de 14 de Noviembre de 1868." *Boletín de la Sociedad de Geografía y Estadística de la República Mexicana,* 2a época, 1 (1869):328.

Riva Palacio, Vicente. *Historia de la administración de D. Sebastián Lerdo de Tejada. Su política, sus leyes, sus contratos, sus hombres.* Mexico City: Imprenta y litografía del Padre Cobos, 1875.

Rivera Cambas, Manuel. *Historia de la intervención europe a y norteamericana en México y del imperio de Maximiliano de Habsburgo.* 1888–95. 2d ed. 3 vols. Mexico City: Editorial Academia Literaria, 1961.

Rivera y Sanromán, Agustín. *Anales mexicanos. La Reforma y el Segundo Imperio.* Mexico City: Comisión Nacional para las Conmemoraciones Cívicas de 1963, 1963.

Romero, Matías. *El estado de Oaxaca.* Barcelona: Tipografía de Espasa y compa., 1886.

Sánchez, Policarpo T. *Memoria de la Escuela Normal de Oaxaca en su inauguración, 29 de Octubre de 1946.* Mexico City (?): n. p., 1946 (?).

Santaella, Luis B. *Discurso pronunciado en la noche del día 15 Setiembre de 1865, en el portal del Palacio de la Prefectura Superior del Departamento*. Oaxaca: Impreso por M. Rincón, 1865.

Santibáñez, Manuel. *Reseña histórica del cuerpo de Ejército de Oriente*. 2 vols. Mexico City: Tipografía de la Oficina Impresora del Timbre, 1892–93.

Scholes, Walter V. *Mexican Politics during the Juárez Regime, 1855–1872*. Columbia: The University of Missouri Studies, 1957.

Segura, José Sebastián. *Boletín de las leyes del imperio mexicano o sea código de la Restauración*. 4 vols. Mexico City: Imprenta literaria, 1863–65.

Sierra, Justo. *The Political Evolution of the Mexican People*. Translated by Charles Ramsdell. Austin: The Univerity of Texas Press, 1969.

Simpson, Eyler N. *The Ejido: Mexico's Way Out*. Chapel Hill: The University of North Carolina Press, 1937.

Simpson, Lesley B. *Many Mexicos*. 1941. 3d ed. rev. and enl. Berkeley: University of California Press, 1952.

Smart, Charles A. *Viva Juárez! A Biography*. Philadelphia: J. B. Lippincott, 1963.

Swierenga, Robert P. *Pioneers and Profits: Land Speculation on the Iowa Frontier*. Ames: Iowa State University Press, 1968.

Tamayo, Jorge L., ed. *Benito Juárez. Documentos, discursos y correspondencia*. 11 vols. Mexico City: Secretaría del Patrimonio Nacional, 1964–67.

Taracena, Angel, ed. "Don Benito Juárez y los Tedeums oficiales, 1857." *Boletín del Archivo General de la Nación* 9:782–86.

Taylor, William B. "Cacicazgos coloniales en el Valle de Oaxaca." *Historia Mexicana* 20:1–41.

———. *Drinking, Homicide and Rebellion in Colonial Mexican Villages*. Stanford: Stanford University Press, 1979.

———. *Landlord and Peasant in Colonial Oaxaca*. Stanford: Stanford University Press, 1972.

Tempsky, G. F. von. *Mitla, A Narrative of Incidents and Personal Adventures on a Journey in Mexico, Guatemala, and Salvador in the Years 1853 to 1855*. Edited by J. S. Bell. London: Longman, Brown, Green, Longmans, & Roberts, 1858.

Toro, Alfonso. *La Iglesia y el estado en México (estudio sobre los conflictos entre el clero católico y los gobiernos mexicanos desde la independencia hasta nuestros días)*. Publicaciones del Archivo General de la Nación. Mexico City: Talleres Gráfico de la Nación, 1927.

Torre Villar, Ernesto de la, ed. *La intervención francesa y el triunfo de la república*. Mexico City: Fondo de Cultura Económica, 1968.

Tutino, John. "Indian Rebellion at the Isthmus of Tehuantepec: A Sociohistorical Perspective." *Actes du XLIIe Congrès International des Americanistes* 3:197–214.

U.S. Congress. House. *Message of the President of the United States, of March 20, 1866, Relating to the Condition of Affairs in Mexico in Answer to a Resolution of the House of December 11, 1865*. Part 1. 39th Cong., 1st sess., Exec. Doc. no. 73. Washington, D. C.: GPO, 1866.

Valadés, Adrián. "La marcha de Díaz hacia Oaxaca durante la Intervención." *Historia Mexicana* 7:92–115.

Valadés, José C. *Historia del pueblo de México desde sus orígenes hasta nuestros días*. 3 vols. Mexico City: Editores Mexicanos unidos, 1967.

Valverde Téllez, Emetrio. *Bio-bibliografía eclesiástica mexicana (1821–1943).* 3 vols. Mexico City: Editorial Jus, 1949.
Vigil, José María. *La Reforma.* Vol. 5 of *México a través de los siglos.* 1887–89. Edited and directed by Vicente Riva Palacio. 10th ed. 5 vols. Mexico City: Editorial Cumbre, 1973.
Whitecotton, Joseph W. *The Zapotecs: Princes, Priests, and Peasants.* Norman: University of Oklahoma Press, 1977.
Williams, J. J. *The Isthmus of Tehuantepec: Being the Results of a Survey for a Railroad to Connect the Atlantic and Pacific Oceans.* New York: D. Appleton & Co., 1852.
Zayas Enríquez, Rafael de. *Benito Juárez: su vida, su obra.* 1906. SepSetentas, no. 1. Mexico City: Secretaría de Educación Pública. 1971.

UNPUBLISHED ARTICLES AND DISSERTATIONS

Chance, John K. "Race and Class in a Colonial Mexican City: A Social History of Antequera, 1521–1800." Ph.D. dissertation, University of Illinois at Urbana–Champaign, 1974.
Falcone, Frank S. "Federal-State Relations during Mexico's Restored Republic: Oaxaca, A Case Study, 1867–1872." Ph.D. dissertation, University of Massachusetts, 1974.
Helms, James E. "Origins and Growth of Protestantism in Mexico to 1929." Ph.D dissertation, The University of Texas at Austin, 1955.
Iturribarría, Jorge Fernando. "Los abogados generales del Instituto de Ciencias y Artes del Estado de Oaxaca y su participación en la Guerra de Reforma y en la defensa de la soberanía nacional." (In Iturribarría's possession.)
Knowlton, Robert, "The Disamortization and Nationalization of Ecclesiastical Property in Mexico, 1856–1910." Ph.D. dissertation, State University of Iowa, 1963.
Luebke, Benjamin H. "Delineation of Rural Communities in the State of Oaxaca, Mexico." Ph.D. dissertation, University of Florida, 1959.
Miller, David Lynn. "Porfirio Díaz and the Army of the East." Ph.D. dissertation, The University of Michigan, 1960.
Perry, Laurens B. "The Dynamics of the Insurrection of Tuxtepec: Mexico in 1876." Ph.D. dissertation, The University of Michigan, 1971.
Taylor, William B. "The Valley of Oaxaca: A Study of Colonial Land Distribution." Ph.D. dissertation, The University of Michigan, 1969.

NEWSPAPERS

Boletín Oficial. Oaxaca, 1857–58.
Boletín Trigarante. Oaxaca, 1858.
El Constituyente. Periódico Oficial del Gobierno de Oaxaca. 1856.
La Democracia. Periódico del Gobierno de Oaxaca. 1857–59.

Diario del Imperio. Mexico City, 1865–67.
El Libertador. Periódico del Gobierno del Estado de Oaxaca. 1856.
Periódico Oficial del Gobierno de Oaxaca. 1855.
El Rayo. Periódico Político y de Variedades. Oaxaca, 1867.
La Victoria. Periódico del Gobierno de Oaxaca. 1861–65.

ACKNOWLEDGMENTS

I AM IN THE DEBT of many people who encouraged me in this study, facilitated my research, and offered constructive criticism: Professors Thomas McGann and Nettie Lee Benson of The University of Texas at Austin; Mr. Cecil Welte, Lic. Luis Castañeda Guzmán, and Sr. Jorge Fernando Iturribarría of Oaxaca; Professors Charles Hale of the University of Iowa, Michael Costeloe of the Univeristy of Bristol, Asunción Lavrin of Howard University, Robert Knowlton of the University of Wisconsin at Stevens Point, and Thomas Preisser of Sinclair Community College, Dayton, Ohio. May all Latin Americanists have a friend such as Miss Jane Garner, Rare Books and Manuscripts Librarian of the Nettie Lee Benson Latin American Collection, who over the years generously took time to track down photographs and bits and pieces of elusive information for me.

I am also indebted to the University of Louisville, where I taught between 1967 and 1971, for funds for clerical assistance; to The University of Texas at Austin for the financial support that allowed me to computerize a large amount of data concerning properties disentailed and nationalized during the Reform; to the University of Bristol, where I served as Leverhulme Visiting Fellow in 1971–72, for facilitating research in the British Museum; to Wright State University for a series of small grants and a semester of a reduced teaching load, which allowed me to finish writing the manuscript; and to the National Endowment for the Humanities for a fellowship in 1971, which made it possible to complete research on the broadened topic.

Most of all, I am indebted to my wife for her tolerance in having books, research notes, writing pads, and stacks of earlier drafts of the manuscript spread throughout the house for inordinately long stretches of time, and to my four sons for their patience with a father who frequently could not go on picnics and fishing expeditions because he had work to complete.

INDEX

271